Yorkshire Terriers For Dummies®

Picking a Breeder

When you go hunting for a breeder, look for one who does the following (Chapter 3 has more details):

- ✔ Breeds only animals who are healthy and have good, stable dispositions
- ✔ Waits to breed until he has a waiting list of buyers for the puppies or is breeding for a new puppy he can show
- ✔ Begins socializing the puppies shortly after they're born
- ✔ Has the puppies undergo health checks by a vet and gets their initial shots
- ✔ Waits until the puppies are a minimum of 12-weeks-old before separating them from their mother
- ✔ Sells puppies out of his own home
- ✔ Investigates the people he sells puppies to
- ✔ Makes health records and medical checks of the dam, sire, and puppy available to you
- ✔ Gives you the registered names and numbers of the puppies' dam and sire
- ✔ Insists on spay/neuter agreement for non-show-quality puppies or specifies limited registration in the American Kennel Club (AKC) for the puppy
- ✔ Offers a written guarantee for the health and temperament of the puppy
- ✔ Does other things (exhibits his dogs, participates in breed clubs, and so on) with the dogs besides breed them

Standard in Brief

Here's a quick rundown of the main points in the Yorkshire Terrier breed standard (go to Chapter 2 for the complete list):

- ✔ **Coat:** Long, straight, and silky
- ✔ **Color:** Blue on back; tan on face, chest, and legs
- ✔ **Size:** No more than 7 pounds
- ✔ **Temperament:** Self-assured and intelligent
- ✔ **Head:** Small and slightly flat on top
- ✔ **Nose:** Black
- ✔ **Ears:** Small, pointed, and erect
- ✔ **Body:** Compact with short, level back
- ✔ **Tail:** Docked and slightly higher than back

For Dummies: Bestselling Book Series for Beginners

Yorkshire Terriers For Dummies®

Quick Guide to Puppy-proofing Your Home

Eliminate or move hazardous chemicals from your home, yard, and garage. Pay special attention to these items:

- Cleaning supplies
- Paints, varnishes, and paint thinners
- Motor oil and antifreeze
- Laundry detergents and bleach
- Fertilizers and insecticides
- Poisonous house and garden plants (for a list, go to www.hsus.org/ace/11777)

Other danger spots include

- Power cords
- Unsteady or wobbly furniture
- Low-hanging table runners or cloths
- Holes or gaps in fences

Emergency Phone Numbers

Cut these numbers out and keep them by your phone or on your refrigerator:

Vet's Office:_____

Emergency Care:_____

Breeder:_____

Animal Poison Control: (888) 426-4235 ($50 consultation fee)

For Dummies: Bestselling Book Series for Beginners

Yorkshire Terriers
FOR
DUMMIES®

by Tracy Barr and
Peter F. Veling, DVM

WILEY

Wiley Publishing, Inc.

Yorkshire Terriers For Dummies®

Published by
Wiley Publishing, Inc.
111 River St.
Hoboken, NJ 07030-5774
www.wiley.com

Copyright © 2004 by Wiley Publishing, Inc., Indianapolis, Indiana

Published by Wiley Publishing, Inc., Indianapolis, Indiana

Published simultaneously in Canada

No part of this publication may be reproduced, stored in a retrieval system, or transmitted in any form or by any means, electronic, mechanical, photocopying, recording, scanning, or otherwise, except as permitted under Sections 107 or 108 of the 1976 United States Copyright Act, without either the prior written permission of the Publisher, or authorization through payment of the appropriate per-copy fee to the Copyright Clearance Center, 222 Rosewood Drive, Danvers, MA 01923, 978-750-8400, fax 978-646-8600. Requests to the Publisher for permission should be addressed to the Legal Department, Wiley Publishing, Inc., 10475 Crosspoint Blvd., Indianapolis, IN 46256, 317-572-3447, fax 317-572-4355, or e-mail brandreview@wiley.com.

Trademarks: Wiley, the Wiley Publishing logo, For Dummies, the Dummies Man logo, A Reference for the Rest of Us!, The Dummies Way, Dummies Daily, The Fun and Easy Way, Dummies.com and related trade dress are trademarks or registered trademarks of John Wiley & Sons, Inc. and/or its affiliates in the United States and other countries, and may not be used without written permission. All other trademarks are the property of their respective owners. Wiley Publishing, Inc., is not associated with any product or vendor mentioned in this book.

For general information on our other products and services or to obtain technical support, please contact our Customer Care Department within the U.S. at 800-762-2974, outside the U.S. at 317-572-3993, or fax 317-572-4002.

Wiley also publishes its books in a variety of electronic formats. Some content that appears in print may not be available in electronic books.

Library of Congress Control Number: 2004107976

ISBN: 978-0-7645-6880-0

Manufactured in the United States of America

10 9 8 7 6

1B/RV/QS/QY/IN

WILEY

About the Authors

Tracy Barr has been part of the Dummies phenomenon for over a decade. In that time, she has served as editor, editorial manager, writer, and consultant to folks who write and edit *For Dummies* books. Most recently, she coauthored *Adoption For Dummies* and wrote *Cast Iron Cooking For Dummies.* A dog lover and owner her whole life, she is especially fond of the littlest terriers.

Peter F. Veling, DVM, a 1981 graduate of the Purdue University Veterinary School, owns Caring Hands Pet Hospital in Indianapolis. He is married to Jane Veling and has three children, Rob, Drew, and Caitlin. They share a home with a variety of four-footed family members including dogs Ruby and Jade, and cats Mungo, Tiger, Nellie, and Bob.

Dedication

To all the animals in our menageries.

Authors' Acknowledgments

We would like to thank the following people for the contributions they made to this book: Jim Hupp, who gave a Yorkie breeder/exhibitor's perspective on the material; Gayle Vautaw of Lyngale Yorkshire Terriers (Logansport, IN), Julie Howard of Jo-Nel Yorkshire Terriers (Kokomo, IN), and exhibitor Cathy Parker, who graciously answered the questions we threw their way; and the editors, Chrissy Guthrie and Michelle Dzurny, for their feedback and suggestions.

And a special thanks goes to artist Mary Carmichael who, despite her affinity for Expressionism, drew Yorkies that actually look like, well, Yorkies.

Publisher's Acknowledgments

We're proud of this book; please send us your comments through our Dummies online registration form located at www.dummies.com/register/.

Some of the people who helped bring this book to market include the following:

Acquisitions, Editorial, and Media Development

Project Editor: Christina Guthrie

Acquisitions Editor: Tracy Boggier

Copy Editor: Michelle Dzurny

Assistant Editor: Holly Gastineau-Grimes

Technical Editor: James J. Hupp

Editorial Manager: Christine Meloy Beck

Editorial Assistants: Courtney Allen, Elizabeth Rea

Cover Photos: © Alice Su, 2003

Cartoons: Rich Tennant, www.the5thwave.com

Composition

Project Coordinator: Maridee Ennis

Layout and Graphics: Joyce Haughey, Heather Ryan, Brent Savage, Jacque Schneider

Special Art: Photos by Isabelle Francais; illustrations by Mary Carmichael

Proofreaders: Brian H. Walls, TECHBOOKS Production Services

Indexer: TECHBOOKS Production Services

Publishing and Editorial for Consumer Dummies

  Diane Graves Steele, Vice President and Publisher, Consumer Dummies

  Joyce Pepple, Acquisitions Director, Consumer Dummies

  Kristin A. Cocks, Product Development Director, Consumer Dummies

  Michael Spring, Vice President and Publisher, Travel

  Brice Gosnell, Associate Publisher, Travel

  Kelly Regan, Editorial Director, Travel

Publishing for Technology Dummies

  Andy Cummings, Vice President and Publisher, Dummies Technology/General User

Composition Services

  Gerry Fahey, Vice President of Production Services

  Debbie Stailey, Director of Composition Services

Contents at a Glance

Table of Contents

Introduction

So you want to adopt or are thinking about adopting a Yorkshire Terrier. Good for you. Your first decision — to educate yourself about these dogs (otherwise, why would you be reading this book right now?) — is a good one. Yorkies can make great pets for people who know enough about the breed to know whether a Yorkie is the right dog for them.

Fortunately, finding out about Yorkies is quite a bit of fun, mainly because they're such a contradiction. Sure, they look like little doll dogs, what with their silky hair and the satin ribbons that usually adorn them, but in their hearts, they're terriers. And that means they're feisty, independent, intensely loyal, and just a tad . . . well, okay, *very* . . . territorial.

The best home for a Yorkie is one in which what they are (terriers) is just as, if not more, important than what they appear to be (Toy dogs). When you adopt a dog, you need to know about more than the inner dog. You also need to know how to best care for the outer dog, too.

About This Book

Basically, this book has two purposes: first, to be an easy-to-use reference that tells you everything you need to know about Yorkies, both before and after you adopt one. In this book, you can find answers to questions like

- ✔ What are the physical characteristics and temperament of the breed?
- ✔ How do I introduce a new Yorkie to my other pets?
- ✔ What's up with the ribbon? Do I have to put one in, and if I decide to, how do I do it?
- ✔ What's an effective way to train Yorkies, and which commands are the most important ones to teach?
- ✔ What health issues are common to Yorkies and what are the symptoms?
- ✔ Lord help me, how do I make it through the first night home with my Yorkie?

Of course, this book has another purpose, too: to give you enough information about Yorkies so that you can make an informed decision about whether a Yorkshire Terrier is a good match for your home and lifestyle. If, after reading this book, you decide, "Nah, a Yorkie isn't for me," great. I just helped you avoid a potentially costly and heartbreaking mistake.

The great thing about this book is that *you* decide where to start and what to read. Jump into and out of it at will. You can head to the table of contents or the index to find the information you want.

Conventions Used in This Book

To help you navigate through this book, I set up a few conventions:

- ✔ *Italic* is used for emphasis and to highlight new words or terms that are defined.
- ✔ **Boldfaced** text is used to indicate the action part of numbered steps.
- ✔ Monofont is used for Web and e-mail addresses.

And in an effort to support gender equality, I (with the help and eagle eye of my copy editor) alternated references from male to female. Unless specified otherwise, all masculine and feminine pronouns apply to both male and female Yorkies.

What You're Not to Read

This book is chock-full of absolutely essential and not-to-be-skipped information. It also includes information of the things-you-might-find-interesting-but-don't-really-need-to-know variety. To help you distinguish between the two, I made the skippable info easy to recognize. The skippable stuff, although interesting and related to the topic at hand, isn't essential for you to know:

- ✔ **Text in sidebars:** The sidebars are the shaded boxes that appear here and there. These boxes contain related but nonessential information. So, they aren't necessary reading.
- ✔ **Anything highlighted with a Technical Stuff icon:** The information in these paragraphs is interesting but not critical to your understanding of Yorkies. Basically, if you avoided every paragraph attached to these icons, you'd still know everything you need to know about Yorkies.

Foolish Assumptions

In writing this book, I made some assumptions about you and the type of information you want to find:

- ✔ You're thinking about adopting a Yorkie and want to find out more about the breed and its care before you take the plunge.

- ✔ Your Yorkie's coming home soon, and you need ideas on how to get ready for her arrival.

- ✔ You're standing, brush in hand, among a mass of ribbons and hair bands, your Yorkie's top knot looks like a 3 year old did it, and you need grooming tips — and you need them *now*.

- ✔ You're having difficulty training your Yorkie and you want training advice and instructions.

- ✔ You don't have a Yorkie and don't plan to get one (at least not in the near future) but love them anyway and want to know more about them.

How This Book Is Organized

This book is organized so that you can find information easily. Each of the five parts is devoted to a particular topic and contains chapters relating to that part.

Part 1: Finding Your Dream Dog

Making the decision to open your home to a dog is a big one — even if the dog is small. The objective of this part is to give you the information that you need to make good decisions: Here you can find out enough about the breed (breed standard, history, needs, and so on.) to determine whether a Yorkie is the right dog for you; what your options are for finding the dog you want (breeder, pet shop, rescue organization); basic decisions you need to make about the dog you're looking for (age, gender, pet or show quality) *before* you begin the actual hunt, and what to look for when you finally go to pick out your dog.

Part 11: The Homecoming

This part helps you get your house ready for your new dog, from puppy-proofing to setting up his areas. It also offers suggestions for the ride home, explaining what you should take with and what you can expect to bring home, besides your Yorkie, that is. And because the first days and initial nights — a period that can set the tone for the whole experience — are so important and hectic, this part also offers advice on what you can do to get off on the right foot.

Part III: Taking Care of Your Yorkie

Yorkies are, by and large, a pretty independent group, but they still need care. This part offers you guidelines for basic Yorkie care: How to keep them happy, healthy, and fit, and how to perform the necessary grooming. In this part, I also explain some of the hereditary conditions that are common to Yorkies and give you guidelines on health conditions and symptoms that require a trip to the vet.

Part IV: Training with TLC

Even small dogs need training. Although they may not be able to do enough damage to cause serious injury (after all, you can pick them up and tuck them under your arm if they get out of hand), a poorly trained dog isn't much fun to be around. Throw small children into the mix or strangers who don't look as benignly on the "little nip" as you do, and you can have a recipe, if not for disaster, at least for a major hassle. This part begins with basic info on the positive training method, explains how to housetrain your Yorkie, and gives you instructions on teaching your dog basic commands that will make him a good citizen in your house and beyond.

Part V: The Part of Tens

The standard *For Dummies* Part of Tens, this part offers you quick lists of information. Here you can find lists of online Yorkie resources, tips for exhibiting your Yorkie in the show ring, and fun Yorkie facts.

Icons Used in This Book

The icons in this book help you find particular kinds of information that may be useful to you:

This icon appears wherever a bit of advice can save you time, money, hassle, or stress.

 This icon points out important information that's worth remembering.

 When you see this icon, pay attention. It highlights info about unscrupulous breeders, unsafe practices, and dangers that can harm your dog.

 You see this icon beside interesting but nonessential information. Feel free to skip these paragraphs; you'll miss neat asides but nothing crucial.

Where to Go from Here

In this book, you can jump in wherever you want and find complete information. Want to know what housetraining challenges await you and what you can do to be successful? Head to Chapter 14. If you're interested in how to find a reputable breeder, go to Chapter 3. Use the table of contents to find broad categories of information or use the index to look up more specific topics.

If you're still contemplating getting a Yorkie, you may want to start with Chapters 1 and 2. These chapters give you all the basic info you need about Yorkies — their breed characteristics, what they need to be happy, and what types of homes are good for them. Beyond that, go wherever your interests and questions take you.

Part I
Finding Your Dream Dog

"It's definitely Yorkshire Gigantis – prehistoric predecessor to the Yorkshire Terrier. You can tell by the bony topknot."

In this part . . .

*W*hen Disney's live–action movie *101 Dalmatians* came out, people rushed to get Dalmatian puppies. *Homeward Bound: The Incredible Journey* spurred interest in Golden Retrievers and Boxers. *Lassie* watchers made rough–coated Collies one of the most popular dogs in the United States. People see (pick an adjective: beautiful/cute/lovable/devoted/preternaturally intelligent) canines and want one for their very own.

Think all this interest had breeders jumping for joy? Think again. Most dog fanciers will tell you that people who base their decisions to adopt a dog on little more than observing animals through cinematographers' lenses or their own rose–colored glasses are usually asking for trouble. So before you adopt a Yorkie because you saw a cute little doggy in the window or got a hoot out of *Best in Show,* take a little time to really find out about the breed.

If, after you have a clear picture of the breed, you're still interested in a Yorkie and are confident that your home would be a good one, take the time to find a reputable breeder. Then take a little more time to find the dog who's right for you.

Chapter 1

Yorkies and You: A Match Made in Heaven?

*N*ot many people can deny that a Yorkshire Terrier puppy — 3 to 4 pounds of personality in a soft, shimmery package of silky hair — is just about one of the cutest canine specimens to ever grace the species. Even all grown up, they have a very high "awww" quotient. As such, Yorkies are sure to nab the attention of many people looking for a small dog. Before you decide that a Yorkie is the dog of your dreams, however, you need to find out more about the breed. This chapter offers you a brief overview of the great things Yorkies offer to the people who love them. I also outline the things Yorkies need to be happy and healthy in your home.

Yorkies in a Coconut Shell

Because of their size and the lifestyle to which they've become accustomed, Yorkies (see Figure 1-1) fall into the Toy group. *Toy breeds* are very small dogs that are bred to be companions. Some Toy dogs look like smaller versions of larger dogs (take the Miniature Poodle, for example); others are just naturally small.

©Isabelle Francais

Figure 1-1: Yorkies are Toy dogs with lots of heart.

Because of their nature and the purposes for which they were originally bred (chasing down and killing vermin — especially useful in
controlling the rats in the mines of England), Yorkies are terriers,
despite the category assigned to them by the American Kennel
Club (AKC). As such, they have the characteristics associated with
terriers: They're clever, brave, determined, feisty, energetic, and
have little tolerance for other animals — big or small, including
other dogs.

So, yes, Yorkies are highly pamper-able dogs. They're small enough
to tuck under your arm, share your pillow, and recline on your lap
during dinner. You can even tote them around in a highly fashion-
able, outfit-matching satchel-cum-dog carrier, if you're so inclined.
But Yorkies are terriers at heart: They're independent, love activity
(especially chasing things), and can be territorial (which means
you have to take care when you introduce them to other animals
or other animals to them). If a squirrel runs across your deck at
breakfast, your Yorkie is more likely to jump in a flurry of flowing
hair and give chase than lollingly accept the scrumptious morsel
that you're offering.

Toy breeds

Yorkies are in good company in the Toy category. Other Toy breeds recognized by the American Kennel Club (AKC) are

- Affenpinscher
- Brussels Griffon
- Cavalier King Charles Spaniel
- Chihuahua
- Chinese Crested
- English Toy Spaniel
- Havanese
- Italian Greyhound
- Japanese Chin
- Maltese
- Miniature Pinscher
- Papillon
- Pekingese
- Pomeranian
- Pug
- Shih Tzu
- Silky Terrier
- Toy Fox Terrier

And what of the Toy Poodle? Well, the AKC classifies all Poodles in the Non-Sporting group but classifies them by size: Standard, Miniature, and Toy. Standard and Miniature Poodles show in the Non-Sporting group. Toy Poodles show in the Toy group. The situation for Toy Manchester Terriers is similar. The AKC classifies them in the Terrier group along with Standard Manchester Terriers, but Toy Manchester Terriers show in the Toy group.

Think of Yorkies as no-nonsense, cut-to-the-chase, just-the-facts-ma'am kind of dogs trapped in mama's-little-baby, cute-as-buttons, kissie-kissie packages. Primp, polish, and beribbon them all you want, but love them for their personalities. That's where the real gold is.

To read about the history of the breed and the *breed standard* (that is, what people in the know and the AKC consider the ideal characteristics and traits that define Yorkshire Terriers), bounce to Chapter 2.

It's a Dog's Life

Yorkies need what all dogs need: love, companionship, food, shelter, and a toy to chew on. All these necessities come from one source: you. Adopt a Yorkie, and you have a Yorkie's lifetime of fun to look forward to — and the responsibility that goes with it. The following sections very briefly outline what these pooches need to live long, healthy, happy lives.

Love and companionship

Despite the independent streak common to all terriers, Yorkies aren't meant to lead solitary lives. Except for those times when you confine your dog to her crate or a small area (for training purposes; head to Chapter 8 and Part IV), your Yorkie will consider herself your boon companion and will follow you from room to room, upstairs to down, and front yard to back.

For many Yorkies, having their humans within sight isn't enough; they need to be near you. Sit, and she'll be on your lap. Wash dishes, and she'll be between your feet and the kitchen cabinet. Go to the bathroom, and she'll be outside the door waiting for you. Yorkies are happiest when their humans crave that interaction as well. They don't do as well in homes where an occasional pat is the norm, they're frequently separated from the family, or they're relegated to the outer edges of family activities. They are, after all, companion dogs, and their favorite companion is you.

Safe shelter

Well, to state the obvious, Yorkies are house dogs. As much as they enjoy the outdoors and all the little surprises (butterflies, squirrels, ants, and so on) that keep their inquisitive minds busy and their little legs pumping, they can't live there. So, *no* doghouses. *Your* house — no matter how small or where it's located — is fine. Yorkies don't need a lot of space, and they do as well in apartments as they do in country homes.

Here are a couple of tips for setting up your dog's home in your house:

- ✔ **Until your Yorkie is trained, he needs a small, quiet area to call his own.** Place his crate, food dishes, and bed in this area. And when you aren't around to make sure that he stays out of trouble, put your Yorkie here to keep him out trouble and danger. Head to Chapter 5 for tips on setting up this home-within-a-home. Of course, after he's trained, he'll probably get the run of the house.

- ✔ **If you adopt a puppy, keep in mind that your house is home to a lot of dangers and you need to puppy-proof it.** Again, go to Chapter 5 for a list of dangers and what you can do to protect your puppy.

Good food

Here's another obvious statement: Yorkies won't eat you out of house and home. A not-so-obvious point is that, because they don't eat a lot, you need to make sure that what they *do* eat gives them the nutrients they need. That means premium-quality dog food and only occasional treats. You can find the details on Yorkie cuisine in Chapter 9.

Exercise and playtime

Yorkies are very inquisitive, active dogs. They need an outlet for all that bundled up energy and curiosity. Fortunately, because of their size, making sure your Yorkie stays active doesn't require much effort or anything fancy on your part. Letting your Yorkie run back and forth from one end of your apartment while chasing a rolling tennis ball or taking a brisk walk once a day usually satisfies that need. Having toys she can push around and play with also helps harness her energy, and a toy that keeps her guessing is all the better. To find activities and games that your Yorkie will love, go to Chapter 9.

Training

Training your Yorkie is important for three reasons: First, it makes for a happier dog. Second, your dog is safer when trained. And third, training makes your dog pleasant to be around:

- ✔ **A trained dog is a happy dog:** Odds are that no dog has ever actually said the words, "Thanks *so* much for that lesson. My life has improved immeasurably since I stopped peeing behind the living-room wingback." So how can people say that a well-trained dog is a happier dog?

  Because a well-trained dog has a more predictable life and his interaction with his humans is more pleasant. No dog likes getting in trouble. And most dogs turn into neurotic messes if they can't figure out why or predict when their usually calm humans will turn an ugly shade of crimson and start shouting "Bad dog! Bad dog! Shame! Shame! Shame!" for no apparent reason.

- ✔ **Safety first!** Training is important for safety reasons. True, a Yorkie isn't big enough to pose much of a threat to the safety and well-being of you or other folks (although I still sport a very faint scar on my lip from trying to kiss my mother's Chihuahua). I'm talking about *the dog's* safety. Coming when called. Stopping on command. Not reacting aggressively to other dogs. These skills can keep your dog safe.

- ✔ **Good citizenship points:** Training isn't about tricks; it's about teaching acceptable responses and behaviors. A well-trained dog makes *your* life easier. You don't want any dog — even a small one — getting overly protective of his food dish, being overly protective of you, snapping at strangers, growling and barking at people you pass on the street, picking fights with other neighborhood dogs, or staying out late and spray-painting graffiti on highway overpasses. Training makes your dog a good citizen.

Head to Part IV to read about training techniques that work well with Yorkies. You'll find instructions on the most important commands.

Medical care

Medical care falls into two categories: the care you give to prevent illness and the care you give when your little gal falls ill:

- ✔ **To prevent illness:** Make sure your puppy gets her shots and makes annual trips to the vet for checkups and necessary follow-up immunizations. Chapter 11 tells you what to expect at well-dog visits and explains the immunization schedule.

- ✔ **To help your dog when she's sick:** Be aware of which symptoms warrant vet attention. Frankly, because Yorkies are small and, as a result, can dehydrate easily and don't have much wiggle room in terms of how much weight they can safely lose, most symptoms of illness warrant a trip to the vet. In addition, Yorkie pups are especially prone to low blood sugar. You can find details and care instructions in Chapter 12.

Yorkies are, as a whole, very healthy little dogs. But like all breeds, they're predisposed to certain conditions and illnesses. For Yorkies, the most common conditions include *porto-systemic shunt* (a condition in which some or all of the dog's blood bypasses the liver and doesn't get cleaned as it should), *Legg-Perthes* (the degeneration of the head of the *femur,* the upper bone on a dog's hind legs, that fits into the pelvis), *luxating patellae* (dislocated kneecaps), *persistent open fontanelle* (an opening in the top of the skull, like a baby's soft spot), and a collapsing trachea (or windpipe). Before you panic, consider these things:

- ✔ Just because Yorkies are predisposed to these conditions doesn't mean that most Yorkies have or develop them.

- ✔ All these conditions have symptoms that you can recognize fairly easily, which can lead to early diagnosis. And, most conditions are treatable. Even the worst of them (the liver shunt) isn't necessarily fatal.

- ✔ You can reduce your risk of adopting a dog with inherited medical conditions by working with reputable breeders who know about any genetically inherited conditions in their bloodlines and work to eliminate these conditions from the puppies they breed. To find out what to look for in a breeder, head to Chapter 3.

For more information on Yorkie medical conditions, including what symptoms are associated with them and what treatment options are available, go to Chapter 12.

Grooming

Whether you keep your Yorkie's coat long or short, your Yorkie needs regular grooming. Grooming consists of brushing his coat, cleaning his teeth, emptying his anal glands, bathing him, checking his ears, clipping his nails, and trimming the hair around his rectum and around the pads of his feet. This laundry list of tasks may sound like a lot of work, and if you've been gazing at long-haired, beribboned Yorkies, you may think, "You've got to be kidding."

The truth, however, is that grooming a Yorkie is actually pretty easy and not necessarily time-consuming; in fact, you can do the daily tasks — brushing and teeth cleaning — in about five minutes. Obviously, the longer the coat, the more time you'll spend grooming. If you're looking to produce the long, silky, show-quality coat, be prepared to spend quite a bit more time and effort primping your pup. For grooming instructions and a suggested grooming schedule, read Chapter 10.

Grooming isn't just a beauty issue, it's a health issue, too. Keeping your dog clean and well-groomed can help you avoid some problems (like ingrown nails and gum infections) altogether and alert you to other problems (like parasites and skin conditions) before they become a major health issue.

Good Doggy! Why Yorkies Are Great Pets

Yorkies are such popular dogs and make such good pets for several reasons. Here are a few:

- ✔ **They're small:** Their size makes them easy to carry around, walk on a leash, or hold in your lap.

  Yorkies, like many other Toy breeds, make good pets for people (especially senior citizens, people with medical issues, and those who haven't enjoyed much success in training their dogs) who may worry about the size and strength of a larger dog.

- ✔ **They adapt happily to apartment living:** Just about any size living space is big enough for Yorkies, and you can potty train them to go indoors or outdoors (see Chapter 14).

- ✔ **They're easier to travel with than larger dogs:** Yorkies usually fit within the weight restrictions placed on canine guests by many hotels that allow pets. An added bonus: Yorkies are usually less expensive to board than larger dogs.

- ✔ **They require less food than larger dogs:** A half to three-quarters cup of kibble a day is usually enough to keep your Yorkie well fed.

- ✔ **They're loving, devoted, and very affectionate:** Because Yorkies have these qualities, they make great personal companions and good family pets. They love interaction with their humans (see Figure 1-2).

- ✔ **Because of the type of coat they have (no undercoat), they don't shed as much as many other breeds:** So, Yorkies can be a good choice for people with allergies.

If you suffer from allergies or if you're allergic to dogs in particular, don't automatically assume that you won't be allergic to Yorkies. Find out before you adopt one whether your allergy's going to be a problem. If a friend has a Yorkie, for example, ask to spend some time with her dog. In the event that the allergy appears later, have a backup plan: Who will adopt your dog if you can no longer care for it? A friend? Your parents? The breeder? (Many reputable breeders allow you to return the dog if you're no longer able to keep it, but be sure to ask about this possibility.) Abandoning your dog isn't an option.

✔ **In general, small dogs live longer than large dogs:** Yorkies, as a rule, have an average life span of 12 to 14 years.

©Isabelle Francais

Figure 1-2: Yorkies, whether puppies or adults, are eminently lovable and cuddle-able dogs.

If I'd Only Known: Why a Yorkie May Not Be for You

As wonderful as Yorkies are, they're not the dog for everyone. You may want to consider another breed for the following reasons. If you're still determined that a Yorkie is the dog for you, at the very least, keep these points in mind so that you can avoid potential problems:

✔ **You have small children.** Take a small dog who's always underfoot and a child who's just learning to walk, and you can see why very young children and Yorkies aren't necessarily a good mix. Kids who haven't yet learned to be gentle with animals or who like rough-housing with the family pet are also problematic. Yorkies love chasing games (head to Chapter 9 for a list of some games that you can play with your Yorkie), but rough-and-tumble play is out.

✔ **You have larger dogs.** Yorkies think they're bigger than they are and, as terriers, they're territorial and not particularly tolerant of other animals. For these reasons, a Yorkie will very likely challenge your larger dog at some point, oblivious to the size disadvantage.

✔ **You travel a lot and can't take your dog with you.** Yorkies need the companionship of their families. They don't handle being kept in a kennel for boarding very well.

✔ **Potty training takes a little longer.** The myth that Yorkies can't be housetrained isn't true. But they won't learn in a week, and they can't learn if you take a slapdash approach. Consistency, patience, and a lot of positive reinforcement are key to potty training your Yorkie. See Chapter 14 for housetraining info.

✔ **You want a guard dog.** You can count on your Yorkie to inform you of an intruder's presence, and the yipping alone could drive the would-be thief away, but let's face it, a 7-pound dog with a red bow on its brow ain't going to fight off a burglar.

✔ **You don't have time (or the desire) to groom.** You can cut down on the upkeep by keeping your dog's hair short. You can even do without the bows altogether. But the Yorkie's coat is a lot like human hair, and you need to brush it daily (see Figure 1-3). Brushing your Yorkie's hair doesn't take long, and the process isn't hard (in fact, if you like brushing hair, you and your dog may even find grooming time relaxing). But if the only "grooming" task you're up for is scratching your dog behind the ears, then a Yorkie isn't for you.

©Isabelle Francais

Figure 1-3: Whether long- or short-haired, you need to brush Yorkie coats daily.

Quick Questions to Help You Decide

The best thing you can do for yourself and any dog that you welcome into your home is to determine whether your needs and the dog's needs are compatible. If they are, then you have a good match. The following sections offer points for you to think about to determine whether you're ready to adopt a Yorkie.

Can I make a lifetime commitment?

Yorkies live for a long time. Adopt a puppy, and you're talking a commitment of possibly 15 years or more. Adopt an older dog, and the number of years may be fewer but the responsibility is the same. If your older Yorkie has been abused or abandoned, a firm commitment is even that much more important because these dogs may present challenges — medical, emotional, and so on — that will test your resolve. Test your commitment by thinking about these issues:

- ✔ **Is this decision an impulsive or thoughtful one?** You know you're acting more on impulse if you hadn't given a moment's thought to getting a dog but then saw one that just stole your heart and now you're absolutely certain that you have to have that dog *right now.* If this describes you, slow down. A hasty decision is one you're more likely to regret, and then both you and your dog will suffer.

- ✔ **Have you really thought about how a dog will change your life?** Having a Yorkie is a lot like having a small child. Your dog needs to be fed, brushed, pottied, played with, exercised, protected, trained, and socialized — *every single day.* And that list doesn't include necessary chores like medical checkups, trips to the groomer for trimming, and so on. If you're a traveler and don't expect to take your dog along, you need to arrange and pay for care during your absences, too.

- ✔ **Are you willing to do what's best for your dog, even when what's best is an inconvenience, an expense, or a heart break for you?** Although much about owning a dog is one big warm-fuzzy, you'll have times when you have to do things you don't want to do, pay for things with money you earmarked for something else, or make a decision that breaks your heart. That's the tradeoff of pet ownership: companionship and unconditional love in exchange for the burden of being ultimately responsible for another living being. Before you adopt a Yorkie, make sure you can accept the conditions of that deal.

Why do I want a Yorkie?

Make sure your reasons for getting a Yorkie are good, solid ones and not passing fancies. Consider the questions that follow.

What do you like about Yorkies?

If you want a Yorkie because your neighbor has one who is well-behaved and calm, fine. Just remember that these traits aren't breed-specific. What you're attracted to is a dog who's been trained and socialized. Adopting a Yorkie yourself and then doing nothing to train or socialize that dog isn't going to get you the dog you want. So first make sure you like the characteristics of the breed (see the earlier section "Yorkies in a Coconut Shell" for a brief description and Chapter 2 for more detail); then make training and socializing a priority.

Who are you buying the dog for?

Many people buy animals to give as gifts. Usually, such a gift is a really bad idea, especially when it comes as a surprise. Unless you absolutely, positively, *without question* know that the recipient wants and can care for the pet, give a scarf instead. Also remember that, as the person who did the selecting and buying, *you're* the one who's ultimately responsible for the pet.

This responsibility is especially true if you're a parent buying a pet for your child. Sure, your 8-year-old may cross her heart and hope to die if she doesn't feed, pick up after, and walk the dog religiously, but when she loses interest in the dirty work — and she probably will — those jobs fall to you. So before you get a puppy or any other pet for your animal-loving offspring, make sure that you want that pet, too, and are as committed to her as you would be if you'd bought her for yourself.

Are you replacing a beloved pet?

Many people adopt animals to replace ones they've lost. Who can blame them? Beloved animals leave holes in your heart and your life when they go. Wanting to fill that hole with another animal is a natural response. But think about these things before you adopt another animal to take the place of the one that you miss:

✔ **The animal you lost had a personality all his own and a relationship with you that was unique.** No other animal — even one of the same breed or from the same dam and sire — can give you back what you lost. Put off adopting another animal until you can love and appreciate the new animal's unique personality and can accept that the new relationship will be different from the old one. Not better or worse. Just different.

✔ **If your loss is the result of having to relinquish your other animal for behavioral issues, be sure that you fully understand what went wrong and know what you need to do differently.** Although the dog usually gets the blame ("She disturbed the neighbors with her barking," "She was uncontrollable," "She snapped at neighborhood children," and so on), the problem usually isn't the dog at all, but the owner who didn't properly train or socialize her. If you adopt another dog without understanding the cause of the original problems, you're just asking for trouble to repeat itself.

Is my home a good one for a small dog?

Yorkies do well in homes with or without children, with or without other pets, with or without a yard, and in the city or in the country. What you need to ask yourself is, does my home have things that would present a danger to a small dog or that would make introducing a small dog so problematic neither the dog nor I would be happy? Ponder these issues:

- ✔ **How easily or well would a Yorkie fit into your life:** If you're gone a lot or your idea of a good pet is one who's out of sight and mind, a Yorkie may not be the best choice. Because they're bred to be companions, they need regular interaction with their families to thrive. Adopting a highly social dog and then relegating him to isolation is just plain cruel.

- ✔ **The personality and size of your other dog(s), if you have one:** Put any two dogs together, and they eventually work out who the *alpha dog* — the leader — is. In the dog world, there's no such thing as a secret ballot. Instead, dogs openly jockey for position. One issues a challenge (being the first one to the food bowl, for example), and the other responds by either asserting dominance or submitting. Sounds civilized enough, but if you've ever watched dogs feint and parry like this, you know that, when two dogs assert their dominance simultaneously, the growls can quickly escalate to fighting. Pair a 6-pound feisty-and-fighting Yorkie against a 60-pound calm-and-usually-easygoing Collie, for example, and the Yorkie still comes out on the bottom — literally. Even when your big and little dogs get along, play can get rough, and the Yorkie can get hurt.

  If you have a larger dog, your Yorkie isn't automatically destined to get hurt. But you need to be especially vigilant and conscious of the hot spots — events and areas that can lead to aggressive behavior by either dog. After your dogs establish the pecking order between them, you have to accept it, whether you like it or not, if you want to offset future problems. Go to Chapter 13 for more information.

- ✔ **Your house is in turmoil all the time:** Dogs take on the personalities of the homes in which they live. Put even the calmest dog in a wild house, and she ends up either hyper and wild or cowering in the corner writing suicide notes. If you don't mind wild (or suicidal), I guess this situation isn't a problem. But if you want a calm dog (and frankly, who doesn't?), you need to take extra care in controlling the interactions your dog has with the other wild creatures (probably children) living in your home. Head to Chapter 13 for ideas on controlling the chaos.

Am I willing to groom or pay to have it done?

All dogs need some grooming. How much (in both time, effort, and money) depends on the breed and the coat style. Yorkies are easier to groom in some respects (they don't have an undercoat that needs to be thinned, for example) and more difficult in other respects (their coat, like human hair, is susceptible to matting if it's not bathed and brushed regularly). Even if you cut down on the amount of grooming by keeping your Yorkie's coat short (called a *puppy cut*), you still need to perform grooming tasks regularly.

If you really don't want to spend any time grooming your dog, you need to be willing to pay a professional to do the bigger tasks (trimming the coat, for example) for you. Don't want to spend the money for a pro? Then consider a short-haired breed.

Do I have enough money to afford a dog?

When you think about the cost of a dog, you may think in terms of the literal cost of the dog — that is, how much you pay the breeder or pet store when you buy it. You need to think more broadly. A dog costs money throughout his life. Before you make your decision to buy a dog, be sure to consider *all* the expenses:

- ✔ **The cost of the dog:** Expect to pay from a few bucks to several hundred dollars for a Yorkie puppy — more, if you're buying a show-quality dog. Flip to Chapter 3 for more information on what you can expect to pay for a Yorkie.

- ✔ **Supplies the dog needs:** Necessary supplies include grooming materials, food and water dishes, traveling crates, dog beds, dog toys, and so on. Go to Chapter 5 for all the stuff you need for your Yorkie.

- ✔ **Food and treats:** You don't need a lot of food and treats, to be sure, but you need to figure them into your budget as a regular expense.

- ✔ **Regular vet checkups, tests, and preventive medication:** Annual vet bills average between $80 and $120 dollars for routine checkups and annual tests. Add to that the expense of having the vet clean your Yorkie's teeth every year or two, which is one of the biggest expenses associated with owning a Toy breed. Expect to pay more if your little gal has health problems that require additional tests or meds.

✔ **Any emergency care:** You never know when your Yorkie may require X-rays, tests, and treatment.

✔ **Other potential expenses:** These expenses include things like

- **Grooming fees:** Bathing, brushing, and trimming can cost anywhere from $20 to $60, depending on the condition of the coat, the salon, and the services you ask for.

- **Boarding costs:** If you travel and keep your dog at the kennel, don't forget to factor in how much a suite at the doggy hotel costs.

- **Travel expenses:** If you take your dog with you, remember that many hotels charge a higher nightly rate for guests with dogs.

- **Higher rent:** Many apartments increase the rent for residents with animals.

Obviously, the initial expenses (the cost of the dog itself, the puppy shots and initial vet visits, and the supplies you need) are usually the highest. Unless your dog has a medical condition that requires special care, you can fairly easily incorporate the other expenses into your budget. If you're strapped already, however, and have to struggle to get together the money for the dog himself, now may not be the time to get a dog.

A Final Word on Initial Thoughts

If you've thought about the issues you need to think about, are sure that your home will be a good one for a little dog and that you'll be a good parent, and are aware of and comfortable with any challenges that having a Yorkie in your life might present, then go for it.

After you make your decision to adopt a Yorkie, you have other important decisions to make, like what kind of Yorkie (young/old, male/female, and show/pet, for example) you want and where you'll find it. You also need to know important things like what clues to look for to determine the health and personality of the puppies you're choosing from. The remaining chapters in this part tell you what you need to know to find the dog of your dreams.

Chapter 2

Good Things Come in Small, Furry Packages

*A*hh. The mystery of canines, a species that has survived from time immemorial and that has witnessed the evolution of Man. Hard-wired with ancient, instinctive impulses and conditioned through the millennia to use those instincts in the service and companionship of humankind, who knows what secrets their souls hide or what lore they would share if they could but speak? "Hi, my name is Petunia, and I just L-O-V-E my snuggle blanket and sitting on the heat register in the winter"? Maybe, maybe not.

Faced with the inscrutability of the canine mind, you may very well wonder, "Can I *truly* know my Yorkie?" Obviously, you must answer that question for yourself. But you can know *about* Yorkies. As you may have guessed, that's the topic of this chapter.

The Breed Standard

Yorkshire Terriers haven't been around forever. In fact, they haven't been around long at all — about only 140 years. Of course, a full-fledged, mop-haired Yorkie wasn't the surprising love-child of an illicit union between two nondescript dogs who happened to make googly eyes at one another across a garbage heap 140 years ago. No, the Yorkshire Terrier, like all dog breeds, was created by humans.

Suffice it to say that two nondescript humans did *not* make googly eyes at one another 140 years ago, with the result being the coincidental (and miraculous) production of a Yorkie. Humans *deliberately* created this particular little terrier through selectively breeding certain dogs (hop to the section "The Illustrious History of the Mighty Yorkie" to get the lowdown on the breed's background). Selective breeding is what makes a breed a breed, which is simply, to quote the American Kennel Club (AKC) definition, a "relatively homogeneous group of animals within a species, developed and maintained by man."

In the AKC definition, the key words are "relatively homogeneous." That means that dogs of a particular breed share certain qualities and characteristics relating to size, coat, color, disposition, and so on. Put all the ideal characteristics that a breed should possess into one document, and you have the *breed standard.* The breed standard outlines the characteristics that reputable breeders aim to reproduce and that judges at dog shows look for.

The following sections explain the breed standard recognized by the AKC. These standards may be slightly different for other kennel clubs.

Kennel clubs that recognize the Yorkshire Terrier breed

The AKC recognizes the Yorkshire Terrier as a breed, as do the following organizations:

- ✔ National Kennel Club (also American)

- ✔ National Canine Association (American, again)

- ✔ Canadian Kennel Club

- ✔ Kennel Club (United Kingdom)

- ✔ Finnish Kennel Club

- ✔ Japan Kennel Club

- ✔ Australian National Kennel Club

- ✔ Federacion Canofila Mexicana

Well, you get the picture. One breed club the Yorkie isn't listed in is the American Rare Breed Club, for obvious reasons: Yorkies aren't rare dogs, despite the fact that yours may be one in a million.

The AKC is *not* the organization that comes up with the breed standards. Each breed's national breed club creates the official standard and any amendments to it. So the Yorkshire Terrier Club of America (YTCA) developed and maintains the breed standard for the Yorkshire Terrier.

General appearance

To recognize a Yorkie as a Yorkie doesn't (or shouldn't) require an up-close and personal examination. Yorkies have a certain look. According to the AKC, the general appearance of the ideal Yorkie includes the following traits:

- ✔ **A long, blue and tan coat that hangs straight and parts down the middle:** Much of the breed standard relates to the condition, quality, and presentation of the coat. You can read more about requirements of the ideal Yorkie coat in the later sections appropriately titled "Coat" and "Colors."

- ✔ **Compact and well-proportioned stature:** Size and body structure matter. The breed standard stipulates that Yorkies must not be over 7 pounds and, on average, adult Yorkies fall between a petite 5–7 pounds. (Remember, however, that some Yorkies are smaller and some are larger.) In terms of body structure, everything should be in proportion and just, well, fit. No points for disproportionately large or small body parts here.

 Want to know about how much your Yorkie pup will weigh when he's full grown? Take his weight at three months and double it. If your 3-month-old Yorkie weighs 3 pounds, he'll weigh close to 6 pounds as an adult. A 4-pound 3-month-old will weigh approximately 8 pounds, and a 14-pound 3-month-old probably ain't a Yorkie at all.

- ✔ **Self-assured manner and carriage:** As terriers, Yorkies have a lot of spunk, confidence, and intelligence — traits that are no more evident than when they move across a room in sassy little steps with their heads held high. You often see this demeanor in dog shows (see Figure 2-1).

 Few, if any Yorkies, actually meet all the standards of the breed. And a 14-pound Yorkie with a silver coat and a floppy ear is as wonderful a companion as the pint-sized prizewinner with the erect ears and dark steel blue silky coat.

©Isabelle Francais

Figure 2-1: The self-assurance (some would say self-importance) of the breed is evident in this dog's demeanor.

Part specifics

After the general description of the breed (explained in the preceding section), the breed standard outlines what the specific body parts should look like. You can find additional detail in the following sections, but for a quick look at the highlights, see Figure 2-2.

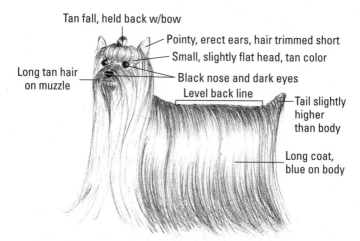

Tan fall, held back w/bow

Pointy, erect ears, hair trimmed short

Small, slightly flat head, tan color

Long tan hair on muzzle

Black nose and dark eyes

Level back line

Tail slightly higher than body

Long coat, blue on body

Figure 2-2: Highlights of the Yorkshire Terrier breed standard.

If you plan to show your Yorkie, get a hold of the actual breed standards from the AKC (or the kennel club that sponsors the show you're competing in). You can access the AKC standard from the AKC Web site at www.akc.org.

Head

The Yorkie's head is small and slightly flat on top. The skull isn't too round, and the muzzle isn't too long. The teeth should be good, and the dog shouldn't have an underbite or a pronounced overbite. The nose is black, the eyes are dark, sparkly, and intelligent, and the ears are small, *v*-shaped, pointed, and erect.

Body

The body should be well proportioned and very compact, with a relatively short, level back (that is, a back that doesn't slope too much from the shoulders to the rump, or one that doesn't look humped back).

Legs, feet, and tail

The front legs *(forelegs)* are straight; the hind legs are straight when seen from behind, but the *stifles* (the upper thighs) of the hind legs are slightly bent when seen from the side. Yorkies' feet are round and have black toenails (Yorkie Goth).

The tail is *docked* (cropped short) and carried slightly higher than the level of the back. (In the U.K., Yorkie tails don't have to be docked.)

Coat

To meet the breed standard, you should keep your Yorkie's hair long (see Figure 2-3). Of course, if you don't plan to show your dog and don't want the hassle of grooming even a moderately long coat, you can keep your Yorkie in a *puppy cut* (a short coat style that many people prefer for convenience). Remember, though, that the long hair is a hallmark of the breed's appearance.

Like human hair, Yorkie hair just keeps growing. In fact, a Yorkie's coat can grow long enough to drag on the ground, if you keep it protected in show wraps (scoot to Chapter 10 for info on wrapping your dog's hair). If you don't wrap your Yorkie's hair, it will break off on the carpet and stay at a length about even with the ground.

Texture is also important. Yorkies' coats should be silky and hang straight down each side of their bodies. The straighter the hair hangs, the better. So no Shirley Temple curls, dreadlocks, or sophisticated upsweeps for this breed.

©Isabelle Francais

Figure 2-3: This show-quality coat is pleasing to the eye, soft to the touch — and time-consuming to maintain.

In addition, Yorkies have one long, straight part that extends the length of their bodies, starting at the base of their skulls and going all the way back to the tips of their ever-wagging tails. Have you ever tried getting a straight part on a pencil-thin wagging tail? Fortunately, when you keep the coat long, the part usually falls into place.

Odd colors aren't A-Okay

Some Yorkies are born all gold, blue, red (or chocolate), or parti-colored (a combination of several different colors all mixed together). The AKC doesn't recognize any of these colors, and responsible breeders don't promote them because they may indicate a genetic problem that could affect the health and well-being of the dog. Some health problems associated with these colors include serious skin conditions, allergies, baldness, and sometimes, prolonged illness.

If you're adopting an off-colored Yorkie, expect to pay less (or nothing at all) and be sure that the puppy has undergone careful health screenings. Also expect the breeder to insist on a spay-neuter clause in the contract so that the dog can't breed.

The breed standard for Yorkies also gives the following styling tips:

- ✔ Keep the coat trimmed to floor length.

- ✔ Tie back the *fall* (the hair just above the eyes) with one bow in the center, or part the hair and tie it back in two bows.

- ✔ Keep the muzzle hair long, but trim the hair around the tips of the ears; go to Chapter 10 for ear-trimming info.

Colors

Although Yorkie pups are born black and tan, their color changes as they mature. The ideal coat color for adult Yorkies is blue (actually a deep, steel gray; no silver, black, or bronze mixed in) and tan. The AKC also recognizes black instead of blue and gold instead of tan. Bottom line? Your Yorkie can be any of these color combinations: blue and gold, blue and tan, black and gold, and black and tan.

Not only are these colors the *only* accepted colors, but they must also appear in the accepted places:

- ✔ **On the body:** Blue or black from the back of the neck to the tip of the tail.

- ✔ **On the head:** Golden tan or gold on the fall, with a richer tan/gold on the ears and muzzle.

- ✔ **On the chest and legs:** Tan or gold on the chest. On the legs, the tan/gold should go no higher than the elbow on the front legs and the stifle on the hind legs.

A word of caution about "Teacup" Yorkies

Yorkies are already small dogs — one of the smallest breeds around. And at 7 pounds, a Yorkie weighs little more than a bag of flour. Some unscrupulous and unethical breeders, however, deliberately try to produce even smaller Yorkies that weigh in the 2- to 3-pound range. Unfortunately, these breeders have had some success. They call these little dogs "Teacup" Yorkies, leading unwitting buyers to believe that Teacups are an actual variety of the Yorkshire Terrier breed. They're not.

What's wrong with having an even smaller Yorkie? Not a thing — if the Yorkie is the product of sound and ethical breeding practices. Periodically, and for no apparent reason at all, very small dogs (*runts* is what they would have been called in years gone by) are born, and they steal your heart because they're so in need of love and care. But be wary of any breeder who advertises or supposedly "specializes" in Teacup Yorkies. Here's why:

- ✔ **There's no such thing as a Teacup Yorkie.** A Teacup Yorkie isn't an officially recognized AKC variety. Anyone who tells you (or implies) otherwise either doesn't know what she's talking about or is lying — neither of which is a quality that recommends this person as someone you can trust.

- ✔ **A Yorkie who weighs 3 pounds or less often requires special care.** Extra-small Yorkies are more prone to serious health problems and birth defects (like porto-systemic shunt or small kidneys — which you won't know about until much later). These Yorkies are more likely to have problems with anesthesia and often require special (and usually expensive) medical tests before doctors can perform procedures. Go to Chapter 12 for info on health problems common to Yorkies.

- ✔ **Although extra-small Yorkies are occasionally born, no responsible breeder breeds for this trait.** Most breeders believe that average Yorkie weight (between 4–7 pounds) maintains the optimum health of the dog and the breed. In fact, many breeders only breed females who weigh at least 5 pounds.

- ✔ **Small size does *not* make these dogs more valuable.** A small Yorkie shouldn't cost more than a healthy, normal-sized one. In fact, if reputable breeders have a very small dog in a litter, they often charge less for the dog and release him only on the condition that you have the dog neutered or spayed.

The first thing you think about when you adopt a Yorkie should be the dog's health and well-being, and it should be the first criteria you use to judge the people who sell you your dog. For information on finding a responsible breeder, head to Chapter 3. To find out what to look for in a healthy puppy, head to Chapter 4.

Personality Plus!

For such little dogs, Yorkies have a lot of personality, possessing many, if not all, of the traits described in the following sections.

Every dog is unique and has her own personality. Although Yorkies as a group are energetic and love to keep busy, for example, that doesn't mean you can't find some couch potatoes among the lot. The following characteristics describe Yorkies in general; they don't describe all Yorkies or your Yorkie in particular.

Intelligent

Yorkies are smart. Ask one for the square root of any non-negative prime number, and he'll look at you with his keen, dark eyes and think, "Is she talking about treats?" Okay, so they're not so smart in math. But they're smart in the things that matter to dogs. They're alert, curious, and quick to figure out how to get what they want — which, when you're a dog, is really all the intelligence you need. Because of their natural smarts and their devotion to their owners, Yorkies are also eminently trainable — as long as they want to learn what you want to teach. In fact, Yorkies are definitely smart enough to train humans.

Independent

Nearly all terriers, Yorkshire Terriers among them, have an independent streak — a tendency that makes them inclined to listen to their own voices rather than to their humans'. If you express confusion about what needs to be done, waffle on your expectations about appropriate canine behavior, or don't follow through consistently when you train your dog, your Yorkie's going to make up and follow his own rules.

Spunky

Yorkies are spirited little dogs who want to know what's going on. They run after any little critter that crosses their path (a natural reaction from an animal originally bred to chase and kill vermin), and they don't shrink from a challenge — even when you wish they would.

As they pursue objects of interest, Yorkies can be oblivious to dangers that are apparent to you. So you need to teach your dog to obey certain fundamental commands and to come when she's called. Head to Chapters 13 and 15 for commands that will keep your Yorkie safe.

Courageous (in a cautious sort of way)

Call it gumption, boldness, nerve, or derring-do, Yorkies have this personality trait in abundant supply. They seem unfazed by things you'd think would scare the bows right off them. Take large dogs, for example; Yorkies are oblivious to the size difference. In fact, because of Yorkies' territorial instincts (an instinct shared by all terriers), they don't hesitate to challenge dogs and other animals that invade their space, and they don't shrink from a fight. For this reason, be especially vigilant when you introduce new pets to your household or when your Yorkie is around strange animals (at the park, for example).

Yet, for all their bravery and spunk, Yorkies are naturally cautious around strange people and unusual sights and sounds. You can get your Yorkie to overcome this natural wariness by properly socializing him. To find out how, head to Chapter 13.

If you don't socialize your Yorkie or if you reinforce her fears (for example, by trying to soothe her when she's upset), you may end up with a dog who snaps and bites.

Affectionate and devoted to their owners

The Yorkshire Terrier is one of the most loving breeds. Yorkies thrive on interaction with and affection from their humans, and they'll tolerate just about any humiliation to make the people they love happy. How else do you explain the bow?

More than many other breeds, Yorkies need human companionship. They don't like being alone for long periods of time, and they express their dissatisfaction through destructive chewing and constant barking. If you work all day and can't come home and spend quality time with your dog, a Yorkie probably isn't the dog for you.

Determined (some would say stubborn)

I can't say it enough: Yorkies are *terriers*. Somewhere in your little dog's genes, beneath that silky coat and lap-cuddling exterior, is a vermin-dispensing dynamo — a trait that requires quickness (to catch the prey), agility (to follow it through small, tight spaces), and determination (to stick with the task until it's done, even when the prey fights back). This determination gives your dog remarkable focus when pursuing an object. It also means that what you want him to do needs to be more compelling than what he wants to do if he's going to obey.

Full of common sense

They may look like high-society dogs, but Yorkies come from a working-class background (they were weavers' dogs; see the section "The Illustrious History of the Mighty Yorkie" in this chapter for details), and they like their lives to be simple and straightforward. Too much pampering and you spoil the independent, vibrant nature that makes them so appealing. And don't we have enough neurotic beauty queens in this world already?

Full of joie de vivre

Although they may snap when they're surprised, mistreated, or scared, Yorkies are, on the whole, good-natured, happy dogs. You can see this quality in their step, their wagging tails, and the enthusiasm with which they greet life.

The Illustrious History of the Mighty Yorkie

Because of the Yorkies' long, gleaming coat, diminutive size, and reliance on human companionship, you may simply assume that this breed was born into high society and has never experienced labor more strenuous than nibbling delectable tidbits from the fingers of adoring ladies and gentlemen. Well, if you assumed this was their lifestyle, you're wrong.

Yorkies started out as scrappy little dogs, the companions of Scottish weavers and miners. Their job? Exterminating vermin. Yorkies were *ratters,* that is, dogs bred to chase and kill rats. And a large part of their character is still shaped by this instinct today.

If you're having a hard time envisioning your little cuddle-muffin killing anything other than the butterflies he just happens to catch in the yard, consider this vignette, which puts a rather poetic spin on the Yorkie's terrier instincts: According to some tales, Yorkies were bred to chase rats away from children during the night. One Yorkie would stay at the foot of the children's bed, another at the head, and they would protect the children as they slept.

Want to know more about the Yorkie's past? Read on.

The first Yorkies

Nobody knows the exact origins of the Yorkshire Terrier. Most people suspect that these little dogs are the product of some intense co-mingling between Scottish and English terriers, an event made possible when Scots displaced by the Industrial Revolution migrated into northern England (Yorkshire) looking for work in the English mines and textile mills. These folks brought their small terriers with them. No small amount of confusion surrounds exactly which dogs the Scots had in tow: the Waterside Terrier (a small, blue-gray dog with fairly long hair), the Skye Terrier (one of the oldest terrier breeds hailing from Scotland), the Clydesdale Terrier (a Scottish terrier with a long, soft coat that tipped the scale at about 18 pounds), the Paisley Terrier (a dog with a blue coat), or the Polka-Dotted Swiss Terrier (just kidding).

Regardless of which type of terrier it was (perhaps a combination of the four), the "Scotch dog," as it was called, was probably bred with any or all of the following dogs in England:

- ✔ **Manchester Terrier:** A sleek, short-haired, small- to medium-sized terrier, also known as the Black and Tan Terrier. This dog is believed to have contributed the general terrier outline (shape of the body) and personality.

- ✔ **Maltese:** A small, white dog with a long, soft coat. The Yorkie's long, silky coat and face shape are attributed to the Maltese.

The Maltese isn't a terrier; it's a spaniel (and for the record, a Maltese doesn't hail from England either; it comes from Italy). But back in the middle 19th century when all this breeding was going on, the Maltese was called the Maltese Terrier, despite its lack of terrier characteristics.

- ✔ **Dandie Dinmont Terrier:** A short-legged, short-haired, mustard (reddish brown)- and pepper (bluish gray)- colored dog with a soft and abundant tuft of hair on the tippy-top of its head. What exactly this little fellow contributed to the Yorkie character is unknown, unless it was the ability to sport an unusual coiffure with aplomb.

The product of all this breeding was a 12- to 14-pound wire-haired Yorkshire Terrier intended to catch rats and ferret out small game. Then, the breeders got busy refining the breed to produce what would eventually become the Yorkie that's so beloved today.

Theories on the Yorkie's small size

The original Yorkshire Terrier was quite a bit larger than today's breed standard would allow. Nowadays, the AKC specifies that the Yorkie should weigh no more than 7 pounds, but the first Yorkies weighed in around 12 to 14 pounds. If you consider that they were working dogs, bred for hunting and killing vermin (a purpose they served for nearly half a century before they became popular in drawing rooms), the desire to reduce their size is a little puzzling. Some fanciers speculate that size became an issue because of the breed's growing popularity in high society: Well-bred ladies wanted classy little dogs. Here are other theories, based on the activities of 19th-century England:

✔ **Poachers wanted smaller dogs.** Yorkies were originally the dogs of people on the lower rungs of the social ladder, who supplemented their diets through poaching small game. These folks needed dogs to chase the game to ground, kill it, and drag it back out of the hole. A small dog can more easily chase a rabbit into its hole and dispatch it there (or flush it out of its hole and into the poacher's net) than a larger dog can.

This theory also provides an explanation for the long coat: Poachers needed something to grab onto to pull a dog out of a rabbit hole if a) the dog got stuck or b) if the constable was heading out to nab poachers, and the poachers and their dogs needed to make a quick getaway.

✔ **Larger size was a handicap in rat-baiting contests.** A popular 19th-century pastime was rat-baiting. Put several rats in cages, let terriers loose among them, and then place bets on which dog could kill its quota of rats in the shortest amount of time. How many rats a dog had to kill was based on the dog's weight. Larger dogs had to kill more rats; smaller dogs had to kill fewer.

Evolving popularity

In the beginning, Yorkies were popular with rich Yorkshire families who admired their hunting capabilities. They were also great money-makers for the poor farmers and workers who raised and sold them. In 1861, the Yorkie, then called a "Broken-Haired Scotch Terrier," appeared in its first bench show in England.

In 1870, the dog was renamed the Yorkshire Terrier in a nod to the region where people had done so much work to create and improve the breed.

Ranking the most popular breeds

Every year, the AKC ranks the popularity of breeds based on the number of registrations. Here's the 2003 list:

1. Labrador Retriever

2. Golden Retriever

3. Beagle

4. German Shepherd Dog

5. Dachshund

6. Yorkshire Terrier

7. Boxer

8. Poodle

9. Shih Tzu

10. Chihuahua

To access the complete list ranking all 150 breeds recognized by the AKC, go to www.akc.org/breeds/reg_stats.cfm.

As Americans became enamored with Victorian England, they became enamored with the Yorkshire Terrier, too. The first Yorkies were brought to the United States in the early 1870s, and they came as parlor dogs — companions to the wealthy families that were so keen on them. Their popularity slowly but steadily grew and then skyrocketed in the 1950s.

Yorkies today

Today's Yorkies are much smaller and more delicate than the original Yorkies were. No longer considered ratters, they're not expected to behave like one. They're pure companions and are immensely popular. For the last few decades, Yorkies ranked among the most popular dogs in the U.S. and the U.K. In 2003, Yorkies ranked as the sixth most popular dog in the U.S., according to the number of AKC registrations.

Chapter 3

Gonna Find Me a Yorkie: Breeders and Rescue Groups

● ●

In This Chapter

▶ Finding a good breeder

▶ Adopting a Yorkie from an animal shelter

▶ Being wary of pet stores and backyard breeders

● ●

After you decide that a Yorkshire Terrier is the puppy you want and are confident that your home is a good one for him, you may think that the next step is to look in the classifieds of your local paper for Yorkie pups for sale. Who knows? If you're lucky, you may be able to bring your little darling home by the weekend or — even better — tonight! Whoa, Nellie!

Don't let your enthusiasm and excitement run roughshod over your good sense. Sure, you want a Yorkie, but you want him to be healthy and well adjusted. You want a warm, cuddly puppy who'll grow into a friendly, loving dog. To find a dog like that, you want to limit your search to responsible breeders — folks who devote a great deal of time and energy to producing sound, healthy puppies and improving the breed. In this chapter, I tell you what you need to know about breeders — what they do, how to find a good one, and everything else. I also explain the things you need to be aware of if you're thinking of buying (or have already bought) your puppy from a pet store.

For those of you looking for an older Yorkie, one who needs a second chance at happiness, this chapter also offers information on working with and finding Yorkie rescue groups.

Distinguishing Hobby Breeders from Backyard Breeders

All puppies are born with potential, based on the traits and characteristics they inherit and the environment in which they're raised. Consideration for those factors separates the serious, dedicated breeders (also called *hobby breeders*) from the nonserious breeders (commonly referred to as *backyard breeders*). Hobby breeders make deliberate choices, based on disposition, health, and genetic history of the dogs they intend to mate; backyard breeders don't give this issue much, if any, thought. Hobby breeders also make sure to properly socialize their puppies and provide necessary medical checks and care before selling them to new homes; backyard breeders generally don't.

Ideally, you want to buy your Yorkie from a skilled and knowledgeable breeder who specializes in Yorkshire Terriers. The key words are *skilled* and *knowledgeable*. The quality of the puppies (disposition, health, conformity to breed standards, and so on) is directly related to the practices of the breeder you select.

There's no qualifying exam to become a breeder, no license necessary to run a kennel, and no inspection process in place to ensure that the animals are well cared for or that the breeder's practices are ethical. Always, always, always check out the breeder yourself, using the guidelines I provide in the following sections.

What Good Breeders Do

As the preceding section explains, anyone who has two Yorkies and matches them up to produce a litter is technically a breeder of Yorkshire Terriers, even though that person may have done nothing more than let his hyperactive Muffy spend an afternoon with the handsome yet timid Butch down the street. So the term *breeder* alone doesn't tell you squat about the breeding practices or the puppies that are produced. You have to look beyond the label to the practices.

Make sound breeding decisions

When making choices about which dogs to breed, responsible breeders consider the following:

✔ **Physical health of the dam (mom) and sire (dad):** Responsible Yorkie breeders only breed animals that are healthy and haven't been afflicted by medical conditions, such as *portosystemic shunt* (a potentially deadly liver condition), *Leggs-Perthes Disease* (a degenerative disease of the femur), *open fontanelle* (a soft spot on the skull that doesn't close), and *luxating patella* (dislocated knee caps). Although Yorkies, as a rule, aren't routinely checked for these conditions unless symptoms warrant it, some show breeders have their top dogs' hips and eyes screened for any debilitating conditions. For information about medical conditions associated with Yorkies, head to Chapter 12.

✔ **Mental health of the dam and sire:** Responsible breeders breed only dogs who have good dispositions — not nervous, shy, timid, aggressive, or hyperactive. For a description of the optimal personality traits of Yorkies, see Chapter 2.

✔ **How closely related the dogs are:** Dogs who are more closely related have a greater chance of passing on inherited diseases. (See the sidebar "Uncle Dad: Why breeding closely related dogs is bad" later in this chapter if you're interested in why this is the case, besides the fact that parent-child, brother-sister matings just tend to freak us humans out; dogs, for their part, seem oblivious to it.)

✔ **The age and well-being of the dam:** As a rule, female dogs become fertile between 6 to 9 months old, and they come in season (become fertile) twice a year after that. Many reputable breeders don't begin breeding their females until they're 2 years old, and they certainly don't breed their females every cycle; many a reputable breeder has only one litter a year from a single female (see Figure 3-1).

What are the benefits of waiting to breed female dogs?

- The dog is still considered a puppy throughout the first year. Breeding a dog who's both physically and emotionally immature doesn't bode well for anyone.

- Waiting until the dog is mature gives the breeder the chance to truly evaluate the dog as a specimen of the breed, both in terms of conformation (meeting the physical characteristics of the breed) and personality.

The benefits of not breeding every cycle are obvious. If they're not, read *The Feminine Mystique*.

✔ **Breeding when they have a waiting list of buyers for the puppies:** To ensure that their puppies have good homes, many breeders wait until enough people express a serious intent to buy a puppy before they breed. For this reason, you may discover that you have a significant wait ahead of you. And, if fewer puppies are born than waiting homes are on the list, your wait is going to be that much longer, because you'll have to wait for the next litter. (In these cases, many breeders will refer you to another reputable breeder who may have puppies on the way or puppies who are waiting for a home.)

©Isabelle Francais

Figure 3-1: Reputable breeders wait until their females are mature before breeding them.

Take care of the puppies they produce

Reputable breeders take responsibility for and look after the health and well-being of every single puppy they breed. They know that how they raise and care for their little charges has a huge impact on how well adjusted and healthy the puppies are and how satisfied the prospective owner is with his or her purchase. Good breeders do the following:

✔ **Begin socializing the pups from day one.** Good breeders expose their puppies (as appropriate) to human touch and interaction, sound, other household pets, areas beyond their kennels, and so on. In fact, most reputable Yorkie breeders have their kennel areas (where they keep the dam and puppies) right in their own houses, so that the pups are exposed to the sights, sounds, and attention of an average home. Some breeders even begin the very early stages of training, like introducing the word "no," putting out newspapers for the pups to go to the bathroom on, and so forth.

✔ **Give the puppies their initial shots and keep track of the dates and types of inoculations given.** You need this medical info when you take your puppy to the vet after you adopt her.

✔ **Have the puppies undergo a health check by the vet.** This exam tests for health problems like parasites, weak stifles (knee caps), or hernias. The breeder may also have the vet do blood work on your pup to look for high ammonia levels, which may indicate porto-systemic shunt (liver shunt); this test, however, isn't routine on healthy puppies produced from healthy parents.

✔ **Don't let the puppies go until they're ready.** Yorkies are usually ready at 12 weeks old. Waiting until week 12 allows the breeder time to evaluate all puppies in the litter for health and temperament, enabling him to make informed recommendations when matching puppies to prospective owners. In addition, puppies who are taken from their mothers too early can have temperament problems. Also, be aware that some states have laws forbidding the sale of puppies under the age of 6 weeks.

✔ **Set conditions for the sale of the puppy.** Good breeders' concern for their puppies extends beyond the date of purchase. And to ensure that their dogs are adequately and appropriately cared for throughout their lives, good breeders make certain requirements about the homes and people they allow to adopt. These requirements are often spelled out in the contract or bill of sale; go to the section "Provide appropriate paperwork" later in this chapter for a brief description and Chapter 6 for more detail about breeder contracts.

✔ **Sell the puppies out of their own homes.** Selling the puppies out of their homes is the only way that breeders can exert any influence over who adopts their dogs (the only criteria pet stores can use is a customer's ability to pay). And let me tell you, to a breeder, their puppies are always their dogs, even after two years pass and your garden is the one the dog digs through. That's how responsible breeders feel toward the puppies they produce.

Uncle Dad: Why breeding closely related dogs is bad

The dog-breeding world has terms to indicate how closely related two mated dogs are:

- ✔ **Inbreeding:** Mating two dogs who are related through one or more common ancestors. Examples of inbreeding include mating a female dog with her sire or mating a male dog with his sister.

- ✔ **Linebreeding:** Another form of inbreeding in which the dogs are more distantly related dogs, like cousin-to-cousin, uncle-to-niece, or grandparent-to-grandchild.

- ✔ **Outcrossing:** Breeding two dogs of the same breed who aren't otherwise related.

Genetic diseases are, by definition, diseases passed on through the genes. When dogs breed, each parent contributes one set of genes to his or her offspring.

Genes carrying the inherited disease can either be dominant or recessive. When the gene is dominant, the condition shows up in one form or another in each successive generation, even if only one of the parents carries the defective gene.

When the defective gene is recessive, *both* parents have to contribute the defective gene in order for the condition to emerge in their offspring. (When one parent passes on a recessive gene and the other passes on a normal gene, the offspring will be a *carrier* of the condition — just like the parent who passed on the bad gene — but won't actually have the disease.)

Here's why inbred dogs have more genetic health problems: When you inbreed dogs, you limit the gene pool, which means that the same genes just keep getting replicated from generation to generation, increasing the likelihood that two dogs with recessive, defective genes will mate and produce a puppy who isn't just a carrier, but a sufferer, of the condition.

Genetics lesson over.

Investigate prospective homes

If you find that you're answering at least as many (often more!) questions than you're asking, take it as a good sign. Responsible breeders don't let people with homes that they deem unsuitable adopt their puppies. So prepare yourself for the interrogation, er, I mean interview. Here are the types of questions you can expect a breeder to ask:

✔ **Have you ever had a Yorkie before?** They want to know what you know about the breed. Believe me, what you don't know, breeders are more than happy to tell you.

✔ **Are you familiar with the problems associated with this breed?** A good breeder explains the negative as well as the positive aspects of owning a Yorkie. The last thing breeders want is to place a puppy with someone who's unprepared or unwilling to deal with the challenges.

✔ **Do you have other pets?** Yorkies can get along fine with other pets (as I mention in Chapter 1), but the size and temperament of your current pets are important, given the Yorkie's size.

✔ **Do you have children? What are their ages?** Breeders want to know the kind of environment they're sending their puppies to. Some breeders even want to meet your children.

Believe it or not, one of the biggest dangers to a Yorkie is a small child. Until your children are old enough to be gentle and steady enough not to toddle over the family pet, your home may not be the best one for a Yorkie.

✔ **Where do you live? Do you have a fenced yard or easy access to a park?** Yorkies don't need a lot of space, but they do need room to run off their excess energy.

✔ **Do you plan to show the dog?** Breeders know what to look for when determining show- versus pet-quality dogs. Knowing what you want can help her identify whether she even has any dogs who will meet your requirements. If you want a show dog, head to Chapter 4 for things to keep in mind.

✔ **Will your dog be a house dog or an outdoor dog?** Come on. You don't really expect "outdoor dog" to be the acceptable answer here, do you? Any Yorkie breeder worth his or her salt will refuse to sell a Yorkie to someone who doesn't want the dog in the house.

✔ **What's the name and phone number of your vet?** Don't be surprised if the breeder asks for the name and contact information of your veterinarian for reference purposes. Some breeders don't let you adopt a dog until you provide this info.

If, for any reason, you can no longer take care of the dog, many reputable breeders will take the dog back (or request to help in the selection of a new home). Because returning the dog to the breeder is a trauma for all involved, breeders go to a lot of trouble to make sure that your home offers the greatest chance for success. Hence, their questions and conditions. They do it to protect their dogs and you.

Breed improver or moneymaker?

To figure out whether the breeder you're talking to is more interested in money than producing healthy, well-adjusted puppies, pay attention to these clues:

✔ He sells dogs of several different breeds.

✔ He doesn't inquire much about you, your home, your knowledge of the breed, and so on. In fact, he doesn't seem interested in much of anything except when you can pick up the dog and drop off the money.

✔ He doesn't answer your questions, or he gives you the wrong answers. See the section "Finding a Reputable Breeder" in this chapter for the questions you should ask and the answers you should get.

✔ He doesn't want you to see the kennel or puts off the visit using lame excuses.

Provide appropriate paperwork

In addition to the precautions they take when breeding and the investigations they perform for finding a pup's prospective home, reputable breeders also amass quite a store of important papers. They keep these papers on the premises, available for your viewing. When you adopt the dog, you get copies of many, if not all, of these papers (see Chapter 6 for details). These documents include

✔ Health records and medical checks for the dam and sire.

✔ Health records for the puppy, showing inoculation schedule, results of any health tests, and so on.

✔ Identification information for the puppy, including breed, gender, and color; date of birth; registered names and numbers of dog's dam and sire; name and address of the breeder.

Under American Kennel Club (AKC) rules, any person who sells a dog who he claims can be registered with the AKC must keep records of this information and give it to you when you take possession of the dog. If your breeder says this info isn't necessary or that you'll receive it later, consider not buying the dog from this breeder.

✔ **An application for registration with the AKC for the pup.** On this form, which the breeder gives you when you buy the dog, the breeder stipulates either full or limited registration. (Limited registration means that your dog's offspring aren't eligible for AKC registration.) For information on which designation is appropriate, flip to Chapter 6.

After you register your dog with the AKC, you can get his *pedigree,* which is basically the dog's family tree, listing ancestors in his line. Your breeder may have already given you the pedigrees of your dog's dam and sire. Because these are essentially your dog's pedigree — minus his name — you don't really even need to order a pedigree from the AKC to find out his family tree. If having the documents merged makes you happier (and you're too cheap to pay the relatively small AKC pedigree application fee), just Scotch tape the two pedigrees together and add your puppy to the list with a magic marker. Voila! — a document suitable for framing.

✔ **A written guarantee explaining how you'll be compensated if undetected genetic problems crop up.** Most breeders allow you to return the puppy for a full refund if you discover that the puppy is unhealthy.

✔ **A breeder contract, outlining conditions of the sale.** The breeder contract outlines the conditions of the sale, such as whether the dog should be altered — that is, neutered or spayed (all reputable breeders insist on this condition for puppies whose health checks have not come back clear)— the type of registration for the puppy, and so on.

Do things with their dog besides breed her

Most people who love their dogs are enamored with their dogs' good qualities and blind to their bad ones. Good breeders aren't. They may love their dogs to distraction, but they don't love them blindly. Breeders are intimately familiar with the good and the bad. This awareness doesn't diminish their affection for their dogs, but it does affect the decisions they make: which dogs they breed, what registration category (limited or full) they recommend for the puppies, and so on.

Participating in breed clubs

One way that breeders continue to test their perceptions and reign in the great, but unfounded, expectations that the rest of us may be prone to is to participate in breed clubs. By hooking up with other fanciers, breeders get the benefits of other's opinions and knowledge about the breed. The Yorkshire Terrier Club of America (YTCA) is the national breed club for Yorkies in the United States, but many local clubs also exist. Through membership, breeders get up-to-date information on the latest breeding practices, general dog care, and health information regarding Yorkshire Terriers.

Entering competitions

Breeders also enter their dogs in dog competitions. Even if a breeder thinks she has a champion, she won't know for sure until her dog is compared to others and wins a competition. The only way that can happen, of course, is to compete. And when a breeder enters one of her dogs in a competition, she's essentially offering up her breeding program for evaluation, too.

Finding a Reputable Breeder

Finding a breeder isn't hard at all. The trick is finding a reputable breeder. The first places you can look or inquire about breeders are (*Note:* No one warrants individual breeders, but these people can at least point you in the right direction):

- ✓ **The Yorkshire Terrier Club of America (YTCA):** You can contact this organization or go to its Web site (www.ytca.org).

- ✓ **Local dog clubs:** You can find local breed clubs by contacting the YTCA (see the preceding item) or the AKC at www.akc.org.

- ✓ **Dog shows where Yorkies are competing:** Here, you can talk to the breeders and other fanciers who are attending the show or exhibiting their dogs. For a list of upcoming shows and competitions in your area, contact your local breed club or the AKC.

- ✓ **Ask your veterinarian for a recommendation:** She may be able to direct you to good breeders or warn you away from bad ones.

- ✓ **Ask for a reference from someone you trust who's bought a Yorkie:** Friends are a great resource you can tap into.

Use the list of breeders you get as your starting point. Armed with names and contact information, you can begin your investigation.

You can also look on the Internet. To find breeders in your state, enter "Yorkshire Terrier breeder *<your state name>*". If you take this route, be sure you do your homework and thoroughly investigate the breeder you contact. Claiming to be a conscientious breeder and having a razzle-dazzle Web site don't indicate the quality of the breeder. And if you use the classifieds in the local newspaper, be aware that most of what you'll find are listings belonging to backyard breeders. For information on backyard breeders, see the section "Distinguishing Hobby Breeders from Backyard Breeders" earlier in this chapter.

Asking the right questions

When you contact a breeder, the first thing you need to do is explain your desire to adopt a Yorkie. Then, in the course of the give-and-take of conversation, be sure to ask the following questions:

✔ **Do you specialize in Yorkies?** The answer has to be yes. If it's not, find another breeder. If the answer is yes, probe a little:

- How long have you been breeding Yorkies?

- How many Yorkies do you have? And so on.

✔ **Do you specialize in any other breeds?** Some reputable breeders, who have the space and the time, breed more than one type of dog. If the breeder does breed other types of dogs, find out how many. One or two other types isn't necessarily a problem — as long as she has only one litter at a time. But if she has several other litters to care for at once, question what kind of attention and care this breeder gives to *any* of the dogs she raises.

✔ **Do you show your dogs?** Often, good breeders compete in dog shows, both for the love of the sport and the knowledge that they can gain through participating.

✔ **When you're planning a litter, do you breed for any particular traits?** Many breeders breed for conformity (how closely the dog adheres to the breed standard; refer to Chapter 2). Some breeders, however, may breed for temperament, health, or another trait that they're particularly interested in promoting or improving.

✔ **Do you have puppies available now or will you in the near future?** Don't be surprised if the breeder says he doesn't have any puppies now and won't have any for several months. Many sought-after breeders have a waiting list of people who want to buy their puppies. Your name would go at the bottom of the list. Having to wait months for your new pup isn't fun, but take it as a sign that the breeder is a good one and breeds his dogs carefully.

If a breeder knows that all his puppies are claimed or knows that he won't be breeding for several months (many only breed their dogs every other heat cycle), he's very likely to give you the names of other breeders who may have puppies available now or in the near future. Reputable breeders will refer you to other reputable breeders.

✔ **Where do you raise your puppies?** The best answer is "right in the house with us." To ice the cake, you also want to hear the breeder explain what he does to socialize the puppies. You don't want to hear that they've been raised outside of regular human contact.

Puppies need to be exposed, almost from birth, to people beyond their breeder, different sights and sounds, and different areas. Without this exposure to new things, the puppy may have a hard time adjusting to the hustle and bustle of your home.

✔ **Is spaying/neutering mandatory?** Reputable breeders often set the condition that you spay or neuter their pet-quality puppies; they also stipulate that these dogs are eligible for limited registration (for more on registration, see the section "Provide appropriate paperwork" in this chapter). These terms may sound harsh, but this practice discourages thoughtless breeding and protects the standards of the breed.

The goal of breeding should be to produce sound puppies and improve the breed. To achieve these goals, only the dogs who are closest to the breed standard (refer to Chapter 2) are bred. Other dogs can be wonderful pets, but they shouldn't be bred.

✔ **Do I need to be aware of any special health issues related to this breed?** Now, if you're reading this book, you should be aware of the relevant health issues (I explain them in Chapter 12). What you're trying to find out here is whether the breeder knows — and is willing to tell you — about these health issues. Reputable breeders spell out very clearly all issues that may be potential problems. They don't want to scare you away, but they will bluntly explain all that you may have to deal with when caring for your particular Yorkie. Breeders think that if you're still interested despite the special issues, maybe *you're* the keeper.

Follow up this question with

- **Which of these health problems have you encountered the most over the years?** If the breeder has bred several litters and says that he's never had any health problems, be skeptical.

- **Has the breeder had the dam and sire tested for these health issues?** Reputable breeders breed only healthy dogs; health checks are the only way to verify whether a dog is clear of certain ailments. The breeder should include these reports in the paperwork you receive when you pick up your dog.

✔ **What guarantees do you offer and under what circumstances are they applicable?** Breeders can't guarantee how your puppy's going to turn out, but some breeders offer guarantees for certain health and temperament issues. Go to Chapter 6 for details.

✔ **Can I visit?** The answer needs to definitely be yes. There's no good reason why you can't see the kennel. If the puppies are still young and not adequately immunized yet, a good breeder may limit your access to the puppies in order to protect their health, but arrangements can and should be made for a visit when the puppies are older.

Some breeders, in fact, insist on meeting you before placing a puppy in your home. Some insist on meeting you twice: once before the puppies are ready to leave (this visit may be when you select your puppy) and again when you pick up the puppy to take him home. And don't be surprised if you're asked to leave your shoes outside or at the door and to wash your hands before touching the puppies so that you don't spread germs to them.

✔ **Can you provide references?** The answer to this question is important for two reasons: First, good breeders are willing to give you names and phone numbers of others who've bought their dogs. Second, being able to provide these names means that they know where their dogs went. If a breeder can't give references, he either doesn't want you talking to other owners or has no idea where his dogs are.

✔ **Will you be available to answer questions in the future?** Good breeders consider the puppies they breed to be their dogs for-ever. The answer here, then, should be yes, the breeder will be available to answer any questions you have throughout your dog's life.

Visiting the kennel

Before you adopt any dog from any breeder, visit the kennel (the area where the breeder keeps the dogs). You want to see a kennel that's clean and has ample room for the dogs. You also want to see dogs who are well cared for: healthy looking, clean, and happy (see Figure 3-2).

For Yorkies, the "kennel" may simply be an area in the breeder's home. If this situation is the case, get over any concern you have that, by requesting to see the kennel, you're invading this person's privacy. You just want to see where the puppies live; you're not asking to rifle through his underwear drawer.

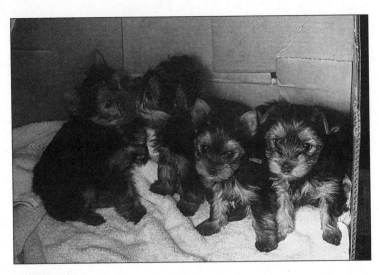

©Isabelle Francais

Figure 3-2: A clean kennel area with energetic pups is a good sign when choosing a breeder.

If the kennel isn't in the main living area (some may be in quiet areas in the nether regions of the house), specifically ask whether the puppies are allowed in the house and what the breeder does to socialize them. You may discover, for example, that the breeder confines the puppies to the kennel at certain times during the day, like mealtime, naptime, when prospective owners come to visit, and so on, but that they're out and about at other times. That kind of arrangement is fine. If you hear that the breeder never allows the puppies into the house or does little to socialize them, consider buying a dog from a different breeder.

If you experience any of the following situations, leave without a puppy:

- ✔ The breeder says that visiting isn't necessary or he won't give you full access to the kennel area.

- ✔ The kennel area is dirty and smelly.

- ✔ Diarrhea or vomit is present anywhere in the kennel area.

- ✔ The puppies are dirty, cower when you approach, or don't respond to your overtures.

Seeing the mama and the papa

When you visit the kennel, ask to see the dam and the sire. Breeders should always keep the dam on the premises. (If she isn't, go elsewhere.) You want to see her health clearances and pedigree; also pay attention to how she looks and behaves. The dam should appear clean and well cared for. In addition, she should seem relaxed with the breeder. Keep in mind that she'll probably be watchful of you; it's normal for a dam to be wary of strangers around her babies. However, she shouldn't be aggressive or fearful.

The breeder may tell you that you can't see the sire because he's not there. This answer is acceptable if the dam was fertilized through artificial insemination or if the breeder used the services of a stud. But you should still be able to see the father's health clearances and pedigree — ask for those papers instead. Alternatively, you can ask for the name and phone number of the sire's owner and arrange a visit so that you can see him for yourself.

Ads to pass by

If you're looking for puppies in the paper, you can get a clue as to the type of breeder by the ad that she writes. Avoid calling ads that include the following, which can indicate ignorance, unethical breeding practices, or someone who's in it for the money:

✔ **Champion-quality:** Only dogs who have actually performed or been shown in the show ring and won can be described as "champion-quality." For that reason, no puppy can be champion-quality.

✔ **Rare color, extra small size, or other descriptors meant to indicate that this dog is "special":** The AKC has definite, precise standards for size and color of every registered breed. Although dogs who don't meet the standards can still certainly be lovable, you're evaluating the breeder here, not the dog. Do you really want to buy a dog from someone who either doesn't know what the breed standard is or who knows and is trying to swindle you?

✔ **Advertising several breeds:** When a breeder advertises several breeds, this indicates that the breeder is more interested in money than producing healthy, sound puppies. If a breeder has puppies from several different breeds, he probably didn't make things like socialization or health checks a priority.

What you can expect to pay a breeder

When you buy a puppy from a breeder, expect to pay, on average, between $500 and $800 (although some charge more, and some charge less). In addition, show-quality Yorkies usually cost more.

You're probably going to spend the same, or close to the same, amount of money for puppies from both the hobby breeder and the backyard breeder. Because you're going to be paying for quality anyway, you need to ensure that you get it. (See Chapter 4 for information on how to select a healthy, well-adjusted puppy.) Whether your dog is show quality or pet quality, he should still be the product of thoughtful and careful breeding.

Taking In an Older Dog

If you want a Yorkie but aren't interested in adopting a puppy, you can look for an older dog. Many, unfortunately, are available. When you adopt an older dog, you're adopting an animal with a history, as well as habits and behaviors that have already been formed. Sometimes the dog is housetrained, healthy, and can do a few tricks — like whip up an omelet on a Sunday morning. Other times, you may find yourself with a dog who no one has bothered to train or, worse, has been abused.

In either case, you and your new charge have some adjusting to do. Obviously with a healthy, trained dog the adjustment period requires little more than letting the dog grow accustomed to you and her new environment. In the case of a dog who hasn't been trained or has been abused, the adjustment is much more challenging.

For the adoption of an older Yorkie to be successful, you need to know as much as you can about the dog's history and the challenges (medical, behavioral, and so on) that you may face. You also need a knowledgeable resource you can turn to for advice and guidance. That's why, if you want to adopt an older Yorkie — and you don't have a dear friend who's moving out of state and can't take her dog with her — you should hook up with a Yorkshire Terrier rescue group. Animal shelters are another option; I provide info on shelters later in this section as well.

Yorkie rescue groups

Yorkshire Terrier rescue groups are organizations made up of Yorkie owners, breeders, and others who love the breed and want to help and protect its most vulnerable dogs: those dogs who've been abandoned, abused, or displaced for whatever reason.

Finding a rescue group

If you're interested in adopting an older Yorkie, consider contacting one of the following organizations:

- ✔ **Yorkie Rescue, Inc.:** This rescue organization is associated with the YTCA and is accessible through its Web site. Go to www.ytca.org and click the "Rescue" link.

- ✔ **Yorkshire Terrier National Rescue, Inc.:** Go to www.yorkshireterrierrescue.com.

- ✔ **Yorkshire Terrier Rescue Network, Inc.:** Go to www.yorkshireterrierrescue.net.

- ✔ **United Yorkie Rescue:** Go to www.unitedyorkierescue.org.

For information about other rescue groups devoted to Yorkshire Terriers, contact your local breed club and ask for rescue groups in your area.

The services rescue groups offer

Rescue groups provide a number of services for abandoned Yorkies, such as

- ✔ **Foster care:** If a Yorkie can't stay with her current owners until a new home is found, a volunteer takes the dog into his own home and cares for her during the wait. By doing so, volunteers learn the temperament and behaviors of the dogs up for adoption.

- ✔ **Veterinary care for abandoned dogs:** Vet checkups alert the rescue volunteers to any medical problems that the dog may have. These visits also bring the dogs' vaccines and heartworm medication up-to-date. Many checkups also provide teeth-cleaning and dental care, as well as grooming.

- ✔ **Spaying and neutering:** Before the Yorkies can be adopted, they're spayed or neutered in an attempt to stop the proliferation of unwanted and homeless animals.

- ✔ **Microchipping or tattooing for identification:** Many rescue organizations have a microchip implanted in the dog or have the dog tattooed with information that identifies the owner. In cases of microchipping, the identification refers back to the rescue group (in the event that the new owners have abandoned the dog or can't be found).

Where the dogs come from

Yorkies available for adoption through rescue groups come from a number of different places:

✔ **Families that can no longer care for them:** If the situation permits, the dogs often remain in their current homes until a new home is found.

✔ **Area shelters:** When a purebred dog is left at a shelter, the shelter often calls a rescue group for help in finding a home for the animal.

✔ **Puppy mills and irresponsible breeders:** Occasionally, puppy mills are raided, and the dogs found there are released to rescue groups. Or an irresponsible breeder whose hoped-for quick turnaround didn't happen, so he abandons his puppies. These are two of the reasons that rescue groups may have puppies to place.

✔ **The mean streets:** Other dogs are just abandoned and found wandering.

However you look at it, it's a pretty sad story.

In providing all this attention and care, the rescue-group volunteers can tell you quite a bit about the dog you're adopting, including the state of his health, his temperament, and so on.

Adopting a rescued Yorkie

Although different rescue groups may have different procedures, the process for adopting a rescued dog is basically the same:

1. **You fill out an application.**

   You may have to pay a small application fee (around $5 or $10).

2. **Your application goes to a screener.**

   The screener, often called a *breed representative* in rescue groups that rescue many different breeds of dogs, has years of experience with Yorkies and knows what to look for in prospective adoptive homes. She looks at your info to see whether your home is suitable for any of the adoptable dogs. She may also call you if she has any questions or needs more information from you.

3. **If the screener finds that your home is suitable, she'll call to give you information about the dogs who would be good matches for you.**

You get all the information the rescue group has about the dogs you're being offered; info like why they were abandoned, what health issues they have, whether they're housebroken, odd behaviors or responses they have that you need to be aware of (for example, a dog who becomes fearful around loud noises), and so on.

If no dogs are available, your name goes on a waiting list.

Sometimes shelters refer abandoned Yorkies to local rescue groups. If you're matched with a shelter dog, you need to act quickly. The situation would just be one tragedy on top of another if you accept a referral for a dog in a shelter, only to discover that the dog has already been euthanized.

4. **You select a dog, pay the fee (or give the appropriate donation), and bring the dog home.**

   In addition to the application fee, rescue groups also either charge a fee or expect a donation for the placement. Usually these donations or fees fall within the $50 to $300 range — which is very reasonable if you think about the care and attention they give to *all* their rescued dogs — not just the ones who are adoptable.

5. **You live happily ever after.**

   To increase the chances of happily ever after, many rescue organizations arrange some kind of contact — letters or visits, for example — after you adopt the dog. They just want to see how everything is going and to be a resource for you if you hit any snags.

Animal shelters

When you adopt an animal from a shelter or the Humane Society, you're certainly doing a good thing: Namely, you're saving a life. If you want an older Yorkie, a shelter may be the place to go. If you choose to adopt from an animal shelter, keep these points in mind:

- **The shelter may or may not have Yorkies available for adoption.** Call the shelters in your area to find out whether a Yorkie's up for adoption.

- **You may be given limited information about the dog.** How much information shelter personnel can provide you with depends on the circumstances under which the Yorkie came to them.

✔ **The dogs receive limited medical care.** Dogs are usually treated for typical ailments, such as parasites, but because of the lack of funds, they don't receive more extensive medical care.

✔ **The shelter must approve you for adoption.** The shelter has to approve you to adopt your dog, based on your willingness to agree to the conditions set by the shelter (for example, you may be required to spay/neuter the Yorkie if the animal is currently unaltered). This approval is necessary even if a Yorkie rescue group referred you to the shelter.

✔ **Shelter fees are pretty affordable.** Shelter fees are usually less than $100.

To find contact information for shelters in your area, look in your local phone directory or go online and enter "animal shelters *<your city name>*" in the search field of your favorite search engine.

Why you should pass up pet stores

All those cute little puppies looking out at you from their cages just makes you want to scoop them up and take them home. Before you do, keep in mind that pet stores, on the whole, are some of the worst places to buy pets. Here's why:

✔ **You have no way of knowing what the dam and sire were like.** Were they timid? Aggressive? The parents' traits are big predictors of your puppy's character when he matures. And that issue doesn't even throw health into the equation. Breed two dogs with health problems, and the offspring are likely to have these health problems, too.

✔ **You don't know how the pups were raised before they were brought to the store.** Were they socialized at all? If they came from a puppy mill, then the answer, is no.

✔ **Pet-store puppies are more likely to be ill.** Starting off with vet bills to pay because the little gal has parasites or a virus is no fun — for you or her.

✔ **Most dogs in pet stores come from puppy mills or backyard breeders.** Reputable breeders would never send their puppies to a pet store to be sold (see the earlier section "What Good Breeders Do" to find out why).

If you buy your Yorkie from a pet store, be prepared to deal with problem behaviors and to spend a lot of time socializing your puppy.

Chapter 4

Dreaming Up and Choosing the Ideal Yorkie

*I*f you're like most people, impatience sets in after you decide on a breed and make the initial contacts with the breeder. After all, you made the big decisions and did the legwork that got you to a reputable breeder. And now you want your dog. To make matters even more hair-pulling, you may have been waiting for what seems like an endless amount of time already. When you're buying a Yorkie, weeks or even months can pass between the time you find a reputable breeder or rescue group and the time you can actually hook up with a particular dog.

Well, patience is a virtue. And you have to be virtuous a little bit longer. Now you have to figure out what kind of Yorkie you want: male or female, show- or pet-quality, Sagittarius or Leo. You also have to know what to look for when you're finally in the hot seat, surrounded by adorable, prancing Yorkies, without a clue how to pick the one who's going to share your life for the next (hopefully) 15 or 16 years. Although your emotions may be running high, you can't let them take over. You must pay attention to clues that indicate whether the cute dog in the corner, the dynamo racing around the pen, or the easygoing guy gnawing contentedly on the squeaky toy is the best fit for your family. In this chapter, I help you figure out which Yorkie will become the love of your life.

Final Decisions before Picking Your Dog

You already know you want a Yorkie. Now you need to think about what kind of Yorkie you want. Do you want a male or a female? Most people have a preference one way or the other. How about a show- or pet-quality dog? Your answer to that question depends on what you want the dog to be able to do: compete in the show ring or just curl up behind your knees when you're lying on the couch. Are you sure you want a puppy? Some people prefer adopting older dogs.

You've already made the big decision: to get a Yorkie. Now, before you run hell-bent for leather to the nearest breeder with cash in hand, take a little time to think about some of these other details.

Male or female?

You hear all sorts of rumors about the differences between male and female dogs. In some circles, the girls get a bad rap (they're more timid, more stubborn, less "showy," moodier — a common complaint about females of any species, it seems — more standoff-ish, and so on), and the boys get the good press (they're more loving, more predictable, more personable, and so on). In other circles, people maintain the opposite is true.

Despite these fervently held opinions, the truth is that you can find out more about a particular dog's disposition by looking at his or her parents than by looking at his or her genitalia.

 If you have a male Yorkie (or another male dog) at home already and you're thinking of adding another to the mix, you may want to consider a female. Established males tend to be less aggressive with new females than they are with new males. Beyond this situation, some differences exist, based primarily on physiology, that may sway your decision.

Sugar and spice and everything nice

If you have an unspayed female, you have to deal with her heat cycles and the slight mess that goes along with it. You also have to put up with all sorts of characters hanging around outside the house hoping to take advantage of her, shall we say, *accommodating* disposition. If you don't want an unplanned pregnancy, you'll have to teach her that nice girls wait for marriage.

We *are* talking about dogs here, aren't we?

Snips and snails and oops

If you have an unneutered male, your challenges will be keeping him from wandering off (see the preceding section to find out why), lifting his leg every chance he gets, or becoming a tad too intimate with your shin, the corner of the divan, and other objects of affection. In addition, unneutered male dogs are much more likely to fight with another dog, and male Yorkies — neutered or otherwise — don't think they're smaller than the other dog, regardless of the other dog's size, and will give the fight a go.

Of course, if you have your Yorkie spayed or neutered, you eliminate these issues. And then you're right back to where you started: trying to decide between a male or a female. The right answer? Whichever one you prefer.

Show or pet?

One of the first decisions you have to make when you're adopting a Yorkie is whether you want a show-quality or a pet-quality dog. If you don't offer this information during your conversation with the breeder, he'll probably ask you your preference. If the topic doesn't come up, he'll presume you want a dog who will be a companion, not a contender in the show ring.

Of course, in things that matter, show-quality and pet-quality Yorkies are exactly the same:

- ✔ Both make wonderful companions.
- ✔ Both have that irrepressible Yorkie temperament.
- ✔ Both can sport the bow, that immediately identifiable symbol of all things Yorkie.

But important differences do exist between pet- and show-quality Yorkies that can impact your decision.

The lowdown on the showdown

Show-quality dogs have what it takes to compete in the show ring: They epitomize the breed standard (refer to Chapter 2); they have the temperament to tolerate crowds and attention; and the best of them possess a special spark that grabs people's attention.

Show-quality puppies also cost significantly more than pet-quality puppies, with the most expensive being the pups who come from a long line of champions and show potential for following in Mom or Dad's footsteps, er, paw prints.

Show-quality Yorkies also require significantly more grooming. Although silky hair is innate to the breed, making it look good and keeping it in show trim takes a lot of work. (Chapter 10 contains general grooming tips; if you want to know how to prepare and maintain a show Yorkie's coat, you need specialized information and guidance from a knowledgeable breeder and exhibitor.)

In addition, identifying a young puppy as having show potential is nearly impossible. The set of the ears, the color of the coat, the temperament, and the size all evolve as the puppy grows. What may look like a promising show dog at 12 weeks may turn out to be an introvert who piddles anytime a stranger comes near. Because puppies change as they grow, if you want a show-quality puppy, you have two choices:

- ✔ Pay a higher price for a promising puppy, and then keep your fingers crossed that he realizes his potential.

- ✔ Wait until a puppy is old enough (which can take as long as 6 months to a year) for the show potential to be more apparent.

Finally, breeders who show their Yorkies usually breed for themselves. Those breeders who actively participate in competitions are likely to keep their most promising pups for themselves. If they used a stud service, they may give the pick of the litter to the *sire's* (dad's) owner as a way to reduce the stud fee. And if someone's never had a Yorkie before and doesn't know the first thing about showing a dog, a breeder is even more reluctant to let her adopt a puppy who shows particular promise for fear that the puppy's potential may be lost to the owner's ignorance. Pair these scenarios with the fact that not all litters produce show-quality dogs, and you can see why asking for one may make your wait even longer.

Pet-icularly mahvelous

Show Yorkies are the jet-setters of the canine class structure, whereas pet-quality Yorkies are the true-blue. They may not conform so perfectly to the breed standard or have that certain somethin' somethin' that impresses judges, but you can't beat them for cuddliness, companionship, and — dare I say it? — inner beauty. If you want a pet-quality Yorkie (and most people do), your wait will be shorter, and your bank account will be safer. Here's why: More pet-quality Yorkies are available than show-quality ones, and pet-quality dogs cost less.

Basically, a pet-quality dog is simply one who has traits or characteristics that prevent her from being successful in the show ring. Maybe she's the wrong color or has too much curl in her hair. Maybe his testicles didn't descend properly. Maybe she's heavier than the maximum 7 pounds allowed in the breed standard. Whatever the reason, a pet-quality Yorkie, if he's able to make it into the show ring at all, won't make it out with any sort of prize.

Enough Yorkies weigh over the 7-pound maximum — and some significantly over it — that people unfamiliar with Yorkies assume that they, like Poodles, come in two varieties: standard and minia-ture. *They don't.*

When you buy a pet-quality Yorkie, expect the breeder to include a spay/neuter clause in the contract and indicate that your puppy's eligible for limited registration with the AKC. (*Limited registration* means that any puppies your dog has or sires aren't eligible for reg-istration at all. For more on registration, see Chapter 6.) Both these measures are designed to discourage you from breeding your pet-quality dog. For more information about these conditions, head to Chapter 12.

Even if your pet-quality dog can't make it in the show ring, that doesn't mean she can't compete: She can participate in obedience, agility, and tracking competitions. Head to Chapter 9 for informa-tion on these events and other things that can keep your Yorkie active and happy.

Young or old?

Although many prospective Yorkie owners prefer adopting a puppy, others are more interested in adopting an older dog. So another factor you have to consider is the dog's age: Do you want a dog you can raise and train from puppyhood, or do you want an older dog who's spent a few (or many!) seasons kicking around the block and can probably teach you a thing or two?

In the following sections, I explain some considerations you should keep in mind when deciding what age dog you want to get. But what you have your heart set on is the only thing that really matters.

Fine young things

When you adopt a puppy, you're adopting potential. How (and whether) that potential is realized depends on you and how you raise your dog. Give her lots of love, attention, and the necessary training and socialization (see Part IV), and you'll end up with the pet you hoped for. Neglect these things, and your puppy will grow into a dog with problems. When you adopt a puppy, remember the following:

✔ **Yorkies can be adopted at 12 weeks old.** Reputable breeders agree that Yorkie pups are old enough for adoption at 12 weeks old. By the 12th week, the breeder has a good idea of the pup's personality and a better idea of his show potential, and the puppy is physically and emotionally ready to separate from his *dam* (mom). Although a few breeders may permit a 10-week-old puppy to go to his new home, no reputable breeder releases puppies much younger than that. If you're talking to someone who's trying to sell 6-week-old Yorkies, you're not talking to a reputable breeder.

✔ **Familiarize yourself with the breed standards.** By becoming familiar with the breed standard (see Chapter 2), talking to other Yorkie owners, or reading books (like this one), you have an idea how a Yorkie puppy will turn out based on the typical characteristics of the breed. Remember, however, that not all puppies are typical representatives of their breed.

✔ **Puppies are a lot of work.** For all that cuteness, you have a big job ahead of you: helping your dog become the dog she's meant to be and the companion that you desire.

Puppies don't stay puppies forever (thank God!). Your puppy will one day grow up to become the dog you've created. Take good care of him, and you'll have a great dog to show for it. Fail to take proper care of him, and you'll pay for your neglect for years.

Sometimes the best of both worlds — a young dog who's past the chewing stage and may have some manners to boot — is to adopt an older puppy. Discuss this possibility with the breeder. Who knows? For a fee, she may be willing to keep the puppy for a few extra weeks and teach him the basic manners and housetrain him.

Pasts imperfect

You may decide that you want an adult Yorkie because you don't have the energy or the time to raise a puppy. A well-cared for older dog who needs a new home may be the answer to your dreams. Maybe you're drawn to an adult dog who was abused or neglected and want to give her a second chance at happiness. (Sadly, a number of adult Yorkies fall into this category.)

When you adopt an older Yorkie, you're adopting a dog whose already formed her habits — good or bad. What you see is pretty much what you get. If the previous owner was a good one, you reap the benefits. If the previous owner was a bad one (or if the dog was abandoned), you deal with the consequences: the fearfulness caused by hardship, the medical issues (major and minor) that resulted from or were exacerbated by neglect, and the behavioral problems that went unchecked.

Letting a mistreated dog into your heart is one of the most rewarding experiences you can have as a pet owner. With love, patience, and commitment, you can give her a good, safe life. Also, many reputable breeders place 5- to 6-year-old females who they no longer want to breed. These dogs can make great companions, and they greatly appreciate the individual love.

You can find older Yorkies by contacting breeders and Yorkie rescue groups (see Chapter 3 for details).

One pup or two?

Two Yorkie pups means twice the fun, right? Sure does. And twice the love? Yep, without a doubt. In fact, if you get two puppies at the same time, just add "twice the" to everything you get: twice the cuddliness. Twice the licks and kisses. Twice the silly little things that make you laugh. But don't forget these things when you tally everything up: twice the messes. Twice the expenses. Twice the training. Twice the work.

When you adopt two Yorkies simultaneously, the pups have constant companionship when you're away or otherwise engaged. Yorkies thrive on interaction and, if left alone frequently or for long periods of time, they can become lonely. Lonely Yorkies reveal their unhappiness through crying, destructive chewing, causing general mayhem, and penning the occasional sad love song. But add a pal to the equation, and their lonely days are over; one puppy usually has a calming effect on the other.

One challenge you face when you have two puppies at the same time is that your puppies often look to each other — and not you — for direction. Which isn't at all bad at 3 a.m. when your puppy's options are to snuggle closer to her littermate or howl until you stumble downstairs. At 3 p.m., however, when your puppy has the choice to continue tugging at the dining room drapes or to come when called — well, that's a different matter entirely.

Because of the challenges inherent in training two puppies at once and the real likelihood that you'll end up with two poorly trained dogs, don't opt for two puppies at the same time unless you're *absolutely* sure of your training skills. If you're confident in your training abilities and can afford the expense, go for it. You'll run yourself ragged, especially during the first months, but the positives — if you're diligent about training and socializing your dogs, and staying in control yourself — can outweigh the negatives.

If you want two Yorkies but aren't sure whether you're up to having twins, consider getting one puppy now and another puppy in a year or two. By doing so, you give each dog your full attention during the crucial puppy months. And your established dog can be a big help in teaching the new dog the rules of the house, which is an added bonus. Sure, you'll have adjustment issues to deal with when the new dog comes home, but even that is often more manageable than simultaneously training two pups.

Let the Inspection Begin!

Oooh, I can feel the anticipation. Few experiences are more fun or exciting than picking out a dog, whether you're looking for a puppy or an older Yorkie. All those cute little button faces. The bold characters who come right up. The shy ones who peak at you from the corners. And the ones who'd rather continue doing what they're doing than bother with you. When every dog's a verifiable heart-stopper, and you have the heart of a marshmallow, how in the world do you choose? You take it a step at a time.

To take the kids or not

The kids want to go. They're dying to go, in fact — begging, pleading, and even dangling the holy grail of kid-bargaining power: to do their chores without arguing and without being asked. That promise is enough to make you give in. But should you? It depends on

- **Your child's age:** An older child can be a big help when you're choosing a puppy. Not only can she give her opinion, but, if you bring the puppy home with you, she can be the extra hands you need to get the pup home safely. Younger children who may be overwhelmed by the excitement of all those puppies in one place should stay at home.

- **Your child's maturity level:** The puppies should be the only babies in the room or in the car for the ride home.

- **How well-behaved your child is:** You need to pay attention to what's going on, which you can't do if you have to continually remind your offspring to behave so that you can judge the dam's offspring.

If you have a child who's too young or too excitable to take with you when you choose your Yorkie, you may want to re-evaluate whether a small Yorkie is the best choice for your family. Maybe a larger, sturdier dog who can better tolerate the attention, clumsiness, and exuberance of a child would be a better choice for your family. Refer to Chapter 1 for help in deciding what kind of dog you should get.

Puppy pickin's

When you're looking for a puppy, do the following:

1. **Evaluate the whole litter as a group.**

   Evaluating the litter as a group lets you observe the dynamics and personalities of the pups in what has become their natural environment. You also get an overall impression of the general characteristics of the bunch. If most pups are rustling around, happy, and curious, that's a good sign. If the majority are cowering or growling, that's a bad sign.

   A puppy who doesn't interact with his littermates and doesn't greet you may grow up to be a fear biter as an adult.

2. **Spend some one-on-one time with each puppy, away from the others.**

   Away from the group, a shy puppy may come out of her shell, and an overly exuberant puppy may calm down. If you eliminate a puppy before having alone time, you may unwittingly overlook the perfect pup for you.

If you're buying a Yorkie from a pet store, you're at a disadvantage when evaluating a puppy, because the information you receive is limited and, to some degree, skewed. Observing a puppy's behavior in a cage (often alone) is far different from observing a puppy among his littermates in an environment that's both stimulating and comfortable. And how can you judge what you see? Is that chewing on the bars, for example, normal puppy chewing, anxiety chewing, or an indication that this dog chews on *anything?* Even when you have some one-on-one time with the pup, you do it in a small, windowed room where the dog has nothing to do *but* pay attention to you. In this situation, do your best to interpret what you see and keep your fingers crossed.

Good signs, favorable portents, and b-a-a-d omens

First, a brief description of what regular, run-of-the-mill Yorkie puppies (if such a thing exists) look like: Obviously, they're small. Even the bigger ones in the bunch don't weigh more than a couple of pounds. Their hair is short, goes in every direction (which makes it look curlier than it really is), and is mostly black with tan tips. Occasionally, a Yorkie puppy has a coat that's a different color, but not often. Their ears are *v*-shaped, but not necessarily erect, and may even flop over or point in different directions. In short, a Yorkie puppy doesn't look much like an adult Yorkie at all (see Figure 4-1).

©Isabelle Francais

Figure 4-1: A Yorkie pup has to grow into her adult appearance. For that reason, don't use looks alone as your criterion for selecting a puppy.

So when you select a puppy, don't focus on appearance as the main criterion. Any of the puppies, with the proper grooming and care, will grow up to look pretty much like the Yorkies you see pictured in books. Instead, look for signs of health and temperament.

Healthy is as healthy does

Healthy puppies are active, bright-eyed, and curious. Their tummies are round but not distended. They may be a little clumsy (weren't you when you were a toddler?), but they're quick. When they play, they can run, hop, and bounce around with the best of them. Basically, a healthy puppy looks like a healthy puppy. Look for these specific things:

- Clear, bright eyes, with no discharge
- A nose that may be damp and even wet, but free of any discharge
- Clean, straight teeth and bright pink gums
- Clean, odor-free ears

✔ A clean, soft coat, and a skin that's free of sores or rashes

✔ A weight that's appropriate for the puppy's size — that is, the puppy's not overly heavy or excessively thin

✔ An active, not lethargic, puppy.

✔ No diarrhea or vomit from *any* puppy and anywhere in the area

Diving into disposition

In a passel of puppies, you'll see quite a few characters. Too bad you can't give them the Meyers-Brigg's Personality Test. Instead, you have to rely on observing the following:

✔ **How the puppies interact within the group:** You can learn a lot about a puppy's personality by watching him with his brothers and sisters. Does he barrel into the others, dragging them into play? Or does he linger around the edges and prefer being left alone? Does he move easily from one group to another? Is he aggressive or more easygoing in play? Just by watching all the puppies mill around together, you can form impressions about who's gentle, who's bossy, who's outgoing, who's shy, who's noisy, and so on.

✔ **How the puppies act toward you:** Although the puppies may be wary of you initially, they should eventually warm up to you and see you as just another object in their environment to play with and then ignore. You can test how alert or curious the puppies are by jingling your car keys, whistling, kneeling, or sitting on the floor — any non-threatening but obvious movement that doesn't directly call them to you but that will draw them near.

Let the puppies come to you. Don't reach for or chase a puppy to get his attention. Yorkies don't care for fast movement and grabby hands, and no one wants to be bullied into submission or chased into a corner.

✔ **Signs of temperament issues:** A few behaviors can indicate that a puppy is a little more high-strung:

• A puppy who cowers in the corner or cringes at sudden movement or noise is likely to grow up to be a fearful, anxious dog.

• A pup who keeps her tail low or between her legs can also grow into a fearful and anxious dog.

• The puppy who growls, nips, and jumps at you during play may grow up to be a handful who needs constant supervision and redirection.

You're looking for a dog who will do well in your home. If you live in a quiet, calm home and have regular routines and lots of love to give, your home may be just the right place for an anxious dog. If you live in a home that has a clear human leader, then your home may be the perfect place for a dominant dog. For most people, however, the best choice is a well-balanced dog who isn't timid, aggressive, or a prima donna — in other words, a puppy who's neither the leader of the pack nor the one who's bringing up the rear.

Letting your puppy choose you

Some people believe that the best way to choose a puppy is to let the puppy choose them. If a puppy comes over to play, inspect, tug at their shoe strings, or nibble on their fingers — well, then, that's just an irrefutable sign of the perfect match. If you're inclined to this method of puppy selection, keep in mind that the puppy who "chose" you is probably one of the more outgoing in the pack. Other puppies — who may have been a better match for your family — didn't get a chance. Additionally, receiving your pup's attention may have had nothing to do with you at all. A curious, outgoing, exuberant puppy will approach any novelty just as enthusiastically. And, in a competition between you and a 3-day-old pizza box, you'd probably lose.

When you choose a puppy before you can take him home

Some breeders expect you to visit the pups before the day you actually take one home. Even those breeders who don't require such a visit usually welcome it. A visit is a great time to get a feel for the breeder, see the dam and the kennel area, and discuss any questions you have about the breed (refer to Chapter 3). During your visit, you can sometimes indicate which puppy you want. If you do select a particular pup, keep these things in mind:

- The younger the puppies are, the harder it is to tell much about them. In fact, many breeders discourage pre-selecting puppies for this very reason.

- Make sure the breeder can identify your puppy from the others — a particularly difficult task when the pups all look the same. Some breeders microchip their puppies for identification purposes. Most don't. Just make sure you can tell yours from the others so that when you come back one, two, or three weeks later, you can still recognize him.

- If your breeder requires that you put a deposit down on the puppy, do so only after he's drawn up a bill of sale with all the conditions of the sale included and the amount already paid recorded. Also make sure that you get a receipt. Head to Chapter 6 for information on the paperwork that accompanies buying a Yorkie.

Matchmaker, Matchmaker, make me a match

Many Yorkie breeders solve your selection problems for you. How? *They* choose your dog. Combining what they've discovered about you through their interviews and what they know about their dogs, they determine which dog you're the best match for.

If your breeder chooses the puppy herself, don't fight it. She knows her dogs better than you can within the hour or two that you may spend with them. She's an expert on Yorkie temperament and what that can mean in terms of their behavior. For example, she may know that Yorkie A is the most aggressive in the group and is more likely to use his teeth when he's inspecting or playing and, therefore, wouldn't be a good choice for a family with small children.

 Breeders who are aware of how a dog's personality can impact what goes on in the home know that they're courting trouble if they allow a puppy to go to the wrong kind of family. In those situations, chances are that that pup will be returned, taken to the pound, resold, or placed in another home. A permanent, happy home for both the puppy and the buyer is the goal of all good breeders. So they use their knowledge to everyone's advantage.

Choosing an older dog

When you adopt an older dog, you look for different things than you do when you adopt a puppy. First, you're not trying to determine potential; you're trying to determine personality. An adult dog is who he is, based on his life experiences and the care and love he got (or didn't get) long before you arrived on the scene. Here's what you need to find out:

- ✔ **The dog's personality (outgoing, loving, timid, shy, dominant, aggressive, and so on) and how these traits translate to behavior:** Does the timid dog snap, for example, or dominant dog challenge or ignore human direction? Does a loving dog need constant human contact? If the dog is aggressive, how and when has the aggression manifested itself?

- ✔ **The dog's health:** If a dog has health problems, you need to know what they are so that you can decide whether you can afford the medical costs of his care or treatment and the commitment to see the problem through.

- ✔ **Any training the dog has gotten previously:** Although having a dog who can run through a whole repertoire of cute tricks is fun, the real question here is, "Is he housetrained?" If he's not, add housetraining to the list of things you need to work on.

The best way to determine what an older dog is like and the type of home that he needs is to rely on the advice and guidance you get from the shelter or rescue personnel. They should be willing to tell you whatever they know about your dog's past life and what they've discovered through personal observation. If you're working with a rescue organization, some of which place animals all across the country, you may not be able to personally meet your dog until the day he arrives. In these cases, working with the breed specialist is even more important.

Paying for That Doggy in the Window

By the time you select your puppy, you should've already discussed the cost and the payment schedule with the breeder. (Refer to Chapter 3 for an idea of how much Yorkies usually cost.)

Many breeders expect payment in full when you come to pick up your puppy. Other breeders require a deposit (usually to ensure that you're serious about adopting a dog). How much of a deposit you have to make depends on the breeder's policy. Some breeders expect half of the total cost, whereas others expect only a small amount. If a deposit is required, make sure you ask whether it's refundable, in the event that you're unable to get the puppy. Also be sure to get a receipt that has the conditions of the deposit written on it.

Most breeders also have a preferred method of payment. Many, for example, require either cash or a cashier's check. Few breeders accept personal checks. Those breeders who do accept personal checks may hold the puppy until your check clears or may require you to pay the amount in advance so that by the time you pick up the puppy, your check has cleared. If this is the case, be sure to get the arrangement in writing.

Part II

The Homecoming

"Okay, before I let the new puppy out, let's remember to be real still so we don't startle him."

In this part . . .

*I*t was the best of times. It was the worst of times. It was homecoming time. Bringing your new Yorkie home is a lot like bringing a baby home: You're excited, fretful, happy, and anxious — all at the same time. If you've been rushing around trying to get everything ready, you're probably tired, too.

The best way to make it through your Yorkie's first day home is to have a plan. Your plan doesn't need to be elaborate, and it shouldn't require a playbook or a detailed schematic. Your plan should simply help you organize what would otherwise be a very chaotic and unpredictable introduction between your new family member and your old ones.

When the first day is done, then you have to make it through the first night — which doesn't require a plan so much as fortitude, patience, and a good pair of earplugs. After the first night passes and dawn shimmers on the horizon (believe me, you'll be up to see it), you're ready to take the next important steps toward getting your Yorkie accustomed to the people and rules of his new environment.

Chapter 5

Getting Ready for the New Arrival

. . . .

In This Chapter

▶ Stocking up on dog supplies

▶ Getting the dog areas ready

▶ Puppy-proofing your home

▶ Checking out vets

▶ Preparing for your dog's first day at home

. . . .

*W*hen you adopt a Yorkie, you usually have at least a few days to get everything ready before you bring her home. Even if you make the decision one day and head to pick up your Yorkie the next, you still have an evening to prepare — and prepare you should! You need to get your house ready, the kids ready, and the dog areas ready. You also need to give a heads-up to your vet (or choose a vet if you don't already have one).

Preparing is as complicated or as simple as you make it. At its most basic, you need to line up a vet and have the essentials you need to care for your dog. Just as important, however, is getting your game plan together so that you know beforehand how you want things to go during your Yorkie's first hours in her new home. With a little prep work, everything will go more smoothly. Trust me.

Necessary Yorkie Supplies

Yorkies, as a rule, don't need much: a warm place to sleep, food, a couple of toys to play with, and a lap to curl up on. Give your Yorkie these things, and you've provided everything that your dog would ask for if he could talk. Of course, as a responsible Yorkie owner, you know that a little more is required — items that your puppy wouldn't ask for but needs anyway, like a collar and leash, a traveling crate, food dishes, and so on. Taking a trip through pet-supply stores, grocery stores, or the pet-supply sections in discount stores can yield what you need. You may even find some of these items by scrounging through your own closets or a neighbor's (with permission, of course).

Pet stores do for pet owners what baby stores do for expectant or new parents: They convince you that your little one needs an abundance of all sorts of fancy gadgets or gizmos. If, in your excitement, you allow yourself to be snagged by all the marketing hooks, you'll spend a fortune on items that your Yorkie doesn't need and you won't use. And if you buy your puppy everything in sight, how can you teach him the value of a dollar?

Get as much of your supplies as you can beforehand; it'll make the homecoming (see Chapter 6) that much easier. If you were looking forward to taking your puppy to the pet mart to pick out his belongings, buy most of what you need beforehand and save a few items to get with your puppy in tow. Good choices to save for your person-and-puppy shopping excursion are puppy food (you may not know what kind you need until after you pick up the puppy) and toys.

Food, glorious food

Deciding what kind of food you're going to feed your dog is one of the most important first decisions you make. Whether you adopt a puppy or an older dog, you need to make careful choices about the food you provide. The following sections tell you what you need to feed your dog when she first comes home.

For a puppy

Your pup's breeder makes the decision about what to feed your puppy an easy one for you: She'll probably give you a care sheet that specifies, among other things, the kind of food your Yorkie's been eating. She may even provide a few days' supply. If you haven't gotten the care sheet or you're stocking up on food in advance, ask your breeder what puppy food she recommends.

If you can't or don't want to follow the breeder's advice, be sure to get food that's specifically designed for puppies because it has the nutrients that growing puppies need. Premium quality brands of puppy food are your best bet because they use better quality protein sources and are easier to digest. For more information on food options and information on appropriate feeding schedules, head to Chapter 9.

Even if you plan to change your puppy's diet from the breeder's suggested brand to one that you prefer, feed your pup the food she's used to during her first few days at home. Changing foods abruptly can upset your puppy's tummy and digestive track. Over the course of a week, gradually switch her diet by mixing the new food in ever-increasing amounts with the old until the old food is gone and the new food is the staple.

Breeders who aren't nutritional experts simply recommend what they feed their Yorkies. Check your puppy's diet out with your vet, who has nutritional training. In addition, unless your vet tells you to do otherwise, your Yorkie pup needs puppy food until she's a year old.

For an adult Yorkie

The important thing to know about feeding an older Yorkie is that you want to make sure you choose the food that's right for his age and his fitness level. If you adopt a senior dog, for example, buy food specifically made for that age group. The person or shelter you adopted him from should be able to tell you what food he's been eating and explain any special dietary needs you need to remember. Of course, if you have any questions about what your specific canine needs, consult your vet.

Dinner dishes

Don't bother getting out the fine china or crystal. Your dog won't appreciate it anyway. After all, this is an animal who's just as pleased to pull tidbits out of the trash or take a few swigs from the toilet bowl. Because your dog doesn't much care *what* you put her food and water in, the choice is yours. Here are a few considerations:

- ✔ **Size:** Don't get a dish so big that your puppy has to practically climb into it to get to his food. Small- to medium-size dishes are fine. Consider a slightly deeper dish for the water (it helps the water stay cooler longer).

   Buy the size dish that your adult dog will use. You don't have to upgrade the dish as your Yorkie grows.

- ✔ **Ceramic, stainless steel, or plastic:** Each option offers its own advantages and disadvantages:

  - • **Plastic bowls:** Plastic bowls are inexpensive and come in various sizes and colors, but they're usually not heavy enough to dissuade puppies from pushing them around, tipping them over, or carrying them through the house. If the plastic gets scratched or chewed (many puppies, and some adult dogs, too, like chewing their food dishes), they're harder to clean. In addition, plastic bowls can lighten the pigment on the dark nose of your Yorkie.

- **Ceramic bowls:** Ceramic bowls come in various sizes, colors, and painted patterns; you can even personalize them with your dog's name or breed. They're also heavy, which is both good (dissuading your Yorkie from carrying it to parts unknown) and bad (drop one and you could hurt yourself or your dog). They're also breakable and more expensive than plastic dishes.

Beware of ceramic bowls made outside the United States; the glazing may contain lead.

- **Stainless steel:** Heavier than plastic and often less expensive than ceramic, stainless-steel bowls may be the best choice. They're easy to clean, discourage chewing (have *you* ever gnawed on a dinner knife?), and don't break when dropped. Some stainless-steel bowls even come with rubber padding that keeps your Yorkie from pushing her food dish across the floor. If stainless-steel bowls have a downside, it's that they're not very sexy.

You may think that you can forgo buying dog dishes entirely and use the plastic butter tubs you've been saving. This solution may save you money, but what you save in cold hard cash, you'll more than make up for cleaning up the messes your dog leaves in her wake. Save the butter tubs, leftover TV dinner trays, and empty microwavable rice bowls for arts-and-crafts projects with your kids because they don't make good dog dishes.

A dog crate

If you've never used a dog crate before (or have used it incorrectly), you may think that confining a puppy to a crate is the ultimate cruelty. In truth, a dog crate is a godsend. It functions as a bed, a car seat, a housetraining center, and a puppy haven all in one. And dogs *love* them. When dogs were wild, they lived in dens, which were simply big enough to comfortably lie down in. Crates re-create that feeling of security and protection for your dog. You can find all the information you need to know about crate training in Chapter 13. In the following paragraphs, I explain what you need to know about choosing the right crate for your Yorkie.

You can find a variety of crates in pet stores, pet-supply stores, dog magazines, and sometimes at lawn-and-garden shops. When you buy a crate, be sure that the latch works and the carrying handle is secure. Depending on the style and manufacturer, expect to spend $40 to $100.

Common styles

Crates come in two basic styles: the solid plastic kind with vented sides (shown in Figure 5-1) and the wire kind that look more like a cage (see Figure 5-2).

- ✔ **Plastic crates:** Plastic crates are more denlike than wire crates, offering more security and shelter but less ventilation (because of the nearly solid sides). As a result, the inside offers more warmth, which is good during winter months but not so good during summer months. Plastic crates are also bulkier (you can't break them down into compact units as you can with many wire crates) but lighter.

- ✔ **Wire crates:** These crates break down into easy-to-store units, but even the smaller versions are heavier than the same-sized plastic crates. With the crate's wire sides and top, your Yorkie has a full view of everything around him (and everything around your Yorkie gets full view of him). Air blows freely through the crate, which is fine during warm weather but not so good during cold weather, when a Yorkie can be easily chilled.

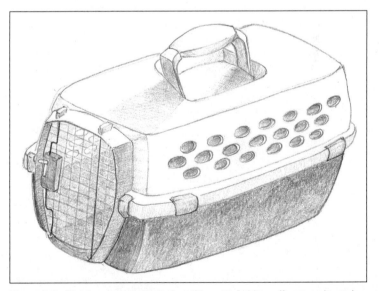

Figure 5-1: Plastic crates, with their solid, vented sides, offer security and a quiet place for your Yorkie to relax.

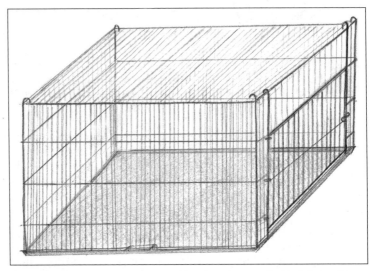

Figure 5-2: Wire crates have open sides that give your Yorkie full visual access to his environment.

Most pet owners have a preference. I, for example, like the plastic crates because of the denlike qualities they provide my dogs. After my dogs earn the run of the house and spots in the bedroom, the crates' primary function becomes a dog haven — a quiet and sheltered place they can walk into and out of at will. People who take their Yorkies on frequent or long car trips, however, often prefer the wire crates, which keep their dogs safely confined yet let them see what's going on around them.

If you plan on taking your Yorkie to far-flung places via plane, make sure that whatever crate you get is approved for air travel.

Just the right size

After you decide on the kind of crate you want, you have to determine the size you need. Make sure that the crate is big enough to allow your Yorkie, at full size, to stand up without hitting his head, turn around without bumping into the sides, and lie down comfortably. The crate shouldn't be so big that it invites your puppy to divide it into a living area and a bathroom area, with enough room left over for a conversation pit.

If the crate is so large that a puppy can sleep in one corner and poop and piddle in another corner, it defeats the purpose of using the crate as a housetraining aid. Once a dog develops the very bad habit of soiling in his sleeping area — a no-no in both human and canine families — housetraining becomes that much harder. See Chapter 14 for housetraining info.

Bedding

When your Yorkie is still a puppy and is spending her nights confined to her crate, line the crate with some bedding. Anything that's soft, comfortable, and not easy to shred or already coming apart can make good bedding. An old baby blanket or towel is perfectly fine, and so is an old pillow that's had so many heads resting on it that it already has a nice hollow that a puppy can curl up in. You can also buy an actual dog bed at any pet-supply store. When you're deciding on bedding, keep these things in mind:

- ✔ **Use bedding that's washable.** You can throw baby blankets and towels into the wash. If you use an actual pillow or dog bed, make sure it has removable, washable slipcovers.

- ✔ **Pay attention to size.** If you're lining the crate, don't cram it full of bedding. You want your dog to be able to move around freely, not fight the bedding for a good spot to lie down.

- ✔ **Watch for shredding.** If your puppy chews on her bedding, be sure to check it regularly for shredding. Then simply trim off the long ends when you find them.

Collar

The right collar for your Yorkie is one that's comfortable and fits well. When you look for a collar, buy one that's made of either nylon or leather.

- ✔ **Nylon collars:** These collars are inexpensive, lightweight, and often adjustable. And an adjustable collar is a good choice for a growing puppy.

- ✔ **Leather collars:** Leather collars are more expensive than nylon collars, but they last a lifetime.

Don't buy a metal collar (a "choker chain") for your puppy. First, a pup the size of a Yorkie has no business wearing a choker chain. You have many other methods at your disposal for controlling your dog besides choking him. Second, the chain wreaks havoc on your dog's coat.

To get the right-sized collar, either take your puppy to a pet-supply store and try the collars on him or measure his neck at home and add two inches to your measurement. Remember, as your Yorkie grows from puppy to adult, his collar size will change. Recheck the collar periodically to make sure that it isn't too tight. A collar that fits well is snug enough to stay on but loose enough to allow you to easily fit two fingers under it.

Although you may be tempted to save a few dollars and buy a big collar that your Yorkie will grow into, this is a bad idea for a couple of reasons:

- ✔ **A loose collar poses a choking hazard.** If the collar catches on something as the puppy runs by or leaps down, the result could be a minor setback (pulling him up short) or a major tragedy (choking him to death).

- ✔ **Your Yorkie will be able to work it off.** If you and your Yorkie get into a tugging match, he could slip right out of it, and then where would you be?

Leash

A leash (or lead) can last throughout your dog's lifetime. For your Yorkie, buy a leash that's lightweight, sturdy, and either 4- or 6-feet long; either nylon or leather is fine. (Avoid chain leashes, which are noisy and uncomfortable to hold.)

Retractable leashes — the leashes that retract and expand as your dog moves toward and away from you — are a great invention. They give your dog more roaming room without the hassle of a long leash. But retractable leashes aren't made for puppies. To use these leashes safely, your dog must already be trained to walk on a leash and reliably come when called (see Chapter 13 for basic commands). Using retractable leashes also requires a human who knows how to "pull in" a recalcitrant pooch. So save these leashes until your Yorkie is full grown and you're both well-trained.

Grooming supplies

If you have a Yorkie, you need a few grooming supplies (or the name and number of a professional groomer). So add the following basic coat-care supplies to your shopping list:

- ✔ **A pin brush with a rubber back:** Make sure the brush's bristles aren't tipped with little balls, which break the dog's hair.

- ✔ **A metal comb:** You need a metal comb with long teeth to get through your Yorkie's coat. Greyhound metal combs come highly recommended, and you order one through dog-grooming supply companies.

- ✔ **A flea comb:** A flea comb is a small metal comb that has very close teeth. Although it's designed to remove flea eggs, you use it to remove gunk from around your Yorkie's eyes.

- **Nail clippers:** Buy nail clippers made specifically for dogs. You can find them in any pet-supply store. They come in different sizes; for a Yorkie, small is fine.

- **Scissors:** You can find basic hair-trimming scissors in the hair-care section of any discount or drug store. Or, if you prefer, buy grooming scissors at pet-supply stores.

- **Dog shampoo:** Make sure the shampoo you buy is suitable for puppies (it says on the bottle) — unless, of course, your dog is full grown. Also buy a tearless variety.

- **Teeth-cleaning kit:** You also need to get your pooch a teeth-cleaning kit, which usually includes dog toothpaste (don't use human toothpaste!), a small, soft, toothbrush, and a finger brush.

For complete grooming instructions, hop to Chapter 10.

Toys

If you don't provide your Yorkie with toys, he'll find his own (like your heirloom pillows or the gerbil you let roam in a plastic bubble). So make sure you include at least one or two of the following toys on your shopping list:

- **Chew toys:** Any toy made of hard rubber can satisfy your puppy's need to chew. You can find hard chews in various shapes — bones, little critters, balls, and so on.

- **Chasing toys:** Yorkies, being terriers, love to chase things. Tennis balls, soft and light enough to carry but large enough to not pose a choking hazard, are ideal chase toys for your little pup.

- **Love-y toys:** Many Yorkies like cuddling and carrying around small stuffed animals.

Don't buy tugging toys. Why? Because you shouldn't play tugging games with your dog. Tugging games teach your dog that fighting you for objects is okay, which only confuses the bejesus out of him when the object you want him to release is the hem of your housecoat. Head to Chapter 9 for good games to play with your Yorkie.

When you look for dog toys, make sure that they don't have any small, detachable pieces that your dog can swallow, no wires he can get caught up in, and no holes for stuffing to come out of. Any of these things can pose a health hazard to your dog.

Baby gate

Periodically during your Yorkie's training period, you're going to want her out of her crate but confined to a small area. At those times, you need a baby gate. After your pup's trained, you may still use a baby gate to cordon off rooms that you don't want your Yorkie in. When buying a baby gate, keep the following issues in mind:

✔ **Style:** Choose a gate that has vertical slats or plastic mesh. Vertical slates keep your Yorkie from climbing because she can't get a foothold.

Avoid the old-fashioned accordion-style gates because your puppy can crawl right through them. Worse, if she tries to jump through, she could get caught and choke to death.

✔ **How it attaches to the wall:** *Mounted gates* attach to the wall. For this reason, they're more permanent and are a better choice if you know that you never want your dog to go into a certain room or area. *Pressure gates,* on the other hand, stay up by using pressure and you can easily move them from one doorway to another.

✔ **Size:** Baby gates come in all widths. Make sure that the gate you choose is wide enough to fit the doorway you want to put it in. Also make sure that the gate is tall enough to discourage your dog from trying to jump over it.

Yard pen and shelter

If your yard doesn't have a shaded or sheltered area, you may want to add a dog shelter — someplace your dog can go to cool down or get out of the weather. This shelter can be a doghouse or a tarp that's secured in the ground and offers shade.

Also, if you don't have a fenced yard, consider getting a yard pen, where you can put your Yorkie to keep him safe while he's outside, whether you're with him or not.

A yard pen is essentially a portable fence that you can set up in your yard. Although it keeps your Yorkie in, it doesn't keep other creatures out. Yorkies, like other Toy dogs, are vulnerable to intruders. It's not uncommon for them to be stolen by humans or attacked by larger dogs and wild predators, such as coyotes and hawks. So if you take your Yorkie outside, even though you may use a yard pen, be sure to keep an eye on him.

Other stuff

To round off the supply list, stock up on the following:

- ✔ **An enzyme-based stain-and-odor remover:** You'll need this remover at some point, no matter how agreeable your dog is to training.

  Don't use ammonia-based cleaners. Cleaning with one of these is like putting up a sign that says "Pee Here!" You may think that ammonia smells clean, but your Yorkie thinks it smells like urine. And a place that smells like urine — even if it's the corner of your antique rose-patterned Oriental carpet — is *the* place to go.

- ✔ **An ID tag:** Make sure your dog's ID tag includes your address, phone number, and your dog's name. Head to Chapter 11 for more identification ideas.

- ✔ **Bitter Apple spray (or another harmless yet unpleasant smelling and tasting concoction, like a vinegar-and-water mix):** Spray these solutions on the belongings you want your puppy to stay away from (like electrical cords).

- ✔ **Don't forget the newspapers:** You can never have too many newspapers at the ready.

  An alternative to newspaper is a rubber mat made especially for indoor potty use. This pad cuts down on urine odor (unlike newspaper, which gets its own "special" smell when wet) and is easy to wash and reuse. You can find these pads at pet-supply stores.

Setting Up the Perfect Space (s)

As you prepare for your puppy's arrival, think about where her areas — the places where you'll put her things and where she'll spend time when she's not with you — will be. You want to make these areas convenient for you and easily accessible to her.

So where are the best places to set up her things? The answer to that question depends on what "things" you're talking about. You'll probably decide to put the food and water dishes in or close to your kitchen. If you're going to have a bathroom area inside, you should definitely put it in an out-of-the way place that your dog can easily get to but that you don't have to look at all the time. Where you place your puppy's crate is a little trickier because it needs to be where she sleeps at night and where you want her to spend quiet time during the day. If these two areas aren't the same, you either need to get two crates or be willing to move your one crate as necessary.

Many people devote one area of their house to their Yorkies. This area is the Yorkie's home within a home — where all his things are, where he dines, reposes, and relieves himself. Other people designate certain areas of their house for certain functions.

However and wherever you arrange your dog's areas (the following sections give you ideas), you need to make your Yorkie feel comfortable, safe, and a part of the family (see Figure 5-3). As long as you're consistent with your expectations, your Yorkie will catch on to what he's supposed to do where.

©Isabelle Francais

Figure 5-3: A cozy setup for a little dog: comfortable, safe, and still close to the family.

Sleeping area

After your Yorkie's housetrained, she can sleep wherever her little heart and your big heart desire — even if that means on the ruffled pillow at the head of your bed. Until then, you need to keep her in her crate during the night. So you need to decide where you want her crate to be at bedtime.

The family bed

When your puppy is first home, you may be tempted to put her in bed with you during the night. I strongly recommend that you resist for a number of reasons:

✔ **It's dangerous.** You can easily roll over onto the puppy and not realize it. Or the puppy can fall off — or jump off the bed — and hurt herself.

✔ **A bed is a big place for a little puppy.** For the same reason that you don't want the crate too big — she'll have enough room to distinguish between her sleeping area and her potty area (refer to the earlier section "Bedding") — you don't want to give her the opportunity to confuse a far-off area of the bed with a bathroom.

✔ **The leader of the pack gets the choicest sleeping area.** It's one of the benefits of being the leader. By restricting access to the bed until your puppy has earned it teaches her that you're boss.

For other tactics you can use to reiterate your alpha-dog status, head to Chapter 13.

In your bedroom, within sight of your bed

Having your puppy room with you is beneficial because he'll be close by, which is good for both you and him. Having him close by is good for you because you can hear when he wakes up at night and needs to go out — an important consideration when he's still too young to last the night without a potty trot. Being close to you is good for him because he feels more secure being near his pack (that would be you).

The disadvantage of your pup sleeping in your room is that, at least initially, he'll cry because he wants to be *with* you, not just *near* you, and you won't have a few rooms' buffer to soften the sound. Also, until he gets used to the bedtime ritual, he'll interpret any move out of bed on your part (even if it's just to relieve your own bladder) as an indication that crate time is up. He'll start crying all over again at the bitter disappointment of being ignored as you stumble back into bed.

In another area of the house

If your dog doesn't room with you at night, you have to decide on another area of the house. Two good alternatives to the bedroom are the daytime quiet area and the bathroom area. If your pup sleeps during the night in the same area where he goes during the day for quiet time and contemplation, he'll associate his crate more quickly with rest, relaxation, and security. The advantage to putting the crate near the bathroom area is that when you let him out in the morning, he'll be right where his papers are — a good thing for a small bladder that's patiently waited through the night and tends to start flowing as soon as the puppy feels the fresh air of freedom.

Daytime quiet area

Part of training your Yorkie is getting her accustomed to quiet time in her crate during those times of the day when you can't be with her, when she's being naughty, or when she needs a nap.

She won't like the arrangement at first and won't hesitate to let you know how unhappy she is, but she'll eventually get used to, and even begin to enjoy, her quiet time. In fact, after she's trained and roaming the house freely, don't be surprised to find her napping or resting in her crate of her own free will.

During the day and early evening, the ideal place for her crate is in a quiet, out-of-the way place in the main living area, where she can still see and hear you, even though she won't be in the thick of the action. If you spend almost as much time in your kitchen as you do in the living room, try putting the crate in a place where the puppy can see both areas.

A bad spot to put the crate is anywhere completely away from you and the rest of the family. Yorkies don't do well in isolation. If you keep this active, people-oriented dog isolated too frequently or for prolonged periods of time, you can end up with a neurotic dog who barks constantly and is overly hyper when he does actually get to be with the family.

The eating area

Put your dog's dishes in an easy-to-clean place where she can easily get to them. Some place in the kitchen or off the kitchen, such as a mudroom, is ideal. But try to avoid high-traffic areas. Your dog should be able to eat in peace.

If you're putting the food dish on carpet, consider getting a large plastic placemat to set under the dishes. It'll make cleaning up spills easier.

The pooping area

If you plan to potty train your puppy using paper, obviously, you need a place to put the papers or pad. Even if you're going to train your Yorkie to go to the bathroom outside, you may decide to start him inside and work him up to the great outdoors. Or maybe your puppy needs to be proficient at both indoor and outdoor waste elimination (see Chapter 14 for housetraining strategies) because you want him to go on the papers or pad during the day when you're gone and outside at night when you're home.

In any case, you need to pick the indoor potty spot. If you're going to keep your Yorkie in a restricted area for extended periods of time (during the day while you're at work, for example), make sure you put the approved potty area in that restricted area. If your lifestyle allows you to be with your dog pretty much all the time, put the potty area in an out-of-the way place that he can get to when he feels the call of nature but that you don't have to look at every time you turn around.

Setting up dog-free zones

After your puppy is adequately trained, she'll probably have the run of the house. Until then, decide where she can and can't go. Before your Yorkie comes home, determine where your dog-free zones are. Limiting access to rooms where you aren't (for example, she shouldn't be in the living room when you're not) and areas where she doesn't need to be (like the garage that has all sorts of dangers lurking for a curious puppy) are your goals. The next step is to figure out how you're going to keep her out of these areas. Closed doors, baby gates, and due diligence are usually the tools at your disposal. If you have kids, share these rules with them.

Puppy-proofing Your Home and Yard

Consider your Yorkie puppy the canine equivalent of a 1-year-old child, and consider your house the playground he's bounding through. He'll examine — by chewing, sniffing, tasting, pulling at, and bouncing around — anything that catches his eye. And any-thing means *anything*: shoes, electrical or power cords, a loosened strip of wallpaper, rotten garbage from the trash can, toys from the kids' rooms, the hem of your drapes, the cleaning products under the sink — you name it. Your task, then, is to puppy-proof your house, not just to keep your belongings safe, but to keep your puppy safe, too.

You don't usually have to go to the same extremes when you bring home an older dog. A mature Yorkie is less likely than a puppy to chew or taste things to figure out what they are. Nevertheless, you do need to keep an eye out to see what behaviors may lead to problems; an anxious dog, for example, may chew just to relieve stress. And some things — like poisons — should always be out of reach to your dog.

Neutralizing poisons

Figure out where the chemical hazards are in your home and take steps to eliminate them. Consider these danger zones:

- ✔ Cleaning supplies under sinks and in lower cabinets.
- ✔ Personal hygiene items in the bathroom (hair-care products, perfume, medicine, and ointments).
- ✔ Motor oil, antifreeze, and car-care products in the garage.

Be especially careful with antifreeze. A thimbleful of antifreeze is enough to permanently wipe out a pet's kidneys in one hour. If your Yorkie (or any animal you have) drinks antifreeze — or even if you just suspect that she has — consider it a medical emergency and go to the vet immediately. To avoid problems, clean up leaks immediately, store the antifreeze on a high shelf, and take old antifreeze to an auto mechanic's shop for proper disposal.

- ✔ Laundry detergent and bleach in the laundry room.
- ✔ Fertilizer, insect killer, and other dangerous chemicals in your yard.
- ✔ Common household and garden plants. For a list of poisonous plants, go to the Humane Society of the United States Web site at www.hsus.org/ace/11777.

Because Mr. Yuck signs are of no use to dogs, you have to find other ways to keep common household poisons away from your Yorkie. Move poisons to higher shelves, put baby locks on your cabinet doors (yes, Yorkies can figure out how to open cabinets), move your plants from the hearth to the mantle, make the garage a dog-free zone, and keep an eye on your puppy until she outgrows the chewing stage.

If your Yorkie does ingest something harmful — or potentially harmful — call your vet immediately. You can also call the ASPCA (the American Society for the Prevention of Cruelty to Animals) Animal Poison Control Center at 888-426-4435. Be aware that you must pay a $50 consultation fee.

Spotting other dangers

Want to know what's going to catch your Yorkie's eye? Crawl around on the floor and pay attention to what you see. A hole in the under-lining of your box spring? A tangle of electrical cords and cables behind your couch? A dust-and-lint-covered chicken nugget beside the toy box? All tantalizingly attractive objects to be pored over.

Also look for wobbly or unsteady furniture, low-hanging table cloths or runners, or anything else that if pulled or bumped could send knick knacks or furniture itself tumbling over on your Yorkie.

Be on the lookout for items in your yard that would be interesting or enticing to a small dog, too. Look for holes or gaps in the fence, wobbly woodpiles, and unstored garden supplies, all of which can prove harmful to your dog.

For folks who have (or want) an invisible fence

Invisible fences are not really invisible. They are underground lines that emit a frequency. The dog wears a collar that, when she gets too close to the wire, gives a warning beep and then a small shock, called a *correction*.

If you're interested in getting an invisible fence, keep these points in mind:

✔ Invisible fences are great for keeping your dog in the yard, but they're not designed to keep any other animals — human, canine, avian, feline, you name it — out. In that way, invisible fences offer only limited protection for your Yorkie. If you can't be outside when she's outside, at least be sure to keep an eye on her.

✔ Your Yorkie must be at least a year old before reputable companies will fit her with the special collar. By that age, she should be reasonably well-trained and know the yard rules, which makes the training period for the fence go more smoothly.

Swimming pools and ponds can pose special dangers to Yorkies. Some Yorkies who have managed their way into swimming pools can't find their way out and, if they're not rescued, they swim to exhaustion and drown. Ponds are a danger to Yorkies because of the algae that may grow in and around them. If dogs ingest algae, it can be toxic.

For a list of food dangers, head to Chapter 9.

Keeping your belongings safe

Preventing your dog from doing harm to himself is certainly the most important reason why puppy-proofing your home is necessary, but it isn't the only reason. Let's not give short shrift to the inevitable pain that comes when you discover one of your favorite slippers has been reduced to a rubber sole with tattered terrycloth shreds clinging to it. And have you ever listened to a frustrated 6-year-old try to dress a Barbie whose chewed up hands and feet keep snagging the insides of her already too-tight clothing?

The best way to protect your belongings is to put them away and out of reach of your Yorkie's exuberant attention. Shoes? In the closet. Kids toys? In the toy box. For those items you can't put away and close the door behind — like drape hems, chair rungs, and so on — consider spraying them with a dog repellant, such as Bitter Apple, a harmless concoction that most dogs find utterly, well, repellant. Or you can use a solution of white vinegar and water, but the vinegar odor lingers, and if you're not careful, your whole house can end up smelling like Easter eggs.

Finding a Vet and Scheduling the First Appointment

As soon as you bring your Yorkie home, you have to schedule an almost-immediate appointment with your vet. Most breeders stipulate a time period (often 24 to 72 hours) during which you should have your vet confirm the puppy's health. Most pet stores also require that you get your puppy's health checked within two days of the date of purchase.

If you can, schedule the appointment within the first 24 hours of bringing your puppy home. And remember to take along a sample of her feces to check for parasites.

So you can hit the ground running, inform your current vet, if you have one, that you're looking forward to a new addition to the family. If you can give your vet a time frame (say, within the next two weeks, for example) for the happy event, all the better. That way he has a head's up and can anticipate your puppy's arrival.

Then you can pick up your puppy, call the vet, and schedule your first appointment. For information on what to expect during this checkup, go to Chapter 11.

If you don't have a vet, now's the time to find one. Ask the breeder of your Yorkie or neighborhood friends (who are more likely to know of vets in your area) for a recommendation. If no one can give you a recommendation, call around to area vets or animal hospitals until you find someone you feel comfortable working with.

Making a First-day Game Plan

Before you find yourself chasing after your new puppy while simultaneously holding the old dog back by his collar, trying to coax the cat down from the top of the kitchen cabinets, and yelling at your kids to settle down, put together a game plan for how your puppy's initial hours in the house are going to go. Make plans for the following and then put them in place before you leave (go to Chapter 7 for practical suggestions):

- ✔ **Where will your current animals be when you bring your Yorkie home, and how will you introduce them to each other?** You need to plan your animals' introduction to each other. So figure out how you can control the timing of their interaction. Do you want your older dog to be on a walk when the Yorkie arrives? If so, arrange to have your spouse, child, or friend keep the old baby occupied while the new baby sniffs around.

- ✔ **What will your kids (if you have any) be doing?** Do you want them to stay out of the way? Can they greet the pup as soon as you walk in the door, or do you want them to stand back until you bring the puppy to them? Whatever you decide, make sure the kids are aware of the plan.

- ✔ **Who's in charge?** Decide who's responsible for calling the shots, controlling the interactions, and setting the rules — and then stick to it. If it's you, congratulations. You're now the alpha dog.

Chapter 6

Picking Up Your Dog

· ·

In This Chapter

▶ What supplies to take along when you get your puppy

▶ A rundown of the information you'll get from the breeder

▶ How to make the trip home smooth and safe

· ·

*W*hen you get a dog, you move through three very predictable stages:

> ✔ **Stage one:** *Picking* your dog
>
> ✔ **Stage two:** Picking *up* your dog
>
> ✔ **Stage three:** Picking up *after* your dog (also known as raising him)

Many people, however — even those who agree that getting a dog requires at least a little preparation and forethought — tend to leap right over stage two and concentrate on stages one and three. Well, in this chapter, I intend to stop the madness.

If you're one of those spontaneous souls who hasn't done *any* preparation at all and yet you're still heading out to get your puppy, follow these directions: Close the book. Turn it so that you can see those cute little Yorkies on the front cover. When you're done admiring them, lift the book so that the bottom edge is even with your nose. Now start whacking yourself until a little sense gets knocked into your thick skull. Then head back to Chapter 5 for ways to get ready for your dog.

The Scouts' Rule: Be Prepared

When you load up the car to head out (presuming of course that your journey will take you a little farther afield than the house down the block), make sure that you have the following items:

- ✔ **A dog crate or carrier:** The best way to keep your puppy safe is to put him in a crate for the trip home. If you don't have a dog crate, find a box big enough to comfortably hold your Yorkie. Make sure the box's sides are high enough to stop him from jumping or crawling out.

  Line the crate or box with an old towel. Doing so makes the crate a little more comfortable for your new puppy and helps him keep his footing so that he doesn't slide around whenever you turn a corner or stop. Add a toy — something to keep your puppy occupied — for good measure.

- ✔ **Paper towels:** Better safe than sorry. Some puppies get carsick. Others may poop or pee in transit.

- ✔ **Trash bag:** See the preceding item. Plastic is better than paper because it doesn't leak, and you can tie it up to eliminate at least some of the smell.

- ✔ **Money:** Don't forget to take along the cashier's check, personal check, cash, or credit card you need to pay for the puppy.

  If you're buying from a breeder, be sure to ask beforehand what type of payment she accepts. Some breeders, having gotten stiffed with personal checks in the past, accept only cash or cashier's checks.

- ✔ **Anything else the breeder requires:** Some breeders, for example, require that you provide the name and phone number of your vet. Be sure you know what else you need to bring for your breeder.

- ✔ **A small bag of kibble (preferably the kind the breeder's been feeding your pup), a bottle of water, and a water dish:** If your trip home is a long one, you'll want to give your hungry traveler a little food and water during the trip home. Although many breeders supply you with a sample of your puppy's chow, don't assume that yours will.

- ✔ **Collar and leash:** If you need to let your pup out of the car to take care of business, bring a collar and leash along. Keep in mind, however, that your pup probably won't be used to a collar and will spend most of his time fighting it instead of relieving himself.

✔ **An extra pair of hands:** Although you don't strictly need a partner with you if you have a crate (you can secure the door and know that your puppy is safe), having someone who can talk to, tend to, and check on the puppy lets you concentrate on driving.

If you don't have a crate, having an extra person in the car with you is a must. A loose puppy in a moving car is a recipe for disaster. And even if the puppy's box doesn't tip over, the puppy doesn't scale the box's side, and the trip home is abnormally free of other drivers, potholes, and sharp corners, puppies are still very distracting.

What You'll Bring Home

If you think that you arrived at the breeder's with a bunch of stuff, just wait until you make the trip back home! In addition to your most prized possession (your puppy, that is), you can expect to tote some pretty extensive paperwork and maybe a few supplies back with you.

When you arrive at the breeder's to pick up your puppy, don't expect to get in and out in 20 minutes. Expect to spend a little time there. Typically, the breeder has a whole host of papers and information to pass on, and much of it he'll want to go over with you in person. If you haven't picked a pup yet, you'll be there even longer. If this meeting is the first time you've seen the breeder or the puppies, refer to Chapter 3 for information on how to evaluate the breeder and Chapter 4 for what to look for in your dog.

Your new puppy — duh!

Of course, the most important thing you take away from this meeting is your dog. If you selected a pup from the litter at an earlier date, now you're just there to pick her up. Do the following:

✔ **Make sure she's the puppy you picked.** If you selected her even just two weeks earlier, she's going to look quite a bit different now than she did then. Fortunately (and amazingly, if you ask me), most breeders can tell one pup from another by their subtle physical differences, which may be indiscernible to you (how a puppy holds her ears, for example, or whether her tail droops at an angle when it's not wagging), and personality differences.

✔ **Make another quick reassessment of her health.** If the healthy, robust puppy you selected a few weeks before shows signs of illness, discuss the situation with the breeder to find out what ails the little gal. (Chapter 4 explains what a healthy puppy looks and acts like.) A reputable breeder may arrange for you to adopt another pup from the litter.

Although you may be tempted to overlook any signs of illness, don't. First, a responsible breeder isn't going to allow anyone to adopt a sick puppy. Second, a sign of illness can indicate a major health problem. For information about medical conditions that can afflict Yorkies, go to Chapter 12.

If you haven't selected a puppy yet, now you get to decide which of the little darlings is going home with you. Refer to Chapter 4 for information on how to choose one cutie out of many.

With your new puppy underarm (underfoot, around your legs, running through the house, and so on), try your hardest to pay attention to the other stuff that the breeder gives you.

A puppy-care kit

Many breeders amass all the stuff you need for your new puppy in a single goodie bag. In addition to all the important info, like paperwork and inoculation dates, discussed in the following sections, you may even get sample packages of food to get you through the first days and possibly a souvenir (a toy, a ribbon, for example) to remind you — and your puppy — of his first home.

Med checks and shots

Most Yorkies go to their new homes when they're around 12 weeks old, which means that, at the least, they should have already received the first two rounds of puppy vaccines and been wormed. The breeder will also have docked the puppies' tails and removed their *dewclaws* (the extra, functionless claw on the inside of the dog's leg, right near her foot). If the breeder had reason to suspect any medical conditions (such as liver shunt; see Chapter 12), she also may have had the puppy tested. So expect to get the following information:

✔ The name of the vaccines used and the dates given

> *Note:* Because the dosage of vaccines is always 1 mL (milliliter), the breeder probably won't indicate dosage.

✔ The type of worming preparation and the date administered

✔ Results of any diagnostic tests

If your puppy has had any other medical care, the breeder includes information (the treatment and why it was necessary) about this, too.

Food facts

The breeder will tell you what kind of puppy food she's used, what her feeding schedule was, and how much food she recommends giving your puppy. She may even provide you with a few days' supply of the puppy food or a few coupons for more of the same brand.

Keep your puppy on the same type of food and feeding schedule during his first few days at home. He'll be stressed out enough anyway at the huge change in his life. You don't want him to have indigestion problems, too.

For information on a healthy diet as your puppy grows into adult-hood, head to Chapter 9.

Grooming instructions

One of your best sources for grooming tips and tricks is your breeder. When you pick up your puppy, your breeder will probably explain the basics of grooming without you even having to ask. He'll tell you what you should do and when, what products you should use (and avoid), and so on. He may even demonstrate proper technique, like how to clean your puppy's ears or how to hold your puppy's paws for nail clipping.

Your puppy probably won't require much in the way of grooming right off the bat. In fact, your initial goal is simply to get her used to being brushed, touched around the paws and ears, and so on. For grooming details, head to Chapter 10.

A bunch of papers and a form or two

Deforestation aside, expect to receive quite a bit of paperwork. Not only do you have the contract itself, but you should also get an American Kennel Club (AKC) registration form, and the breeder may give you copies of the *pedigrees* (or the family trees) of the dam and sire. Keep all these papers on file at home for future reference.

You won't get your puppy's pedigree when you pick him up. You apply for that yourself when (or after) you register your dog. Still, looking at your dog's parents' pedigrees can yield interesting information about his background. See the section "The pedigree: Your dog's family tree" in this chapter for details about the info included on a pedigree.

Breeder contracts and guarantees

The contract you get from your breeder should, at a minimum, include the following information:

- ✓ **Terms of the sale:** This information should include the amount of payment and the date of sale.

- ✓ **Names and addresses of both buyer and breeder:** Just to be clear, the contract should also contain this info.

- ✓ **The puppy's identifying information:** This info *must* include the following:

  - The breed, color, and sex of the dog

  - The dog's birth date

  - The registered names of both the dam and the sire, as well as their registration numbers

  - The name and address of the breeder — in case that info isn't included elsewhere in the contract

Many contracts also contain this information:

- ✓ **Health (and possibly temperament) guarantee:** Many breeders guarantee that the puppy is physically and mentally healthy. To confirm that your puppy is healthy, a breeder requires that you schedule an appointment with your vet. If your puppy *isn't* healthy, you can often return him for a refund or exchange him for another puppy. You generally have to schedule the first vet appointment within 72 hours of purchasing your puppy.

- ✓ **Spay/neuter agreement:** If your puppy is pet-quality rather than show-quality (see Chapter 4 for a description of each type), your breeder will probably require that you have it spayed or neutered within a certain period of time. Some breeders even hold the registration form until you prove that you had your dog fixed.

If your breeder's contract includes a spay/neuter agreement, don't assume that this clause means anything dire about your dog's health or temperament. Such a clause simply means that your dog has a conformation fault — something that stops him from either competing in AKC-sponsored conformation events or from winning those events. An example of a conformation fault is a testicle that hasn't properly descended. Head to Chapter 2 for a rundown of the important points of the breed standard.

- ✓ **The type of registration (limited or full) your puppy is eligible for:** Breeders determine whether your puppy gets full or

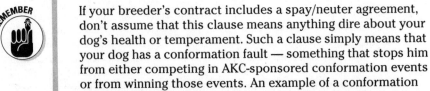

limited registration with the AKC. Breeders often stipulate limited registration for their pet-quality dogs. To find out why, head to the section "Ain't I blue? The registration papers" later in this chapter.

Don't breed pet-quality dogs. Love them. Cherish them. Buy them matching outfits and crochet little snuggle toys, if you must, but *don't* breed them. That's the position that responsible breeders take, and it's the reason that they include spay/neuter agreements in their contracts and offer only limited, rather than full, registration for these dogs.

✔ **What your responsibilities are if you can no longer keep the dog:** Most responsible breeders accept the return of their puppies throughout the puppies' lives. In the contract, breeders include a statement that if, for whatever reason, you can no longer care for this animal, you either return it to them or involve them in finding the dog another home.

✔ **Possibly a list of the inheritable conditions or diseases that are common to Yorkies:** Like all purebred dogs, Yorkies are susceptible to certain illnesses and conditions (see Chapter 12). To make sure that you're aware of these conditions — and not able to come back and say that you were misinformed — your breeder may list them in excruciating detail.

A signed contract protects both you and your breeder. *Don't* come away without one.

Fun with fees

When registering your dog with the AKC, being timely pays. If you register your dog within 12 months of the date that the breeder registered the litter, you pay these fees:

✔ Dog registration only: $15

✔ Registration plus pedigree: $32

If you register after the first 12 months, here's what you fork over:

✔ Dog registration only: $50

✔ Registration plus pedigree: $67

Wait until more than 24 months pass, and not only do you have to pay these inflated prices, but you also need to explain in writing why you took so %^#@&! long to get your derriere in gear:

✔ Dog registration only: $80

✔ Registration plus pedigree: $97

Ain't 1 blue? The registration papers

The breeder is the only person who can determine whether your puppy is eligible for full or limited registration in the AKC. In almost all instances, breeders offer full registration to show-quality dogs — those puppies who closely conform to the breed standard. Those puppies who aren't considered show-quality, for whatever reason — and the reason is often as minor as having an incorrect bite — get limited registration. Here's the difference:

- ✔ **Full registration:** You can register any of your puppy's future offspring with the AKC, and your dog can participate in any AKC-sponsored event that Yorkies are eligible for. If the breeder says your pup is eligible for full registration, you get the standard dog registration form, shown in Figure 6-1.

- ✔ **Limited registration:** With a limited registration, you *can't* register your puppy's future offspring with the AKC. This type of registration breaks the pedigree chain for your dog. Additionally, in dog shows, your Yorkie can only participate in obedience, tracking, and agility contests. Your dog can't compete in *conformation events* (events that judge how closely the dog represents the breed standard). Breeders who don't want their pet-quality dogs to breed give these dogs a dog registration application with the "limited" box checked.

When you pick up your puppy, your breeder informs you which type of registration your pup's eligible for and gives you the appropriate form to fill out.

Some breeders, to put a little more muscle behind any spay/neuter agreement that they have in their contracts, hold the dog registration form, also called the *blue slip,* for limited registration until you provide proof that you had your Yorkie altered.

The blue slip itself is pretty self-explanatory. Simply fill in the missing information and then send the form, along with the registration fee, to the AKC. In a few weeks, you get either a full registration certificate or a limited registration certificate. These certificates are nearly identical, except for the colors of the border (limited registration has an orange border; full registration has a purple one) and that the limited registration certificate includes the statement "Offspring of this dog not eligible for registration."

If you intend to register your dog with the AKC, don't wait too long. After 12 months, you have to pay a penalty. Wait two years, and you have to pay an arm and a leg. See the sidebar "Fun with fees" in this chapter for details.

The pedigree: Your dog's family tree

A *pedigree* is simply your Yorkie's family tree. One difference you may notice between this family tree and the one your human family may have hanging in the hallway is that you read the dog's pedigree from left to right rather than from the bottom up (see Figure 6-1).

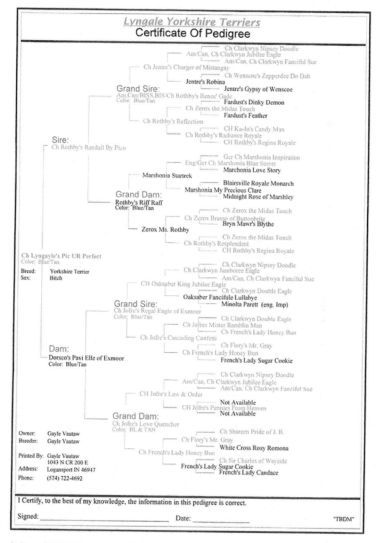

Pedigree reprinted with permission of Gayle Vautaw, Lyngale Yorkshire Terriers

Figure 6-1: A sample pedigree.

To make sense of your pup's pedigree and the information it includes, keep these points in mind:

- The sire is always listed on the top; the dam on the bottom.

- Any titles a particular dog earned in competition appear as abbreviations beside her name. Titles that come before the name are prefix titles (go figure); titles after the name are — drum roll, please — suffix titles.

- To make sense of the titles — and therefore be able to glean important information the pedigree has to offer — you have to know what the abbreviations mean. Here's a list of a few of the titles you may see and what they mean:

Abbreviation	Meaning
AX	Agility Excellent
CD	Companion Dog
CDX	Companion Dog Excellent
Ch.	Champion
MACH	Master Agility Champion
NOC	National Obedience Champion
OD	Outstanding Dam
OS	Outstanding Sire
OTCH	Obedience Trial Champion

- On some pedigrees, a series of almost indecipherable numbers and letters appear beneath the name. This important info includes

    - The dog's registration number.

    - The stud-book date (the date when the dog was first bred).

    - Orthopedic Foundation for Animals (OFA) certifications regarding medical checks on the dog's hips and elbows.

If the pedigree doesn't indicate an OFA certification, don't despair. Although Yorkshire Terriers can be OFA certified, most breeders don't routinely have their Yorkies checked. (As a rule, OFA certification is more important in larger breeds).

- Abbreviations for colors and markings.

To get your dog's pedigree, simply check the appropriate box on the front of the dog registration application (it's the form that says "Check here for registration and pedigree"). In a few weeks, the AKC sends you your dog's pedigree. You can also apply for a pedigree online. Simply go to the AKC Web site (www.akc.org).

A pedigree looks pretty impressive, but keep in mind that simply having a list of names doesn't tell you anything about your dog. Besides the health certifications, the titles are probably the most important information in the document because they can reveal, for example, that your dog's great-great-great granddaddy was a real pro at agility or his great-grandma was a whiz at obedience. But before you get all worked up over the stars in your dog's bloodline and think that your pup will have the same luster, consider this: Frank Sinatra, Jr.

Over the River and Through the Woods: Making the Trip Home

With papers and puppy in hand, you're ready to begin the trip home. If you have the necessary supplies (refer to the earlier section "The Scouts' Rule: Be Prepared" for a list) and heed the following advice, your trip home will go more smoothly:

- ✔ **Get your puppy comfortably settled in her crate or box.** Make sure she has a comfy towel and the toy you brought along (see Figure 6-2).

- ✔ **Secure the crate in the back seat of the car by fastening the seatbelt around it.** The back seat is the best place for your dog because it's the safest. If you have someone along to help, have that person sit in the back, too.

Seatbelts are designed to secure people of a certain height and weight. Fastening a seatbelt around the crate may stop the crate from sliding around, but it doesn't offer much protection if you have an accident. If you drive a van or other vehicle with individual back seats (sometimes called "captain's seats"), you can use a luggage strap to secure the crate against the seat.

Although your pup may not like being in the crate and may let you know by crying or whining, don't let her out. Instead, stick your fingers through the crate door so that she can smell you, give her a few pieces of kibble, or, if you're going solo, share your life story with her. If you must let her out, pull over and take a break.

✔ **Keep your pup confined at all times when the car's moving.** A roaming Yorkie can get into all sorts of dangerous situations in a moving car and cause many more. Hey, to a puppy, every new place is a wonderland to explore: You'll find her under the seats (where the mechanisms for adjusting the seats are), around the accelerator or break pedals, between the doors and interiors, and so on. Even if your pup just wants to stand up to look out the window, she can get hurt if she rolls backward or falls forward when you turn or come to a stop.

If you're driving, your lap is the most dangerous place for your puppy. Not only is she a distraction, but if you get into an accident, she can also be seriously harmed or killed if you fall into her or the airbag deploys.

✔ **If your drive home is a long one, stop periodically to let the puppy out of her crate.** Even pulling over into an industrial park can give you both a break from the road. During these stops, you can hold and cuddle your puppy all you want — safely.

©Isabelle Francais

Figure 6-2: A dog in a dog crate for the trip home.

Chapter 7

Welcoming Your Dog to His New Pad

● ●

In This Chapter

▶ Letting your puppy make a reconnaissance of your house

▶ Introducing your pup to your kids and other animals

▶ Tips for making it through the first night

● ●

*B*etween the time that you pull into your driveway and the time that you carry your puppy into the house, a world of potential is before you. This potential — for your puppy to become the sweet, loving, stable, and trainable companion you want — will either be realized or lost, based on your actions and the interactions that your puppy has with his new environment and the people and other creatures in it. And, generally speaking, your puppy's first hours inside your home will give you a pretty accurate idea of how that potential will shape up.

Turn any puppy loose in the middle of a maelstrom of overly eager kids, barking dogs, and a hissing cat or two with the expectation that he'll eventually get used to the mayhem and "fit right in," and you set the stage for your pup to grow into an adult dog with issues. A shy, meek puppy can end up a nervous, fearful wreck. An outgoing, friendly pup can end up overly excitable and wild. And an aggressive pup only becomes more so. But if you calmly and methodically intro-duce your pup to his new environment (and socialize him properly in the weeks and months to come; see Chapter 8), you'll end up with a calm, well-adjusted, happy dog who's a pleasure to be around.

So your first challenge is to use the introduction period to set the stage for success. Let your pup explore, let your kids be excited (but not chase after the puppy), let your other animals sniff around, and have fun — but be in control. By gently guiding your puppy through the introductions to your other family members, you take the first important step toward teaching him that you're the boss, the protector, and the one to please.

Introducing Your Dog to Her New Digs

Young pups in a new environment have absolutely no concept of proper bathroom behavior. They poop and pee like birds — wherever they are when the urge strikes. So before you head inside the house, give your puppy a chance to relieve herself outside. She isn't old enough to understand the real meaning of going potty outside, but you can buy yourself some time for exploring the great indoors. (Head to Chapter 14 for housetraining instructions.)

Once inside, your puppy, depending on her personality, will either hit the ground running or explore a little more trepidatiously. Either approach is fine. Give her a chance to discover and examine her environment at her own speed.

Try to time your arrival so that the puppy has some time alone to explore the new house. If that's impossible because you have young children, instruct them to stay back as the puppy explores. Before they know it, she'll be crawling all over them for a good look-see. Head to the section "Hello, kiddie" in this chapter for tips on making puppy-child introductions.

Showing her the most important places first

The first places you want to take your puppy to are her food-and-water-dish area and her indoor potty area (if you have one). She needs to know where to go to find her "things." Of course, she'll probably be too curious with all the new sights and sounds to do more than sniff around the area, but if she wants to eat, fine.

Introducing her to her crate is also important, if it isn't the same one she traveled home in. If you are using the crate she traveled home in, then simply put it where it's going to be (refer to Chapter 5 for suggested locations) and leave the door open so that she can wander in and out at will. If she hasn't seen the crate before and doesn't seem inclined to go in, try luring her inside with a small treat or a toy, and praise her if she goes in. Then let her come back out when she's ready.

Don't force your puppy into the crate or lock her in after she's inside. If you do, you'll make her fearful of the very place you want her to associate with comfort and security. For now, just letting her sniff around and step in and out is fine.

Put any toys you have for her in a place where she can find them — near the crate is fine. Show her the toys; even offer to play for a couple of minutes, if she wants to, but let her move on when she's ready.

Letting him snoop around safely

After you show your puppy where to find his possessions, let him explore the rest of the house. As your puppy roams from room to room, make sure that you stay with him. You don't have to get down on the floor, commenting on and admiring every little object he discovers, but you do need to be close enough to step in if he approaches something dangerous or does something you don't want him to do.

The key to training a dog is consistency. Make sure you apply the house rules the same way every time. Wavering just confuses your dog and makes eliciting the right behavior from him that much more difficult. So from the minute you bring your pup into the house, don't let him do anything that you don't want him to do as an adult — be it chew on the table leg, tug on your daughter's long hair, or feint aggression at the tabby — no matter how cute and harmless these antics may appear at first.

If your puppy approaches something he shouldn't (and moving the item — such as a power cord — out of the way isn't an option), say "no" in a firm voice, and then pick him up and move him away from the temptation. If he goes back to it, say "no" and move him again. If he keeps going back to the item, tap him lightly on the nose (lightly is the key here) as you say "no" and then take him to another room where he can explore.

Similarly, don't let your puppy explore rooms you don't intend to let him in. If the dining room is a dog-free zone, for example, make sure you block it off. Allowing him to explore the room is the equivalent of an open invitation. Also be sure to block off unsafe areas — like stairways leading down.

One benefit of following your puppy around is that you'll know when he has to go to the bathroom. If signs show that a bathroom deposit is imminent, pick him up and take him immediately to the approved bathroom area (either newspapers or outside). If he goes, praise him and let him get back to exploring. If he doesn't go after a few minutes, let him explore some more but be especially watchful so that you can bring him back to the bathroom area, when necessary. Remember, success breeds success — and there's no better time to start than the present! For information on how to housetrain, go to Chapter 14.

By being consistent from the get-go about what is and isn't allowed, you're taking the first step to successfully training your dog.

Meeting the Other Family Members

Your human children, if you have any, are probably beside themselves with glee that the new puppy is finally home. Your canine or feline friends are probably much less enthusiastic. They may not be humming dirges, but you can bet they have a dimmer view of the new kid in the house. Your task, then, is twofold: Make the necessary introductions and make sure the interactions don't get out of hand. The following sections tell you how.

Hello, kitty!

Introducing your pup to her new housemates may be the one thing (besides wondering how the night will go) that's causing you the most stress. But it shouldn't, and it won't, if you know what kind of behavior to expect from both your animals.

The presence of the puppy alone is going to introduce stress for your other animals until they figure out what they're going to have to deal with. To make the stress as minimal as possible, choose a relatively quiet time and location to introduce your animals to one another.

Dog-eek!-dog introductions

Here's a little peek at normal canine greeting rituals. In addition to sniffing, you may see a lot of bluffing: the showing of teeth, raising hackles, and shoulder pawing. Don't panic, even though your older dog may look like he's just barely tolerating the precocious puppy skidding around him. Your dogs are doing what dogs do when they first meet: sizing one another up in order to determine who's dominant. It's an essential first step if you ever hope for harmony in your dogs' relationship.

If your other dog is much larger than your Yorkie, the shoulder pawing may be a problem just because of the sheer weight and power of the bigger dog. To reduce the risk that your Yorkie will get hurt, be extra vigilant. In fact, if you have a much larger dog — especially one who still displays puppy behavior himself, is very exuberant, or isn't particularly well trained — a Yorkie probably isn't a good choice for your family. (Head to Chapter 1 to find out whether your house is a good one for such a small dog.)

Here are some suggestions for keeping the initial meetings between your pets calm:

- ✔ **Stay close by but don't interfere unless you think that the bluffing is escalating to aggression (see the next item).** Your dogs have to come to their own conclusions about each other, and they can't do that with you cooing "Be nice" like a mantra or pacing back and forth, wringing your hands.

- ✔ **If you notice any signs of aggression, end the introductions immediately.** Signs of aggression include

    - Crouching and hugging the ground, with ears pinned back to the head

    - Glaring (hard stares)

    - Deep-throated growling

    - A general, tense stillness

- ✔ If you're not sure how your older dog is going to react, put both dogs on leashes before the introduction and have someone there who can help you pull the two dogs apart if things get out of hand.

- ✔ **Don't force the dogs to interact.** Some dogs rush up to sniff at the new puppy; others stand back and observe for a while. Similarly, when your older dog is ready to leave, let him. Don't force him to stay and submit to any more juvenile antics. If the puppy tries to follow him, hold the pup back. After all, even *mothers* of toddlers can take only so much of toddlers.

- ✔ **Let the dogs establish their hierarchy and then abide by it.** Until the puppy earns a higher place in the pack, she's the low woman on the totem pole as far as your other dog is concerned. Although she may become the dominant dog later, she's not now. Don't undermine this hierarchy — even unwittingly. Follow these suggestions:

    - Don't hold the puppy up for introductions. Height equals status to dogs. The higher dog is the more dominant one. So let the dogs greet each other at their natural levels.

    - To help your older dog come to terms with the new arrival, reinforce his dominant status by greeting him first and giving him the most attention.

After your dogs settle the dog hierarchy and accept their individual status (as either dominant or submissive), your home is going to be pretty peaceful. But as your puppy grows and her personality becomes more apparent, the dynamics between the two dogs continue to shift. Occasionally, they get along fine; other times they snap and argue with one another. You usually see these upsets at hot spots — places where dominance challenges are likely to happen: food dishes, doorways, favorite pillows, treat time, and so on.

When you have a Yorkie, especially if your other dog is much larger, be aware of where the hot spots are so that you can eliminate any problems or intervene if things get rough. For example, you can feed the dogs separately, if necessary.

Here, kitty, kitty

Maybe your cat will become great friends with your new puppy (a likelier scenario if she's a kitten when he's a pup). Maybe she'll consider him nothing more than a toy to wind up and let go. Maybe she'll avoid him entirely. As unfair as the situation may be from the canine perspective, the creature in control of this relationship is the cat. Why? Because she doesn't have to stick around any longer than she wants to, and she has the tools — the speed and the agility — to escape.

The introduction between your puppy and your cat is likely to be brief, consisting of however long it takes the cat to decide she's seen enough — an opinion she may very well form from the top of the refrigerator without bothering to get up close and personal.

To aid inter-species harmony, keep these tips in mind:

- ✔ **Keep the puppy on a leash when the cat comes near.** If the cat runs, your Yorkie may give chase.

- ✔ **If the cat hisses or swats at your Yorkie, stay calm.** Don't scold her and don't baby him. Simply call an end to the introduction (if the cat hasn't done so already).

When your cat is ready to leave, let her go. The goal of the first meeting is simply to make introductions, not friends — yet. That may come with time — and without you interfering. And if all you manage to achieve is noncombatant status, that's fine, too.

Other animals in your menagerie

If you have birds, gerbils, hamsters, iguanas, geckos, or other such pets, you need to make introductions (that is, let the animals see one another) only if you let the other critters out to roam the house — even if they roam in a critter cruiser — or if your Yorkie can access their living environment. Introduce them to each other a few days after your puppy's homecoming, when she's had a chance to get used to her environment but you're still closely supervising her. Keep these pointers in mind:

✔ **Make sure you don't unintentionally encourage inappropriate behavior.** Laughing at her behavior, trying to coax her out of it, or giving her anything she can construe as positive attention will give her the impression that jumping and barking at the guinea pigs in the guinea pig cage is just A-okay with you. Instead, say "no" in a firm voice and take her away from the cage. If she persists, give her a few minutes of timeout in her crate.

✔ **Remember that Yorkies are terriers.** A small animal — especially one who runs away — is an almost impossible-to-resist temptation. Unless you train your Yorkie to leave your small pets alone — and she's consistently proved that you can trust her — never let your small critter run free when your Yorkie's around and unsupervised.

Hello, kiddie

You may worry about your cat and dog's reactions to the Yorkie, but you should worry the most about your young children's reactions. Yorkie puppies are fairly hardy — for small dogs — but they're no match for exuberant children. Without meaning to, a playful or clumsy child can seriously hurt a puppy who himself is too playful and clumsy to be very adept at getting out of the way. For this reason, be very specific about what your children are and aren't allowed to do with the puppy. Consider the guidelines in the following sections.

Training toddlers

If you have a very young child (a toddler or preschooler), follow these steps:

1. **Hold the puppy and invite your child to you.**

   Don't let your toddler walk up to your puppy. The combination of an unsteady child and a playful puppy can easily lead to a fall. Similarly, a steady-on-her-feet preschooler may approach your puppy too quickly.

2. **Let your child pet the puppy under your supervision.**

   Remind (or explain) the concept of gentle touches and show your child what a gentle touch is.

3. **When the puppy's had enough, end the interaction.**

   In this instance, you need to take your puppy's lead and not your child's. Forcing a dog to interact when he'd rather do something else doesn't breed familiarity; it breeds contempt.

Here are some other tips to smooth over any rough edges of the toddler-puppy interaction:

- ✔ If the puppy mouths your child (and he probably will), have a toy nearby that you can give him instead. Comfort your child if she's upset, but don't punish the puppy — by word or deed in front of your toddler. Toddlers are great imitators; if you're not careful, you may end up with a 3-year-old who considers canine discipline her responsibility.

- ✔ If your child wants to hold the puppy, treat the situation the same way you would if your child wanted to hold a human baby (your pup may not be human, but he's definitely a baby!): Have your child sit down, put the puppy in her lap, and stay close enough to help her hold the puppy carefully and gently.

At this age, children are really too young to be left alone with a small dog. And reciting a laundry list of rules to your child doesn't do anyone any good. So make sure that whenever the two of them are together, you or another adult is around to keep an eye on things.

Channeling your older kids' energy

You know your child(ren) better than anyone and can judge better than anyone how they'll react to a new puppy. As a general rule, calm kids get excited. Excitable kids are beside themselves with nearly uncontrollable joy. Everyone's excited, including the puppy. So, how do you make introductions when your kids want to rush the puppy, and the puppy wants to run to the hills? Consider playing a modified version of the kids' game Statue (this strategy is ideal if you have more than one child). Playing Statue allows your puppy to check your children out in a calm, safe setting. Here's how it works:

1. **Have the child(ren) sit on the floor.**

   Use whatever room you want, although I don't recommend using the one where the puppy's food dishes are or where her bathroom area is. Those places aren't for play.

2. **Bring the puppy into the room and let her explore.**

   See the earlier section "Introducing Your Dog to Her New Digs" for tips.

3. **While the puppy is in the room, your children sit still and stay quiet.**

   They can't call the dog's name, lure her with toys, or do anything else to attract her attention.

4. **When the puppy approaches a child for a sniff, that child comes "alive."**

Becoming "alive" means that your child can pet and talk to the puppy but can't pick her up or hold her. The puppy can crawl into a lap, as long as she's free to leave when she's ready to.

5. **When the puppy's ready to move on, the child lets the puppy go and turns into a statue again.**

It's very unlikely that your puppy will leave any child unexplored. But if that happens (usually because something outside the room catches the puppy's eye and off she goes), say something like "Saved the best for last" and place the puppy in the child's lap.

Every game needs a winner, and the winner of this game isn't the one the puppy goes to the most, but the one who follows the rules the best. The prize? A special dog-related task that the child is old enough to perform and likely to enjoy. If all your kids are winners (the best scenario), come up with as many fun jobs as you have kids and let them draw lots. Ideas include filling the food bowls, minding the puppy on car rides, keeping shoes and toys picked up, being on potty lookout (or the one to clean up the mess), fluffing the dog blanket, taking the dog for walks, and so on. The job and level of adult supervision depend on your kids' ages and maturity levels.

The fact is, until your kids are old enough to know which jobs are the bad ones, any job that lets them "take care of the dog" is good. By the time they figure out that using the pooper scooper is *not* the prize position they thought it was, you'll have other ways (read threats and coercion) to motivate them.

Here are some other things to keep in mind as your puppy gets acquainted with the human side of your family:

✔ **Puppies use their mouths to explore, and their teeth are very sharp.** Prime your kids on what to do when the dog mouths them: Younger kids may react reflexively, pushing the dog away or hitting (see the earlier section "Training toddlers" for info on what to do when this happens); older kids can probably handle the little nips.

✔ **Yorkie puppies are the perfect size to carry around, but that doesn't mean they should be.** So make a rule about who, if anyone, can pick up the puppy and under what circumstances.

✔ **Remind young children not to be rowdy with the puppy.** With younger children — who may get overly exuberant in giving their attention to the puppy — be sure to remind them not to tug on the puppy's hair, legs, ears, tails, or any other body parts.

✔ **Tell your children to give the puppy her space.** Kids tend to think that the way to make a dog love them is to keep her with them all the time. But that strategy does exactly the opposite. So tell your kids that if they want the dog to hang around them, they have to let the dog go when she's ready.

✔ **Older kids (adolescents, teens, and even mature elementary-age kids) can be a tremendous help.** If you explain what the rules are to your older children as well as how they need to teach and enforce them, you've just recruited your puppy training assistants. Head to Chapter 13 for the training tasks that the whole family should be in on.

The best introduction plan lets your child enjoy the puppy and keeps the puppy safe and from being over-stimulated. Use whatever tactics work.

Surviving the First Night

To not put too fine a point on it, the first night is hell. Oh, sure, many dog books imply that if you do certain things — like let the puppy room with you, put a soft stuffed animal in the crate to simulate the feel of littermates, or croon lullabies every two hours — the night will pass easily. But they're wrong. The first night is never easy, but it's definitely manageable. You just have to resign yourself to the facts.

Buckle your seatbelts; it's going to be a bumpy night

Your puppy misses his mom and his siblings. You've been a fun distraction for most of the day, but now that it's bedtime, your puppy keenly feels the absence of the pack he belonged to. Add the fact that he's in a new place, and top the whole shebang off with a stupid towel in a stupid crate that doesn't smell right anyway. For all these reasons, your puppy's going to spend most of the night crying.

You, on the other hand, spend most of the night awake with a pillow wrapped around your head. You may get suckered in by the intermittent moments of silence and think "Ah, he's finally asleep," only to jerk fully awake again when the crying starts back up.

The goal of the first night isn't to get your puppy to sleep through it (although that'd be really great); it's to establish the nighttime routine. Until he gets used to it, the evenings are going to be hard; after he's used to the routine, you'll all sleep like babies.

Putting your puppy to bed

On your puppy's first night home, you want to begin the routine you intend to follow for the next several months. (I say months because you won't change this routine until your puppy is fully housetrained and trustworthy.) Follow these steps:

1. **About a half hour before bedtime, give your pup her last meal of the day.**

    This last meal is only for puppies under 12 weeks old, who still need four meals a day. If your pup is older than that, skip the meal and head to Step 2.

2. **Take your puppy outside to do her business.**

    If she doesn't go to the bathroom right away, take her back in. If she doesn't show signs of having to go on her own, wait for about a half hour and then take her out again. You'll be in a holding pattern until your dog goes to the bathroom, so make sure that you're not so dog-tired that you fall asleep on the couch and miss the prime moment, so to speak.

3. **As soon as she's gone to the bathroom, take her to her crate, say "Bedtime" as you put her in, and then close the door.**

    You should already have set up the crate with a towel for comfort and a stuffed animal for company. (Lullabies are optional.)

4. **Turn out the lights and go to bed yourself.**

5. **When the puppy cries (and she will), you can comfort her but don't let her out.**

    Comforting your puppy is much easier when you keep the crate in the bedroom with you. Talk softly to your puppy, put your fingers through the crate door, and so on.

6. **After a few hours, take your puppy outside to go to the bathroom.**

    Pick her up and carry her to the bathroom area. Once there, don't talk to her, play with her, or do anything that gives her the impression that this time is for anything other than bathroom business.

7. **As soon as she goes to the bathroom, praise her and then take her immediately back to the crate. Say "Bedtime" again, close the door again, and go back to bed (again).**

8. **When she starts crying again, comfort her but don't let her out.**

As you create your bedtime routine, keep these things in mind:

- ✔ **Because of how long this first night seems — and the second one will only be a little shorter — consider bringing your puppy home on a Friday.** Being sleep deprived is no fun, but stumbling through a weekend day bleary-eyed is better than stumbling through an important meeting at work.

- ✔ **Taking the bathroom run is important because dogs have a natural desire to keep their dens (which is what the crate is) clean.** Combine that instinct with planned confinement, and you teach your puppy to hold her bladder and bowel, which is one of the keys to successfully housetraining your dog. Head to Chapter 14 for step-by-step instructions on how to house-train your Yorkie.

  If you don't let her out of the crate to go the bathroom while she's still too young to hold it through the night, you can subvert the very instinct that your housetraining relies upon.

- ✔ **Don't give in to the crying and let your dog out of the crate just for some cuddle time.** Worse, don't swap the crate for a spot on your bed — at least not yet. The day will come when your Yorkie has earned her place at the foot or head of your bed, but this isn't it. If you give in to her plaintive wails, you teach her that she can get what she wants by complaining.

- ✔ **Although being tired may make you irritable, don't take it out on your dog.** Don't yell at her and don't banish her to the nether regions of the house. Remember, the only source of comfort she has on this first night is you — even if you're across the room in the bed — and the little bit of familiarity she gained from exploring her environment. Moving the crate to a far off region of the house so you don't have to hear her whining is harsh punishment for any dog; and to a little dog who feels all alone, it's just cruel.

Admittedly, the first night is going to be a long one. But the next night will go better, and the following night will go even better than that. If you're consistent, before long your puppy will know the routine and settle right in when you say those magic words "Bedtime."

Chapter 8

Good First Steps

. . . .

In This Chapter

▶ Introducing your Yorkie to new people and animals

▶ Handling common canine fears

▶ Creating daily routines for your dog

▶ Setting the foundation for future training

. . . .

*W*hen your puppy first comes home, everything is new to her, and anything is possible. Your first goal, then, is to provide some structure to what would otherwise be her random and completely spontaneous actions. Essentially, you want to teach her very basic lessons: You do this here; you do that there. You can chew on this, but not on that. This room is a dog-free zone; this is the puppy play area. And so on. In short, you want to prepare her for the life she's going to lead with you, and you want the instruction to start as soon as she sets paw over your threshold.

Of course, puppies don't learn these lessons by being told. They learn by being shown over and over and over again, until the repetition becomes the rule. Right now you're simply redirecting her from inappropriate behavior to appropriate behavior. But eventually you'll move into more formal training, where your goal is to either teach appropriate responses or modify unacceptable behaviors (see Part IV). Key components of these early lessons are socializing your dog and setting up predictable routines and expectations that you can both count on.

Socializing Your Puppy

There's a certain period during a dog's mental development when he discovers the world around him. During this time, called *socialization,* he learns who his social companions are. These early impressions are important because they affect how your dog will behave as an adult toward unfamiliar people, animals, and events.

Dogs have a very keen sense of what is and isn't familiar, a sense formed during socialization. When you socialize your puppy, therefore, you want to deliberately and carefully introduce him to all sorts of stimuli (people, places, noises, events such as car rides, and so on) in order to make him comfortable in different situations and around different people. After all, part of being a well-adjusted canine (or human for that matter) is understanding that, in life, encountering the unfamiliar is normal.

Here are a couple of important points to remember about socialization:

✔ Animal behaviorists believe that the sensitive period of socialization occurs between 5 and 12 weeks old, but that continuing to socialize your puppy throughout the first year is also vitally important because a puppy's social development doesn't stop after week 12.

✔ Socialization is important for all dogs, but it's especially important for puppies who are naturally shy or timid. Without proper socialization, these personality traits can become more pronounced and develop into fear-related aggression.

The 5- to 12-week window for optimum early socialization has important implications for puppies sold through pet stores or agents. These puppies often come from disreputable breeders or puppy mills, where little or no effort is made to properly socialize them. If you're still in the just-thinking-about-it phase of getting a Yorkie pup, make sure you stay away from these sources and contact reputable breeders in your area (see Chapter 3 for details). If you already purchased a puppy from a pet store or careless breeder, be aware that you may need to work that much harder to overcome his early experiences. Depending on the circumstances and your puppy's personality, you may never be able to completely compensate for your puppy's early neglect.

Meeting and greeting other people

When you socialize your Yorkie, don't limit her introductions just to the people in your family. You want her to meet and encounter as many other people as possible, and you want the interaction to be safe and pleasant in order to teach her that strange people are just part and parcel of her world and not something to fear. Follow these suggestions to broaden your pup's exposure:

✔ Invite your friends over for a visit.

✔ Take your puppy with you when you visit extended family or friends.

✔ Go shopping at a pet market that allows dogs (after your puppy is properly vaccinated and wormed, of course).

✔ Take a walk around your neighborhood during a time when you're bound to pass other walkers, bicyclists, and children playing.

✔ Go to the park.

Yorkies don't get the last of their immunization shots until around 15 or 16 weeks, which means you need to be careful how far out into the wild world you take your new puppy. Until she receives her final immunization, make sure that she meets lots of new people at home and plan outings to safe places like your neighbor's fenced backyard. You simply want your puppy to continue learning that her social network extends beyond her family and the house that she lives in.

As you socialize your puppy, keep these pointers in mind:

✔ Expose her to people of different ethnicities, shapes, sizes, ages, and physical characteristics. Dogs have a very keen sense of what is and what isn't familiar, and a dog who's never seen a bearded man, for example, may react in fear to a man with a beard.

Dogs often react to an unusual or eye-catching feature rather than the person: A friend wearing a big, floppy hat may seem threatening, while the same person without the hat on would be seen as friendly. If you notice your puppy reacting to particular items or people in a fearful way, you can take steps to modify that response. Talk to your vet or the breeder for ideas on how to help your puppy overcome her unreasonable reactions or sign your pup up for a socialization class.

✔ In order to be successful, your puppy doesn't have to run up to greet strangers with a friendly wag of her tail. Simply watching calmly — not cowering, not hiding behind your legs, and not barking — is enough to warrant praise.

✔ If your puppy reacts with fear, don't try to soothe her ("Don't be scared. It's just a nice man" in a cooing baby voice, for example) and don't pet her. In fact, don't react obviously to the dog at all. Any sort of reaction (even scolding) is attention that simply heightens her initial impression. A firm but calm "no" and a trip to the crate, if necessary, for a short timeout are better responses. If your hesitant puppy responds appropriately when around other people, however, praise her or give her a treat so that she associates strangers with good things.

Ideally, you want your puppy to be curious and friendly. You don't want her to show aggression or fear, especially when it's not warranted. The goal of socialization isn't to desensitize your dog to real threats (a stranger running toward her with arms outstretched would freak out any dog — or person for that matter), but you don't want her to react fearfully to situations that aren't threatening. A child running by chasing a ball isn't threatening. Nor is a long-lost friend who comes up to greet you.

If your Yorkie has trouble meeting people, ask your vet for advice or enroll her in a puppy socialization class. See the section "Enrolling in 'puppy socials'" for details.

Dealing with strange animals

You don't want your dog to have a hissy fit every time he sees a strange animal — be it the neighbor's cat, dogs in the park, or your pet parakeet. So in your socialization efforts, you need to make sure that your puppy meets other animals that he's likely to encounter in day-to-day life. If you live on a dairy farm, for example, you want your Yorkie to be as comfortable with the cows as he is with the cat who he shares the house with.

To expose your pup to other animals, you can

- ✔ **Invite your friends to your house with their dogs.** You may want to start with one visitor and his dog at a time. For suggestions on introducing your dogs to others, refer to Chapter 7.

  If your puppy is older, make a play date in a neutral setting — like a park or empty field — where territorial instincts won't come into play.

- ✔ **Take a walk through a park.** You often see other pet owners walking their dogs as well. To increase your chances of meeting other dogs, go to a dog park — for safety's sake, make sure it's one that requires all animals to be on a leash.

- ✔ **Enroll your Yorkie in a puppy or dog socialization class.** See the next section, "Enrolling in 'puppy socials,'" for details on what these classes offer and how to find one in your area.

Until your puppy has all his immunizations, be careful not to expose him to dogs who haven't been immunized. Postpone the trips to the dog park and pet markets until you get your vet's okay. Also remember that your puppy is required to be fully immunized before you can enroll him in puppy socialization classes.

Enrolling in "puppy socials"

Often called "puppy socials" or "puppy school," *puppy socialization classes* are different from training classes in that they focus on fostering appropriate interaction between the dogs and encouraging play. They also provide a safe environment where your Yorkie can meet all sorts of other dogs.

During these classes, you have to be present (it isn't doggy day care, after all), and you may get guidance on how to properly socialize your dog and advice if your dog has problems. The main thing you'll learn, however, is how to stand back and let your dog do what dogs do when they meet, greet, and play together and how to recognize and respond to trouble when interactions don't go well.

Because all socialization classes are different, when you're searching for a class, be sure to ask

- ✔ **Who's running the class?** Try to find a class offered by a trainer or animal behaviorist. People who specialize in animal behavior can help you understand why dogs act the way they do and can offer help if your Yorkie is having difficulty behaving.

- ✔ **What's the focus of the class?** You want a class that helps your puppy get accustomed to other types of dogs and learn good canine manners: how to approach another dog, what is acceptable behavior with other dogs, what other breeds look like, and so on. Avoid classes that just throw dogs together and call what ensues socialization.

- ✔ **What's the criteria for enrolling?** Many socialization classes (or any dog-training classes, for that matter) usually require that the puppies have their full set of shots and that adult dogs be current on their immunizations.

- ✔ **How are dogs introduced into the class?** The goal of these classes is to make encountering and interacting with other dogs a pleasant experience for all involved. For that reason, new dogs or puppies are usually introduced slowly — first by sniffing, for example, and then by limited contact.

To find classes in your area, check with your vet, a local all-breed dog club, your dog's groomer, or other pet professionals in your area.

Calming Common Puppy Fears

Many young puppies go through a period when they're naturally cautious of certain things. This vigilance usually becomes apparent when they begin their initial forays away from their mothers, and their cautious behavior is a potentially live-saving response to the unknown. Puppies reaching adolescence, who may have never been apprehensive before, may all of a sudden respond fearfully or timidly in certain situations. Sometimes dogs simply become fearful after a traumatic event — and to a dog, a traumatic event can be anything from a near-drowning (real trauma) to a balloon popping.

Fearful puppies who don't get the necessary help they need grow into fearful adults who are more likely to snap and bite. The key is to help your Yorkie overcome whatever fears he has *while he's still a puppy* so that he can grow into a well-adjusted, confident dog. One way you can help your puppy is to properly socialize him — expand the pool of candidates he perceives as acceptable social companions (see the preceding section). The other way to help your puppy is to address the hesitance or fear he has toward particular situations and events.

Interestingly, many of the same things trigger fear responses in puppies. In the following sections, I explain what some of these common triggers are and offer suggestions for overcoming them.

Oh, the noise noise noise noise!

A normal, busy household offers an assortment of noises, from the soothing to the hair-raising. Your pup may respond negatively to the sounds emitted by phones, pagers, alarm clocks, blenders, doorbells, smoke detectors, and so on. And those noises are just the sounds inside your house. The sounds outside your house that a dog may react negatively to include those you have no control over: thunder, sirens, fireworks, neighbor kids, birds, dogs, and so on.

All these sounds are ones that your dog's going to have to either get used to or accept, however begrudgingly. You can help her by doing the following:

- ✔ **Don't turn down the volume.** You can't help your pup get used to everyday noises — and some not-so-everyday noises — if you create an artificially quiet environment. So don't muffle the doorbell, instruct the kids to tip toe through the house (good luck with that one anyway), or change what the normal hubbub of your everyday life is. (Of course, if your dog reacts negatively to your singing, you may want to consider that a good reason to stop.)

Dogs in general and Yorkies in particular have very acute hearing. Sounds that are loud to you sound very loud to them, and sounds that you don't hear at all may be crystal clear to your pooch. Keep this info in mind when your dog reacts to certain sounds; she may be reacting out of pain rather than fear.

✔ **Don't reinforce your puppy's reaction.** Your goal is to teach your dog that all sorts of noises are normal parts of the environment and not something to get all worked up about. So if a doorbell makes her dance around and yip, don't say in an exaggerated, happy voice, "Oh Goodie! Someone's at the door." Even though you may think you're telling her that a ringing doorbell is a good thing, she's reading your expression, body language, and tone of voice, and thinking, "She's excited; this must *really* be something to get worked up about!" Instead, clap your hands sharply once or give a shake to a penny-filled aluminum can. The sudden distraction quiets your puppy for an instant. Grab that second to say "Quiet" or "Settle" in a calm voice, praise her for her moment of restraint (no matter that it was the result of you distracting her), and then answer the door.

✔ **Figure out what noises cause problems and work to desensitize your dog to them.** If your dog begins to shake and shiver every time you play your Elvis Presley CD, for example, slowly acclimate her to the sound of Elvis's voice. Play Elvis at a volume low enough so that the music doesn't trigger your Yorkie's negative response. Then, over the course of a few days — or even weeks — *slowly* increase the volume. (Of course, if what your Yorkie's doing is singing along, twisting from her hips, or shimmying, then forget desensitizing her and contact the Stupid Pet Tricks folks at the "Late Show with David Letterman.")

Ignore the inappropriate response (that is, don't scold or soothe your puppy; in fact, don't say anything or interact with your dog in any way) and praise appropriate behavior.

Very scary things: Blow dryers and vacuums

Some dogs react strongly to certain noises produced by appliances, particularly vacuum cleaners and blow dryers. I suspect that these appliances elicit such strong reactions because they not only make noise, but they also invade your dog's space.

Think about it from your dog's perspective: Vacuums approach and retreat. Your dog doesn't look at you when you vacuum; he looks at the vacuum. As far as he's concerned, he dodges the creature when he falls back and scares it off when he lunges forward. Blow dryers not only make noise, but they also blow air. And if you have the heat setting on high, they can burn your dog as well.

You can use the following tactics to eliminate or forestall problems.

Vacuums

If your dog doesn't have negative reactions to the vacuum, consider yourself lucky; then praise and treat your dog when she's quiet. Do so while the vacuum cleaner is on so that she associates the noise with good things (a treat or praise).

Too much of a good thing is usually bad, so be careful not to lavish the praise on too thickly. Overdoing it (getting down on your knees to croon, "Oooh, you're such a brave boy to ignore that dirty old rotten vacuum cleaner while Daddy's vacuuming!" while petting her like a maniac) simply agitates your puppy and undermines the whole point of the praise in the first place: to reinforce her calm demeanor while the vacuum's on.

If your dog does have a negative reaction, don't try to soothe or calm her out of it. Instead, try desensitizing her to the sound and movement:

1. **Leave the vacuum out (and unplugged) where the puppy can see it and get used to it.**

2. **After she's used to the vacuum itself, work on getting her accustomed to the sound without the movement.**

   Turn the vacuum on but don't actually vacuum. Then turn it off before she can react negatively. Initially, she may react negatively within only a second or two, but as you praise her for each success, the amount of time she tolerates the noise will increase.

3. **When she's used to the sound — that is, she's not reacting to it anymore, other than with anticipation because it means a treat — add the movement.**

   Vacuum a small area initially and gradually increase the area. Be sure to praise your puppy after each successful run.

An apple a day

Dogs can become fearful of the strangest things. I once had a dog who barked to high heaven anytime she saw a red apple. The reason was because one dark and stormy night when she was a puppy, I dropped an apple on the kitchen floor, and she ran to scoop it up. Just as she clamped down on the apple, a tremendous thunderclap broke. She practically flung the apple from her mouth and ran away from it, never to be persuaded again that apples were not the enemy. Too bad I didn't have the same reaction to that pint of chocolate ice cream I was putting away.

The trick is to take all these steps slowly — so slowly in fact, that your puppy can't help but succeed.

If your puppy never gets past her fear of the vacuum and continues to parry with it, make sure that you keep her confined to a safe area when you vacuum. A dog lunging at a moving vacuum can be dangerous, especially if the dog is as small as a Yorkie, who can easily get a paw caught.

Never ever, *ever* chase a puppy with a vacuum or a vacuum cleaner attachment. A puppy who runs for her life and then turns to attack isn't cute — she's terrified. You can play all sorts of games with your Yorkie (head to Chapter 9 for some ideas), but Chase the Doggy with the Vacuum isn't one of them.

Blow dryers

As a Yorkie owner, your blow dryer is probably the one appliance you need your dog to make friends with. Given the care require-ments of the Yorkie coat, especially if you plan on growing the coat long, you're going to use a blow dryer on your dog pretty regularly, and your dog needs to get used to it. Even if you don't plan to do the grooming yourself, teaching your dog to tolerate a blow dryer makes the professional grooming go more smoothly, and it could save you money because many groomers tack on an extra fee for difficult-to-groom dogs.

Unfortunately, most dogs don't like having air blown at them. (Don't believe me? Try puffing directly into your dog's face. He'll flinch and pull back.) So you have to help your Yorkie get used to it, and the best time to start is when he's a puppy.

Before you turn the blow dryer on your dog, simply keep him in the bathroom with you while you dry your own hair. Doing this gets him used to the noise of the dryer before he has to deal with the blast of air, too. Then, when the time comes to introduce that blast of air to your dog, follow these tips:

✔ Give your puppy a chance to get used to the dryer being close to him. Hold the blow dryer up so that he can sniff at it but don't turn it on.

✔ When you first turn the dryer on, keep both the heat and temperature settings on low (they're quieter, gentler, and won't burn your pup). Also keep the nozzle turned away from your puppy. He may not be able to handle the dryer's noise, vibration, and blowing air all at once and in such close proximity.

✔ Blow the area around your puppy's shoulders and back first, just a few seconds. Then call the session done, turn off the dryer, and give your pup a treat. Over the next few days, increase the time and the area you blow dry, but always follow each session with a treat.

✔ Don't blow the air directly into his face (no one likes to be blasted in the kisser) or around his tail (would you like somebody blowing anything up your wazoo?). Those areas can come later when you have a little more finesse and he's more accustomed to the whole experience.

Car rides

Even if you don't plan to vacation with your dog, you're going to have times when she has to travel in a car. Fortunately, many dogs love riding in cars. Even dogs who are a little less enthusiastic can learn to enjoy it. You can use the following tricks to keep enthusiastic car riders happy and to increase the pleasure of their less enthusiastic brothers and sisters:

✔ **Take short trips.** This tactic is especially important for dogs who don't care for car rides. Sometimes even a trip to the end of the driveway is a victory for a little guy who has a particular dislike of cars.

✔ **Go to fun places.** If you limit your dog's car rides to trips to the vet or to the boarding kennel, your dog, creature of habit that she is, is going to associate the two. So take your dog to some fun places, too. To the park. To an ice cream shop for a very occasional treat. To a friend's house. Even riding around the block just to get back home can be a fun trip, if the company's good.

Check out local banks and coffee shops. Some offer little dog treats at the drive up windows.

Always make sure your dog is appropriately restrained in your car. Use a dog carrier, dog crate, or one of the dog harnesses that function like seatbelts. And never let your dog sit on your lap or stick her head out the window. Refer to Chapter 9 for information on safely traveling with your Yorkie.

Setting Up Your Daily Routines

Setting up a routine to structure your dog's day is good for a couple of reasons: First, a routine makes the day more predictable, and your Yorkie will feel more secure and calm if he knows what happens when. Second, it teaches your pup that good things come to dogs who wait. If, for example, your puppy knows that as soon as he gets up he heads outside to go the bathroom and that breakfast (yippee!) comes after that, he's more able to wait to relieve himself. And, once outside, he's more motivated to take care of his business so that he can partake in the yummy breakfast you've painstakingly prepared.

One thing you have going for you, if you know how to take advantage of it, is that dogs are creatures of habit. They thrive on routine, and they learn through repetition. By setting up a daily routine that you stick with, and by enforcing the rules and expectations in the same way *every time,* your puppy can't help but learn how to behave. The key is *consistency.*

Dining schedule

Although many people leave dry food out all day long and let their pets graze, for a variety of reasons, this strategy isn't such a good one for puppies in general, or Yorkie pups in particular:

- ✔ **Regular meals mean (more) predictable bathroom breaks:** Housetraining a puppy is that much harder if you have no idea when to anticipate a potty break. If you understand that puppies usually have to eliminate within a few minutes after eating, you can more accurately time your treks outside.

✔ **Yorkie pups are susceptible to *hypoglycemia* (low blood sugar):** By serving your puppy regularly scheduled meals throughout the day, you can 1) ensure that she gets the appropriate nutrients throughout the day and 2) monitor how much she eats — potentially important information if you have to take her to the vet for a hypoglycemic episode. See Chapter 12 for more information on recognizing and treating hypoglycemia in Yorkies.

✔ **You reinforce your status:** For later puppy training to be successful, you need to be the leader, and your dog needs to recognize your leadership. One of the easiest ways to demonstrate your leadership is to control the food. Simply filling the dish, holding it up until your puppy calms down or sits, and then putting it in front of her is a powerful message for the little gal: You are boss and bestower of good things — in other words, the one to please.

When you set up a feeding schedule, keep in mind that Yorkies under 12 weeks old should get four small meals a day; puppies between 12 and 24 weeks should get three small meals daily. (After 24 weeks, your puppy can probably move to the two meals a day that adults get.) Following is a suggested feeding schedule for your puppy; note that if she's over 12 weeks old, you can cut out the meal before bedtime:

✔ **First meal:** In the morning, right after his first bathroom break

✔ **Second meal:** Around noon

If you can't arrange to come home at noon for the second meal (or have someone else do it for you), leave enough food in the breakfast bowl to take care of both breakfast and lunch.

✔ **Third meal:** Early evening

✔ **Fourth meal (for puppies under 12 weeks):** About a half hour before bed, followed by one last bathroom break

Regardless of whether you let your puppy graze or eat only at designated times, make sure fresh water is available to her at *all* times. Head to Chapter 9 for more information on what and when to feed your Yorkie.

If you let your puppy graze, keep a close watch on how much she eats. Some puppies overeat, and the rapid weight gain isn't good for your Yorkie.

© Isabelle Francais

When thinking of a Yorkshire Terrier, many people picture a dog with the traditional long coat, a top knot, and a bow — an image that often erroneously leads people to believe that these dogs are all show and no substance.

With coats that continue to grow, Yorkies can become canine Rapunzels — if you have the dedication required to grow and care for such a coat. Most Yorkie owners, however, keep their long-coated dogs trimmed to floor length.

© Isabelle Francais

© Isabelle Francais

Not all Yorkies sport the long coat. Some, like this dog, are kept in shorter styles, which are easier to maintain and just as attractive.

If you keep your Yorkie's hair long and don't tie it back with a bow, you could end up with a dog that has a hard time seeing — and in this photo you can see why. With hair that falls into his eyes and impedes his vision, your dog is prone to mishaps, missteps, and being misconstrued as a Veronica Lake wannabe.

© Isabelle Francais

Although Yorkies have copious amounts of long hair, it doesn't offer much protection from the cold. The reason is that Yorkies are a single-coated breed, which means that they lack the undercoat most other breeds have. Their hair, in fact, is a lot like human hair and offers little protection from the cold. If you live in cold climates or have cold winters, consider putting your dog in a coat for warmth and — dare I say it? — style.

Most breeders agree that Yorkies are old enough to go to their new homes when they're between 10 and 12 weeks old, with 12 weeks being preferable. Although these puppies are old enough to be adopted, Mom still keeps an eye on them.

© Isabelle Francais

Yorkie pups don't look much like the adult dogs they'll become. The tan points on the otherwise dark coat will eventually become more predominant and the colors will change slightly, until this little guy has the blue and tan coat characteristic of the breed.

© Isabelle Francais

Yorkies are inquisitive, active dogs that need safe toys — especially during puppyhood when the urge to chew and investigate is the prime directive. If left to her own devices, a puppy will invariably turn her attention to objects that can hurt her: electrical cords, stuffed animals, items in the trash, and so on. So supply your pup with items that keep her happy and busy. Doing so not only protects your possessions (a puppy can make short work of your suede boots or comfy slippers), but it's one of the first steps you can take to protect your dog.

Yorkies' size and their devotion to their humans make them the ultimate lap dog.

© Isabelle Francais

© Isabelle Francais

Even full-grown, Yorkies are small enough to be carried around easily.

All Yorkies are small, but occasionally, even sound breeding programs produce a Yorkie that is smaller than average. No reputable breeder, however, breeds for this trait. So steer clear of breeders hawking "teacup Yorkies," "tinies," or "minis."

© Isabelle Francais

A child can be a Yorkie's best friend. The key?
Begin training early — the child that is. The lesson?
To be gentle and careful around these small dogs.

Although Yorkies are possessive of their owners and territories, they can get along well with other pets. The key is to let the interaction between your pets come naturally — not force it — and to stay close by during introductions. You can find more suggestions for ensuring peace in your house in Chapter 7.

A crate is necessary when you go traveling with your Yorkie, but it's more than just a way to get him there and back safely. It can also be his home-away-from-home while he's on the road.

Yorkies are active, curious dogs, but as far as "formal" exercise goes, a short walk is all they really need. They can get the rest just by following you around the house or playing dog-friendly games with your children.

Although they're small and have a reputation for being difficult to train, Yorkies are smart and thrive when their owners take the time to teach them basic commands and tricks.

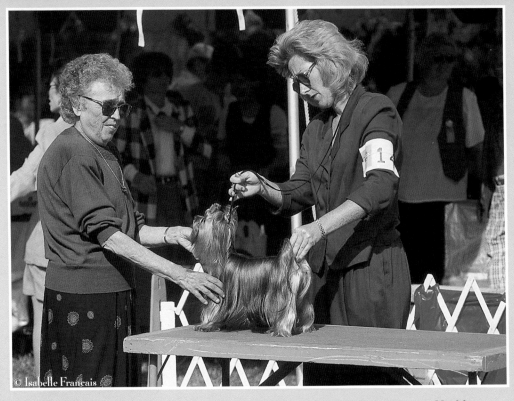

Yorkies are a favorite in the show ring. If you plan to show your Yorkie, head to Chapter 17 for tips and explanations about a few differences between U.S and European shows.

Despite being primped and polished, Yorkies are feisty, curious, fun-loving dogs who are still Terriers at heart.

Potty breaks

When your Yorkie puppy is young, you're expecting too much if you expect him to be potty trained in a couple of weeks. First, *no* puppy can be potty trained until he's physically ready. Second, Yorkies generally take longer to potty train than other breeds. Some people claim this difficulty is an inherent trait of the breed. Others claim that it's a matter of inconsistent or careless humans. The truth probably lies somewhere in between.

However, this difficulty doesn't mean that you should take a fatalistic approach and assume that whatever will happen will happen, and you can't do anything about it. You can do a lot of things to set yourself up for potty-training success, and one of the most important strategies is to schedule regular potty breaks early on. At the very least, take your puppy out at the following times:

- ✔ **Shortly after a meal:** The digestive process in puppies is amazingly fast. A few minutes after your pup eats, head to the bathroom area.

- ✔ **At regular intervals throughout the day:** The younger your pup is, the shorter these intervals should be. Start out at every hour, for example, and then as your puppy matures, extend the breaks to every hour and a half, then every two hours, and so on.

- ✔ **Immediately before bed at night and immediately after rising in the morning:** From bedtime to morning is a long time for a little puppy to wait.

Of course, you should also take your puppy out whenever he shows signs of needing to go. What are the signs? Usually a little squatting motion or a slight hunching of the back. If he's in his crate, he may cry to let you know. Head to Chapter 14 for more details. As he gets older and gains more control, he'll be able to wait longer.

If you're gone for most of the day and plan to keep your pup in his crate, his potty routine is going to be dictated more by your schedule than by his bladder. In that case, make sure you give him a chance to eliminate immediately before he gets into his crate and as soon as he gets out. If you can, try to arrange to come home around noon to let him out for a potty break then.

By scheduling regular bathroom breaks, you teach your puppy where the appropriate bathroom area is and reduce or eliminate accidents in the house — both good starts for the housetraining that comes later.

Bedtime rituals

Bedtime is another time when predictability is important. You don't have to put your pup to bed at the same time every night, but you do need to set up a bedtime routine that you follow every night. Your bedtime ritual should include three elements:

- ✔ **Settle down time:** Everybody likes to relax a little before bedtime, so give your puppy a chance to do just that. At least a half hour before bed, stop all playing.

- ✔ **Bathroom break:** Right before you put your puppy to bed, take her outside to go to the bathroom. If she doesn't go after a reasonable amount of time, take her back in (don't let her turn this time into playtime). Wait a while — keep your eyes peeled! — and then try again.

- ✔ **Bedtime announcement:** As soon as you bring your puppy in from going to the bathroom, put her in her crate and say "Bedtime." Until she associates the word with the action, you have to tuck her in.

You can devise any bedtime routine that suits you and your puppy. If you want to read her *Goodnight Moon* or hum Brahms' "Lullaby," go right ahead. Just remember that you don't want to get her worked up right before bed, and you want to let her empty her bladder and bowel before the lights go out.

Let the (Pre-) Training Begin!

In addition to the suggestions I outline in the preceding sections, you can do a few other things to get training off on the right foot. And by getting off on the right foot, I mean making it more likely that you'll be able to enjoy your puppy, your dog will be happier and more secure, and your training efforts will be successful.

Me and my shadow: Keeping your puppy close by

When your puppy first comes home, he doesn't know any of your house rules and will break them one by one, or all simultaneously, if you leave him to his own devices. So you need to make sure that, whenever your puppy isn't confined to his area or his crate, he's with you.

How do you do that without following your puppy from room to room to room? Easy. You make *him* follow *you.*

Get yourself a leash with a clasp at both ends. Attach one end to your puppy's collar; attach the other end to your belt loop. Then wherever you go, he goes. This technique

- ✔ **Teaches your puppy to follow you:** Leaders lead. Your dog will be happier and more likely to follow your lead (and your rules) if you make it clear that you're the boss. In dog parlance, you're the alpha dog.

- ✔ **Keeps him safe:** You can't watch a puppy who's in another room and out of your sight.

- ✔ **Lets you keep an eye out for signs that he needs to go to the bathroom:** The best tool for housebreaking Yorkies is *your* consistency and diligence.

If you use this strategy, keep these pointers in mind:

- ✔ **Make following you a good thing.** Don't drag him and don't jerk him around. Call him to you and praise him for coming.

- ✔ **Be careful where you step.** Never forget that you have a little gal following you around.

- ✔ **Make sure that the leash is long enough to give the puppy a little roaming room.** He doesn't have to be in the heel position to make this technique successful.

- ✔ **Give him frequent breaks.** Let him off the leash so he can explore and play. When you stop in a room for a period of time, for example, you can let him off the leash if you can stay close by and have time to watch him. If you can't watch him (you have work to do, for example, or a phone call to make), anchor him to an immovable piece of furniture or to a bolt you've screwed into the wall for this purpose. Make sure he has toys and a comfy place to lie down.

- ✔ **Keep him tethered to you until you can trust him on his own.** This stage may last weeks. The more trustworthy your puppy becomes, the less time he needs to spend tethered to you. Eventually, you'll cut the tether strings entirely.

A few words of warning: Don't let your children imitate this move. Don't leave the leash on your puppy to drag around the house. And *never* leave a restrained puppy alone. Yorkies are pretty adept climbers, and a dragging leash can easily become a hangman's rope.

Setting boundaries

If you don't know how you expect your puppy to behave (or if you have no expectations), how will your puppy know what's appropriate? Barring any compelling reason not to act instinctively, a dog does what comes naturally. And often what comes naturally to a dog is at odds with what we humans consider acceptable behavior. So the first thing you need to do is figure out how you want your adult dog to behave — know what is and isn't acceptable to you.

After you know what your expectations are, enforce the rules religiously. If your puppy can sometimes chew on your son's favorite action figure and other times gets in trouble for it, she won't learn that chewing on the action figure is wrong. What she'll learn is that she shouldn't chew on it in front of you — not the lesson you intended.

So when you communicate your expectations to your puppy, communicate them consistently. If kids toys are off limits, *every time* you see her with (or eyeing) a kid's toy, you give her a puppy toy instead. If you don't want her to beg for table scraps, *never* feed her from the table. If you don't intend to allow her into your living room with your antique Persian carpet, don't let her walk through with you or watch TV in there with the kids.

What you do in the first days and weeks that your puppy's home tells your dog what to expect. If you don't start off with your rules firmly in place, future training becomes that much more difficult. Not only will you have to teach her what you want her to do, but you'll also have to help her break the bad habits she's already acquired.

Enlisting your kids' help

With some preparation and guidance, your children can be a tremendous help in your efforts to set boundaries and rules for your puppy. To bring your kids on board, explain what your expectations and rules are so that they know what is and isn't appropriate. If you plan to keep the puppy downstairs except for bedtime, for example, when he goes in his crate by your bed, tell your kids that until you say otherwise, they're not to take him upstairs or put him in their beds. Other important rules to share include the following:

- ✔ **No rough-housing with the puppy:** First, rough-and-tumble play, as well as tugging games, are dangerous for a small dog. Second, they reinforce inappropriate behavior. See Chapter 9 for better games to play with Yorkies.

- ✔ **No feeding any sort of treat without your permission:** Because of their size, Yorkies need to get a big nutritional punch out of the little bit of food they eat. Combine that with the extra nutritional requirements for a growing puppy, and you can see why your pup *must* get a balanced, nutritious meal. Snacking on the wrong kinds of food doesn't leave room for the healthy stuff.

Deputizing your lieutenants

In addition to outlining your house rules, tell your kids how they can help. Following are ideas:

- ✔ **Tell your kids how they can reinforce your rules:** Explain what you want them to say or do if they see the puppy doing something she shouldn't be. Most older kids thrive when given the opportunity to be responsible.

  Using the same signals and responses consistently is the key to being effective. Tell the kids what commands and responses you use so that they can use the same ones. And be specific; instead of saying, "Don't let Muffy chew on things," say "If Muffy chews on the pillows (or something else she isn't supposed to), say 'Muffy, no,' and then give her one of her toys instead."

- ✔ **Have your kids take over the puppy house-cleaning duties:** House-cleaning chores include changing the soiled papers (if your puppy has an indoor bathroom area), scooping up the messes outside, cleaning the food dishes, and shaking out the bedding. True, these jobs lose their luster pretty quickly, but owning a pet is a big responsibility; that's one of the important lessons you and your Yorkie can teach your kids.

Cooling down hot spots

A wild house makes for a wild dog. Families with young children especially have a hard time keeping things calm, and the result can be a frantic or fearful dog — neither of which is good.

If you have young or rambunctious children, limit the dog's exposure to them: This suggestion may sound harsh, but it really isn't. It's a way of keeping your puppy out of the chaos, which keeps him calmer as a result.

How long do you have to limit and control your kids' interactions with the puppy? Until both dog and children learn the rules and apply them consistently. This restraint is nearly impossible to achieve during the first days that your dog's home when your children are overly excited and the puppy is just beginning to learn what's expected of him. As your children calm down and the puppy gets better at behaving, then you can loosen the tether strings.

Keep the dog with you most of the time (see the section "Me and my shadow: Keeping your puppy close by" earlier in this chapter for details) and set up a time when the children are allowed to play with him. During these times, structure the activities and set up the ground rules: no rough-housing or fighting over the dog. Then stay close by to supervise.

Following this strategy teaches your children how to treat the dog and, because time with him is limited, helps them appreciate the time they do get to spend together. It also keeps your puppy out of the fray while he's learning the house rules, helps him learn how to play with children, and reinforces your leader status. It's a win-win-win.

Part III
Taking Care of Your Yorkie

The 5th Wave   By Rich Tennant

@RICHTENNANT

"Let me guess—the vet's analysis of the Yorkie's fleas showed them to be of the 100 percent fresh ground Colombian decaf variety."

In this part . . .

Yorkies require what all pets require: food, shelter, healthcare, and periodic trips to the styling salon and day spa. The devil, as they say, is in the details. What's a good diet for such a little dog? How often does a Yorkie puppy need to eat? How do you care for the coat? How on earth do you trim those tiny little toenails? And when are the puppy shots due? Well, the details are in this part.

Chapter 9

Eat, Drink, and Be Merry!

*T*aking care of your Yorkie is a fairly easy task. Make sure she gets the right food, enough water, and the play and mental stimulation she needs to stay fit and happy. Simply doing these things almost guarantees a cheerful, healthy dog. (The other component is necessary medical care, which you can read about in Chapter 11.)

But what constitutes the "right" food? How much is enough water? And beyond taking your puppy for walks or letting her follow you around the house, what kinds of adrenaline-inducing, mind-stimulating activities do you engage in with a little fluff ball whose most endearing quality is that she fits so comfortably in your lap?

Well, stop worrying. In this chapter, I explain the basics of feeding, watering, and playing with your Yorkie.

The Main Menu, Garcon

Like all dogs, Yorkshire Terriers need certain nutrients to stay healthy:

✔ **Protein:** Protein is essential to the healthy functioning of your dog's body. It impacts his metabolism, growth and development, digestion and reproduction, and blood flow.

✔ **Carbohydrates:** Carbohydrates provide energy and are a source of fiber.

✔ **Fats:** Fats provide energy and keep your Yorkie's skin and coat healthy. They also improve the taste of the food and make your Yorkie's tummy feel full.

✔ **Vitamins and minerals:** These provide a myriad of benefits: They help your Yorkie fight disease, improve his body's functioning, and are vital for healthy bones and teeth (a sore spot — literally and figuratively — in many Yorkies).

✔ **Water:** You may not think of water as a nutrient, but it is — and it's the most important one of them all. Every cell in your dog's body and every bodily function depend on water.

The food you select needs to not only include these vital components in the best combination, but also needs to include the choicest ingredients, be easy to digest (not all dog foods are), and be one that your Yorkie will eat.

Deciphering dog-food packages

To understand what goes into your Yorkie's stomach, you first need to understand what goes into the food that you feed her. To do that, you must become a label reader. Dog-food labels (see Figure 9-1 for an example) include various bits of info you need to pay attention to.

Guaranteed analysis

The *guaranteed analysis* lists, among other things, the minimum percentage of crude protein, the minimum percentage of crude fat, the maximum percentages of crude fiber, and the maximum moisture content. These numbers give you an idea of the overall composition of the food, but they don't indicate the quality of the ingredients used (to figure that out, you have to read the ingredients list).

Too much protein can strain your Yorkie's kidneys. For adult Yorkies, look for foods with a maximum protein content of around 22 percent; a puppy requires slightly more protein, but the amount shouldn't exceed 27 or 28 percent. Pay particular attention to the amount of protein indicated in the guaranteed analysis.

Ingredients list

Like nutrition labels on human food, pet-food labels are regulated by the U.S. Food and Drug Administration (FDA) and the Department of Agriculture (USDA) and have to follow the stringent guidelines set by these organizations. Pet-food manufacturers must list all the ingredients in the food in descending order. Therefore, the item that appears first comprises the biggest part of the food, by weight, and the item that appears last comprises the least. By reading this list, you can see what kinds of protein, carbohydrates, fats, fiber, vitamins and minerals, and other things — like preservatives, artificial coloring, and so on — are in your dog's food.

Ingredients: Chicken, Corn Meal, Ground Whole Grain Sorghum, Chicken By-Product Meal, Ground Whole Grain Barley, Chicken Fat (preserved with Mixed Tocopherols, a source of Vitamin E, and Citric Acid), Fish Meal (source of fish oil), Chicken Meal, Dried Beet Pulp (sugar removed), Natural Chicken Flavor, Potassium Chloride, Dried Egg Product, Brewers Dried Yeast, Salt, Flax Meal, Sodium Hexametaphosphate, Vitamins [Vitamin E Supplement, Ascorbic Acid, Vitamin A Acetate, Calcium Pantothenate, Biotin, Thiamine Mononitrate (source of vitamin B1), Vitamin B12 Supplement, Niacin, Riboflavin Supplement (source of vitamin B2), Inositol, Pyridoxine Hydrochloride (source of vitamin B6), Vitamin D3 Supplement, Folic Acid], Choline Chloride, Minerals [Ferrous Sulfate, Zinc Oxide, Manganese Sulfate, Copper Sulfate, Manganous Oxide, Potassium Iodide, Cobalt Carbonate], Calcium Carbonate, DL-Methionine, Rosemary Extract.

Manufactured under U.S. Patent No. 5,616,569, 5,932,258, 6,093,418 and 6,238,708; other U.S. and foreign patents pending.

Guaranteed Analysis

Crude Protein not less than	26.0%
Crude Fat not less than	15.0%
Crude Fiber not more than	4.0%
Moisture not more than	10.0%
Omega-6 Fatty Acids not less than	2.5%
Omega-3 Fatty Acids not less than	0.25%*
Clucosamine not less than	350ppm*

*Not recognized as an essential nutrient by the AAFCO Dog Food Nutrient Profiles

Animal feeding tests using Association of American Feed Control Officials procedures substantiate that Iams MiniChunks provides complete and balanced nutrition for All Life Stages.

PET FOOD ONLY

Figure 9-1: A dog-food nutrition label.

Manufacturers also have to use common names for the ingredients. When you look on a human food label, you can usually recognize the first ingredients on the list; things don't get too hazy until you get to the ingredients with names like sodium ascorbate or pyridoxine hydrochloride. This isn't necessarily the case with dog-food ingredients, when your guesswork may begin with the very first item listed. After all, what is "chicken by-product meal" and is it something you want your dog to eat?

The key to comprehending dog-food labels is to understand what the different terms mean. Following are explanations of the ingredients that may not mean what you think they mean or that you're most likely to be confused by. *Note:* These explanations are based on definitions from the *Association of American Feed Control Officials* (AAFCO), which sets guidelines and definitions for animal feed and pet foods in the United States:

- **Chicken or beef:** These terms are pretty straightforward, but don't confuse the chicken or beef you eat with the chicken or beef that your dog can healthfully eat:

    - **Chicken:** Includes flesh, skin, and sometimes bone. Doesn't include feathers, heads, feet, and entrails.

    - **Beef:** Includes a combination of flesh off the bone and from the tongue, heart, esophagus, and diaphragm. May include overlying fat and portions of the skin, sinew, and nerve and blood vessels normally found in the flesh.

- **Meat by-products:** Meat by-products are the non-rendered clean parts of slaughtered animals (not including the meat), such as lungs, spleen, kidneys, brain, liver, blood, bone, and emptied stomachs. Meat by-products, contrary to what you may hear or read, don't include hair, horns, teeth, or hooves.

- **Chicken by-product:** Chicken by-product includes clean parts of the chicken (not including the flesh), such as necks, feet, undeveloped eggs, and intestines. It doesn't include feathers.

- **Chicken meal:** Chicken (see the earlier definition) that's been ground up into particle size.

- **Meat meal:** Meat meal is made up of whatever is left over from the rendering process, *not* including blood, hair, hoof, horn, hide trimmings, manure, and the stomach and its contents. Meat and bone meal is essentially the same as meat meal except that the bones are included.

✔ **Digest of <whatever>:** This indicates material that's rendered through a chemical process. Digest of beef, therefore, is beef (see the earlier definition) that results from this rendering process.

Just because dog food includes a lot of things that don't sound appealing to *you* doesn't mean that they aren't good for your dog. In fact, some of the things you may be wrinkling your nose at right now — meat meal, for example, or chicken by-product — are actually loaded with nutrients that are beneficial to your dog and are part of most dog foods, name-brand and premium alike.

That all-important nutritional adequacy statement

Dog-food packages should also include a *nutritional adequacy statement.* Essentially, this statement says that the food meets or exceeds the AAFCO nutritional guidelines and indicates which stage of your dog's life the food is meant for: maintenance, growth, or all stages, for example.

Don't buy a dog food that doesn't include a nutritional adequacy statement. You can't consider that foods without this statement are complete and balanced; using them may lead to nutritional deficiencies in your Yorkie.

Feeding directions

Dog-food packages include feeding guidelines that indicate how much food a dog of a particular size needs to eat each day to maintain optimum health. Keep in mind, however, that these guidelines are general enough to apply to the vast majority of dogs. What your Yorkie actually needs depends on her age, size, activity level, and so on. So use the information in this panel as a guide, not a rule.

Product names: Reading between the lines

Because commercial dog-food manufacturers want their products to sound good to *you,* you often see ingredients touted as part of a product name — "Beef for Dogs" or "Dog food with Chicken and Liver," for example — which may lead you to wrongly believe that the food is mostly made up of the named ingredient. Well, here are the AAFCO rules for how much of an ingredient must be in the product in order for it to be used as part of the name:

✔ **The 95 percent rule:** If the named ingredient comprises 95 percent of the food, then manufacturers can call it "Beef for Dogs," for example, or "Beef Dog Food." If the name includes a combination of ingredients (like "Beef and Chicken Dog Food"), then the two items together must make up 95 percent of the product. Also, the first ingredient listed (in this example, beef) has to make up the majority of the 95 percent — but this rule applies only to ingredients of animal origin. So, if the name is "Beef and Rice Food for Dogs," then 95 percent of the product still must be beef.

✔ **The 25 percent rule:** If the named ingredients make up 25 percent of the product, then manufacturers can call it a "dinner," as in "Beef Dinner for Dogs" or "Chicken Dinner for Dogs." Other words — *nuggets, formula, platter,* and so on — can replace the word *dinner,* but the meaning is the same: The named ingredient makes up only 25 percent of the product. If more than one ingredient is named, combined they have to equal 25 percent of the food. Alone, each named ingredient must make up at least 3 percent of the total.

This rule, unlike the 95 percent rule, applies to any ingredient in the food. So in a "Chicken and Rice Formula for Dogs," the combination of chicken and rice has to make up at least 25 percent of the total.

✔ **The 3 percent rule:** If a name indicates that the food is "with" an ingredient ("Dog Food with Beef," for example), the ingredient must make up 3 percent of the total.

Make sure that you don't confuse the naming conventions of dog-food nutrition labels. There's a big difference nutrition-wise between "Beef Dog Food" and "Dog Food with Beef." The first product includes 95 percent beef. The latter product includes only 3 percent.

Bottom line? Which food to buy

For the optimum health of your Yorkie, make sure her dog food is complete, balanced, and appropriate to her life stage. Also make sure that the food contains high-quality ingredients and is one that your Yorkie will eat. Any dog food that meets these requirements is fine; rarely, however, can you find that combo in the cheapest foods. Your best bet for finding all these benefits? A high-quality store brand or a premium brand dog food.

When you select food for your Yorkie, keep these points in mind:

✔ Although premium brands cost more, dogs need to eat less of them to get the nutrition they need. In the long run, then, the cost difference isn't as great as you may think. In addition, premium brands usually use higher quality, more digestible ingredients, with meat as the primary source of protein instead of grains or soybeans.

✔ Yorkies have higher metabolism rates per pound than larger dogs, and their small mouths can't comfortably accommodate large chunks of food. Choosing a food that's specially formulated for small-breed dogs is the easiest way to make sure your dog's getting the right balance of nutrients in the smaller chunk size.

A generic brand food with small chunks probably isn't adequate for your Yorkie. Without the necessary nutrients, she ends up filling up before she gets the good stuff she needs.

If your Yorkie has special health conditions, consult your vet to find out the best diet and dog food for her.

Steer clear of foods that

✔ Include soybeans in combination with grains as the main protein source. Your Yorkie can have a hard time digesting these foods, and they can cause gas.

A few reported cases indicate that foods containing soybeans may cause *bloat,* a life-threatening condition in which gas from fermenting food rapidly fills a dog's stomach. (Before you panic, bloat can affect any breed — including Yorkies — but it's most common in large and giant breeds.)

✔ List inferior meat sources, like meat by-products, as the primary ingredient. Go for real meat instead.

How much food is enough?

How much food your Yorkie needs depends on his age, size, and activity level. Less active and older dogs generally need less chow, while younger and more active dogs need more.

Start with the recommended amount of food on the dog-food package and divide it by the number of meals you're feeding your dog. Then pay attention to how your dog looks and acts. If he's bright-eyed and active, has a good appetite, and has a silky, shiny coat, he's getting the food he needs.

Two, three, or four squares a day?

When deciding how many daily meals to feed your Yorkie, use these guidelines (but, of course, adjust them to your dog's needs and your vet's recommendations):

- ✔ **Puppies:** Feed puppies up to 12 weeks old four small meals a day. For puppies between 13 and 24 weeks, three meals a day is fine. Older puppies can transition to the two meals a day that adult Yorkies eat. See Figure 9-2.

- ✔ **Adult dogs:** Feed your adult dog two meals a day.

You're probably going to give your Yorkie an occasional (or not-so-occasional) snack or treat. When you do, be sure to adjust his dinner helpings, as necessary. Otherwise, you can end up with an overweight or obese dog. Remember: Too many treats can throw off a balanced diet, and for a dog as small as a Yorkie, a milkbone is practically equivalent to dinner rations. See the section "Snack Time!" in this chapter for information on good and bad treats for your Yorkie.

©Isabelle Francais

Figure 9-2: To be healthy, a Yorkie needs a balanced diet.

Underweight, overweight, or j-u-u-s-t right

One way to judge whether your Yorkie is eating too much or too little is to look at the outline of her body. Ideally, a Yorkie's torso tapers gradually from the shoulders to the hips, and you're able to feel the rib cage easily but not see it. If her torso doesn't taper or you can't feel her ribs without pushing in, she's overweight. If the taper is extreme and tucks into the hips or you can see or easily feel her backbone, she's underweight.

The watering hole

Buying a dog food that's complete and balanced gives your Yorkie all the nutrients she needs, except one: water. Including water in your dog's diet is a no-brainer: no rationing, measuring, or doling out in appropriate portion sizes here. Give your Yorkie access to as much water as she wants whenever she wants it. In other words, keep the water dish full and the water fresh. And remember to clean the bowl weekly.

Snack Time!

Dogs love treats almost as much as their humans love giving them. So don't deny yourself or your dog the pleasure of an occasional goodie. Just make sure that what you offer is good for your dog. And keep in mind that, for a Yorkie, a little goes a long way.

Keep track of how many treats you dole out during the course of a day. A little treat while you're preparing dinner, a little treat while you're eating dinner, and a little treat (or two) when you're cleaning up after dinner — in addition to any treats you may have given earlier in the day — equals a *big* treat for a little dog. In this section, I tell you how to keep your pooch from becoming a porky Yorkie.

Tabling the table scraps

Sharing our food with our pets is human nature. I remember my mother saving the last bite of every sandwich she ate for her Chihuahua. If you want to feed your dog table scraps, go ahead, but keep these rules in mind:

- ✔ **Be selective in what you give your dog.** Human food, as a rule, is way too rich for dogs. Skip the sauces and gravies, the spicy mixes, and the sugary stuff. Find a bit of plain meat, a little piece of bread, or a leftover bite of vegetable. Your dog will think it's manna from heaven because it came from the table, and you won't be wreaking havoc on his digestive system.

- ✔ **Give him only a tiny bit.** Your dog has his own dinner. Sure, he may not be as interested in it as he is in the feast you've prepared, but his meal is healthier for him. As a good parent, you need to have a little backbone.

✔ **Don't feed him food directly from the table.** If you don't want your Yorkie underfoot or whining throughout dinner, don't feed him table scraps while you're eating and don't take the food directly from the table and put it in his mouth. Wait until the table is cleared and you're away from it before you hand over the treat.

✔ **Make your Yorkie work for the treat.** He doesn't have to lay track, but he can sit or perform some little trick before you hand over the goods. It may be a treat, but it doesn't have to be free.

Good treats

Beyond the assortment of treats made especially for dogs that you can buy in any grocery store, here are several other good treats you can give your Yorkie:

✔ Cooked, boneless chicken or turkey meat. An occasional treat of cooked liver is also great for your Yorkie.

Don't allow your dog to eat too much liver, which contains a lot of Vitamin A. Ingesting too much Vitamin A can lead to Vitamin A toxicity, or *hypervitaminosis A.*

✔ Cooked eggs, which are a great source of protein. However, don't allow your dog to eat raw eggs. In addition to the egg possibly being contaminated with bacteria such as salmonella, raw egg whites contain a protein that can deplete one of the B Vitamins that's essential for strong bones and a shiny coat.

✔ A variety of cooked vegetables, including carrots, green beans, lettuce, potatoes, and yams.

Yorkies' tiny digestive systems can't easily digest large chunks of uncooked vegetables, so make sure that the veggies are cut into bite-sized pieces (for a Yorkie, that is) and are cooked until they're soft.

✔ Fresh fruit, such as apples, pears, bananas, and strawberries, cut into bite-sized pieces.

If you let your Yorkie eat fruit, be sure to remove the seeds. Apple seeds, peach pits, cherry stones, and so on, contain cyanide, which is poisonous to both humans and pets. Chances are you know to stop at the core or pit, but your dog doesn't.

Bad treats

Several foods that humans enjoy and can eat without any negative side effects (except for things like bad breath and extra love handles) are bad for dogs. Here's a list of no-no's:

- ✔ **Alcohol:** Fortunately, most dogs reject the taste of alcohol. But mixed drinks can camouflage the taste and smell of alcohol. Only a small amount of alcohol — about a quarter of an ounce, an amount easily left in a cocktail glass — can make a dog as small as a Yorkie seriously ill. An ounce may be deadly.

- ✔ **Bones:** The problem with bones is that they splinter and can get lodged in your dog's mouth, throat, stomach, or intestines. Some bones are worse than others, and chicken bones are the worst culprit. If you want to give your dog bones (which, because of the marrow, can be a very nutritious treat), cook them long enough and at a high enough temperature so that they're soft (you can do this in a pressure cooker).

- ✔ **Chocolate:** The fat content in chocolate causes dogs to have diarrhea and vomiting. The caffeine causes restlessness, twitching muscles, frequent urination, and excessive panting. Beyond these possibilities, chocolate also contains a substance, theobromine, that's poisonous to dogs. Theobromine restricts blood flow to the brain, increases blood pressure and heart rate, possibly leading to heart attack or stroke. As a rule, the darker the chocolate, the more theobromine it contains and the more dangerous it is for your dog.

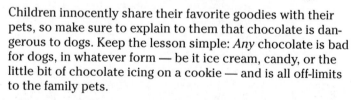

Children innocently share their favorite goodies with their pets, so make sure to explain to them that chocolate is dangerous to dogs. Keep the lesson simple: *Any* chocolate is bad for dogs, in whatever form — be it ice cream, candy, or the little bit of chocolate icing on a cookie — and is all off-limits to the family pets.

- ✔ **Dairy products:** Dairy products themselves aren't particularly dangerous to dogs, but they do pose a problem because many dogs are *lactose intolerant* (they lack an enzyme required to digest milk products). Give dairy products to a lactose-intolerant dog, and you get a dog with gas cramps and diarrhea. Unfortunately, you won't know whether your dog has a problem with dairy products until you try them. So, if you want to treat your dog to cheese, start with a little bit and see how he does.

- **Grapes and raisins:** For unknown reasons, a few dogs have gone into kidney failure after ingesting grapes.

- **Macadamia nuts:** Macadamia nuts can be toxic to dogs. The reason why is unclear, but some dogs have had a negative reaction after eating as few as six nuts. These reactions included pale gums, weakness, lameness and difficulty walking, stiffness, vomiting, tremors, and abdominal pain.

- **Onions:** Whether raw or cooked, onions contain a substance that can damage the red blood cells (which carry oxygen to all parts of the body) in several animals, including dogs. This condition is called *Heinz body hemolytic anemia.*

Other food dangers

Dogs don't know what's bad for them and will eat anything that smells good, seems interesting, or appears tasty to someone else (like you). So even though you may have no intention of sharing the following food items with your Yorkie, she may still get into them, especially if you leave them out and about where she has easy access to them:

- **Baking powder and baking soda:** In your Yorkie, these leavening agents can lead to low potassium, low calcium, and high sodium, as well as congestive heart failure or muscle spasms.

- **Coffee grounds and beans:** Dogs who eat coffee grounds or beans can get caffeine toxicity. The symptoms are very similar to those of chocolate toxicity and can be just as serious. Refer to the section "Bad treats" for details on the problems with chocolate.

- **Moldy or spoiled food:** For the very reasons you want your Yorkie to stay out of the trash, she wants to get into it — to snag whatever delectable treat is causing such an enticing odor. Well, if that "delectable treat" is spoiled or moldy food, you have a problem, because eating certain types of mold can cause tremors in your dog. Plus eating moldy or spoiled food is just plain disgusting.

- **Cat food:** What dog can resist cat food? None that I've ever seen. As a rule, cat food has too much protein and too many fats for your dog. The solution? Keep the cat food out of your Yorkie's reach.

Hangin' with Your Yorkie

Yorkies are such joyful little dogs. They don't require much to be happy: good food to eat, a comfy place to sleep, a little exercise, and lots of love and attention. Of course, you shouldn't stop at the creature comforts. In addition to being super cuddly and oh-so-very pamper-able, Yorkies are also active, curious dogs who love mental and physical challenges (see Figure 9-3).

©Isabelle Francais

Figure 9-3: The best combo for playtime is a safe toy and time with you.

Good activities for your Yorkie are those that

- ✔ **Let your dog use his natural abilities.** In the not-so-distant past, Yorkies were *ratters* — that is, they were bred to sniff out and give chase to rats and other vermin. So any challenge that lets them use these skills is great fun. (To find out more about the history of Yorkshire Terriers, head to Chapter 2.)

- ✔ **Involve interaction with you.** Yorkies are companion dogs. Sure, gnawing on a chew toy is better than nothing, but it's not nearly as fun or rewarding as doing something with you. If your Yorkie's playtime is limited to games he plays alone, you're cheating him and yourself out of some serious fun.

✔ **Don't reward your dog for undesirable behaviors, like aggression or possessiveness.** Some play — such as tugging games or rough-housing — brings out the worst in any dog, even those dogs who are no bigger than a bread box.

Take a gander at the following sections to find fun and stimulating games you and your Yorkie can play together.

Fun at home

You can play all sorts of games with your Yorkie. Here are just a few:

✔ **Chase the Ball:** Put a terrier within proximity of a moving tennis ball, and you have hours of cheap fun. You can play this game inside or out, and it works just as well whether you roll the ball or throw it.

✔ **Go Fish:** No, this game isn't the card game. To play Go Fish, tie a squeaky toy to the end of a rope and tie the rope to a pole. (You can use anything as a pole: an old broom or mop handle, a dowel rod, you get the idea.) Then bounce the toy in front of your dog. When he gives chase, move the "fish" out of reach, letting him catch it often enough to keep the game fun.

✔ **Hide-and-Seek:** Go to a different room and call your dog; if you have a treat cup with you (see Chapter 13 for information on treat cups), give it a shake. When he comes, praise him and give him a treat. In addition to having fun, you're teaching your dog to come when you call him.

✔ **Find So-and-So:** You can teach your Yorkie the names of the other people in the house (if he doesn't already know them); this game is great to play if you have kids. Have your kids sit in a circle, and give each of them a treat cup. Put the Yorkie in the middle of the circle and say, "Find Mary" (or whoever). At the cue, Mary shakes her treat cup, drawing the dog to her. Then say, "Find Alex," for example, and then Alex shakes his cup. Gradually have the children move apart until they're no longer in the same room and eliminate the treats. Before you know it, your dog can round up your children for you.

Make sure that any game you play with your Yorkie is one that reinforces a behavior or action you want. Games are also great training tools. Go to Chapters 13 and 15 for ways to make training time fun.

Fun in competition

Performing in competition has several benefits: The thrill of competing aside, these competitions are fun, you get to meet other people who love their Yorkies as much as you love yours, and you can learn a thing or two from the "pros" who are there. In the following sections, I outline the American Kennel Club (AKC)-sponsored events that Yorkies can participate in.

To find out about competitions in your area, contact your local kennel club. You can also visit the Yorkshire Terrier Club of America (YCTA) Web site (www.ytca.org) and click the "Specialty Show Calendar" link to see shows offered around the country.

Conformation events

In *conformation events,* your Yorkie is judged on how well she conforms to the breed standard (refer to Chapter 2). To be eligible to enter a conformation event, your Yorkie has to meet certain requirements, among them she must be registered with the AKC and be at least 6 months old. (For a complete rundown of requirements, head to Chapter 17.)

Obedience events

In *obedience events,* your Yorkie is judged on how well she performs a prescribed set of exercises, such as heeling both on and off leash, coming when called, staying, standing still for a simple physical exam, and jumping and retrieving objects. To be eligible, you must register your Yorkie with the AKC, and your Yorkie must be at least 6 months of age. For complete information on obedience events, visit the AKC Web site at www.akc.org.

Agility events

In *agility events,* your Yorkie is judged on how well and how quickly she can follow your cues to make it through an obstacle course that includes jumps, tunnels, weave poles, and other challenges. To be eligible to enter agility events, your Yorkie must be AKC-registered and be at least 1 year old.

The AKC published a very helpful booklet for beginners: Go to www.akc.org and click "Dog Events," "Companion Dog Events," and "Agility" to access a downloadable copy of *A Beginner's Guide to Agility.*

Car ride! Staying safe

Yorkies are so easy to travel with that, even when you don't have a dog-related destination in mind (like the vet's or the park), you're still likely to take your Yorkie along on quick errands. But even if you don't have an errand to run, you can still take your Yorkie for a ride. Why? Just for the plain fun of it. Dogs, as a rule, *love* car rides. A moving car, blowing wind, and all sorts of new sights and smells . . . well, it's practically dog paradise. So when you try to think of fun things to do together with your Yorkie, add cruising to your list. To keep your Yorkie safe during your excursions, keep these points in mind:

✔ Always, always, always make sure she's safely confined in a traveling crate or with a doggy restraint that functions like a seatbelt. You can find these restraints at pet-supply stores; see Chapter 5 for more info about crates.

✔ Don't let your Yorkie stick her head out the window. If your dog loves fresh air and you want to keep the window down so she can enjoy it, buy a window screen that you can install precisely for this purpose. You can find these at pet-supply stores, too.

✔ Don't leave your Yorkie unattended in the car. In the summer, the heat can be deadly; during warm weather, the inside of a car can heat up to over 140 degrees in less than 5 minutes. In the winter, the cold can chill her to the bone.

Tracking events

In *tracking events,* the AKC version of canine search and rescue, your Yorkie is judged on how well she can track and find objects. The tasks build in difficulty, beginning with the dog using scent (aged between 30 minutes and 2 hours) to find an object that the *tracklayer* has "dropped" between 440 to 500 yards from the starting position. At each level, the scent gets older, the track gets longer, and the directional changes become more numerous.

Although your Yorkie's eligible to enter tracking events for experience and practice at 4 months old, she must be certified by an approved tracking judge and be at least 6 months old before she can compete in a tracking test.

Chapter 10

Doing the 'Do: Grooming

· ·

· ·

*G*rooming your Yorkie is important for two reasons: The first reason is a vanity thing. A well-kept coat just looks and feels good, no matter what the style. Go beyond well-kept, and you can have a real beauty or cutie on your hands. The second reason, though, is the one that really matters: health.

Regular grooming makes for a healthier dog. Not because a doggy-'do is intrinsically healthful, but because of the simple act of grooming itself: When you take the time to care for your dog's coat, ears, teeth, and nails — yes, these parts need grooming, too — you're more likely to prevent problems (infected gums, for example) before they start and discover problems (like skin conditions or lumps) before they get out of hand. And don't forget that the time you spend grooming is quality time you spend bonding with your dog. And a happier dog is often a healthier dog.

If you haven't groomed a dog before or if you have some experience grooming but want specific tips on how to groom a Yorkie, keep reading.

The Long and the Short of It: Grooming Options

Just because many standard photos of Yorkies show the long hair and top knot doesn't mean that that's the only acceptable coat style. It's not. In fact, any clean, brushed Yorkie is a cutie. But the long coat and the puppy cut are the two most popular coat styles.

The long coat

The long coat is the style you typically see in breed books and on many Yorkie Web sites. It's also the standard style at dog shows. The reason the long coat is so ubiquitous is because the Yorkshire Terrier coat is one of the defining characteristics of the breed. Its color, texture, and length are outlined in the breed standard — as is the preferred coiffure (the single or double top knot). As cute as a shorter cut is (see the next section), it doesn't show off the coat to best advantage.

If you want to keep your Yorkie's coat long, keep these points in mind:

✔ **Achieving the long, silky coat takes dedication and care.** Your Yorkie supplies the coat, which, like human hair, continues to grow. Everything else — the daily brushing, the weekly shampooing and conditioning, the wrapping it up to keep it off the ground, and more — is up to you. If you fail to do these tasks religiously, then that beautiful coat ends up a tangled mess.

Wrapping your Yorkie's coat (that is, winding the ends around folded papers and securing them with a band) is a task you don't really need to do unless you're trying to grow a coat suitable for the show ring. But if you *are* trying to grow a show coat, then keep your dog in wraps 24/7 and only take the wraps out for the show ring. Wrapping protects the coat, allows it to grow, and also helps keep it clean, especially important for the boys, who get urine on themselves. You can start wrapping your dog as soon as the hair is long enough — usually when your Yorkie's around 9 to 10 months. See the section "Wrapping it up" in this chapter for instructions on how to wrap a Yorkie's coat.

✔ **The top knot and bow are musts.** You can choose between a single bow right in the middle or two bows on either side of a straight part, but a bow you will have — and you have to know how to put it in. See the section "The piece de resistance: Adding the bow" in this chapter for instructions.

✔ **If your Yorkie's coat is soft instead of silky, you may not be able to achieve the look you want.** Soft hair mats more, is more difficult to keep clean, and breaks more easily. The sheer work of grooming a soft coat to the breed standard probably isn't worth the trouble. You may have to resign yourself to a shorter cut.

If you plan to show your Yorkie, keep him in the traditional long coat. It's part of the breed standard (refer to Chapter 2).

The short coat

The alternative to a long coat is obviously a short coat. One of the more popular short coat styles is the *puppy cut.* Look at a Yorkie puppy, and you get a pretty good idea what that style is. Essentially for a puppy cut, you (or a professional groomer) trim the coat into short layers all over the body and around the face.

Other short-style options include the modified *Schnauzer cut,* where the coat is trimmed short on the torso and left longer on the legs, and the face is trimmed in the traditional Schnauzer mustache, or the modified *Westie cut,* which is similar to the modified Schnauzer cut except that the hair on the head and face is trimmed to frame the face. You can see examples of these styles in the color insert.

If you opt for a shorter style, keep these points in mind:

- ✔ **Shorter cuts mean less time grooming.** If you love everything about Yorkies except for the grooming chores, go with a shorter cut.

- ✔ **You'll probably need a professional groomer to achieve the look you want.** Although you can certainly do the work yourself, trimming a dog takes quite a bit of skill, the right equipment (clippers with blades of various sizes), and a practiced technique. Unless you want to learn how to do it yourself and can stand your Yorkie looking a little (or a lot) rough around the edges until your skill improves, hire a professional.

- ✔ **A short cut doesn't get you entirely off the grooming hook.** You still need to groom your Yorkie regularly. Of course, everything's relative: *Regularly* with a short cut is a lot less frequent and time intensive than *regularly* with a long cut. Giving her a quick brush every day or every other day, a bath about every week, and a trip to the groomer once every month or two is fine.

- ✔ **What you gain in ease of care, you lose in the traditional Yorkie appearance.** These short cuts cut the blue part of the coat right off. If you plan to show your Yorkie, go with the long coat; see the preceding section. Save the short cut for when her showing days are over.

Setting Up a Grooming Schedule

To keep your Yorkie in the pink, grooming is going to be part of your regular routine. How regular? Depends on the task. Certain tasks, like brushing, teeth cleaning, and cleaning the area where urine collects on males (simply use a damp cloth and warm water), you do daily. Other tasks, such as ear trimming and nail clipping, you do on an as-needed basis. Table 10-1 outlines how frequently you need to perform the various grooming tasks.

Table 10-1	Grooming Timetable
Task	*How Frequently*
Bathing	Weekly or bi-weekly, depending on how dirty your dog gets (**Note:** Wipe urine from males daily)
Teeth cleaning	Daily, if possible; otherwise, at least twice weekly
Ear trimming	At every coat trim or as needed to keep the ears erect and pointed. **Note:** Trim the ears more frequently for puppies because the hair's weight can cause the ears to droop
Nail clipping	Check nails at every bath and trim as necessary
Coat trimming	Monthly or bi-monthly for short coats and as needed for long coats

Caring for the Coat

Yorkies are single-coated dogs, which means that, unlike many dogs, they don't have an undercoat. In this way, your Yorkie's coat is a lot like human hair, and like human hair, it continues to grow. The texture of the coat combined with its length and the Yorkie's tendency to be active make mats and snarls inevitable. And that's where you come in: You get to tame the tresses.

Whether your Yorkie has a long or a short cut, you have to attend to it regularly, if you want to keep it in good condition. The only mandatory tasks you need to perform when grooming the coat are bathing, brushing, and periodically trimming. Of course, many Yorkie owners don't stop there: They wrap and band, too.

Bathing beauties

Bathing your dog doesn't have to be the disaster that's often portrayed in the funny pages or on TV commercials. With a little planning and know-how, bath time can actually proceed quite uneventfully.

Training your Yorkie for grooming

Yorkies aren't born with an innate fondness of having brushes pulled through their hair, water dumped over their heads, and soap worked into a lather all over their bodies. They need to be trained to like grooming time and to stand still for it. Here are some suggestions and tips:

✔ **Start early:** You can begin training your puppy to tolerate (and hopefully, eventually enjoy) grooming as soon as you first bring him home, without ever turning on water or pulling out a snarl.

✔ **Start elsewhere:** When you groom, you touch your dog in places that you miss when you're just petting him: the inside of his ears, his paws, under his tail, around his eyes, and so on. So getting your puppy used to being touched in these areas is one of your first tasks.

The best place to get your pup accustomed to being touched in new areas is away from the grooming table, sink, or countertop. And the best time to do so is when he's relaxed — or even napping — in your lap. Take this quiet time to gently massage his feet, around his eyes, in and around his ears, and so on. Also lift his tail. Talk in a soothing voice and give him treats for accepting your ministrations.

✔ **Start slow:** Pick a single task — like brushing — and do a little of it (be sure to stop before your pup's had enough), and then give him a treat. Repeat this process frequently throughout a day and gradually extend the amount of time spent on the task. When you actually do begin grooming, don't make the first "real" session a tour de force of all you know: Do only those things that cause the least stress. No de-matting, no fishing for wax in the ear — nothing that will make him not like being groomed.

✔ **Stay safe:** No matter how much your Yorkie accepts your touch, all your work goes out the window if he feels insecure when you lift him to a countertop or put him in a slick tub. Be sure to use a heavy towel for him to sit on so that he doesn't slip all over the place, and keep an eye and a hand on him so that he doesn't launch himself off the counter.

First, get your supplies together. A wet dog shivering in the sink and plotting his escape — which invariably involves leaping the distance from the sink or counter to the floor — isn't a good time to go hunting for the shampoo. Here's what you need on hand before you start washing your dog:

✔ A sink or tub
✔ Dog shampoo and conditioner

Don't use human shampoo or conditioner on your Yorkie. His pH levels are different, and shampoo made for your hair is too harsh for his coat and skin.

✔ Mineral oil to protect his eyes

✔ Cotton balls to keep water out of his ears and to clean the eye mucous

✔ A big, fluffy towel (for drying) and a smaller towel (for the dog to sit on while he's in the sink to keep him from slipping)

You also need to prepare your Yorkie's coat for bathing. And that means gently removing tangles with your fingers while the hair is still dry. If you get the hair wet before you remove the mat, you end up with a knot that's almost impossible to remove and a very unhappy Yorkie. By pre-grooming for mats and tangles before bathing your dog, your Yorkie will enjoy a bath and may love the attention, making the experience more pleasant for both of you.

After pre-grooming, you're ready to bathe your Yorkie. Let the water run until it's the right temperature (warm), and then follow these steps:

1. **Put the cotton balls in your Yorkie's ears, one drop of mineral oil in each of your Yorkie's eyes, and your Yorkie on the small towel in the sink.**

   If you lined the sink with a towel, be sure that the towel doesn't cover the drain. Yorkies — and every other animal I can think of — don't like water rising toward their heads.

2. **Thoroughly wet down your Yorkie's coat with warm water.**

3. **Apply the shampoo to the back of your dog's head and, with gentle strokes, work the shampoo down his back to his tail (see Figure 10-1).**

4. **Let the shampoo soak for a few minutes and then rinse thoroughly.**

   To rinse your dog, spray the water in the direction that the coat naturally lays. Don't forget to rinse under his tail and on his tummy.

   If you're working in a tub or a sink without a spray nozzle, use a large plastic cup to rinse rather than force your dog to sit under the tap of running water.

5. **To clean your Yorkie's face, put a small amount of tearless shampoo in your hands, rub them together to form a**

slight lather, and then use your fingers to carefully clean the hair around the ears and muzzle; rinse.

When rinsing the face, being careful is particularly important. I recommend using a cup filled with fresh water (not the bathwater) rather than your sink's spray nozzle. You have more control over the flow and the pressure.

6. **Remove the eye mucous.**

   Being careful, use your fingers, a damp cloth or cotton ball, or your fine-toothed flea comb.

7. **Apply the conditioner according to the directions, and rinse thoroughly using a spray nozzle or a cup.**

   Be sure to get all the conditioner out. If you don't, your Yorkie's coat becomes a magnet for dirt and grime.

8. **When you're done, squeeze out the excess water from the coat and then wrap your dog in the big fluffy towel.**

Hold your towel-wrapped dog for a bit so that the towel absorbs most of the water. Then let him go and watch in amazement as he simultaneously shakes himself and literally runs circles around the house. When he calms down and you stop laughing, it's time to brush his coat.

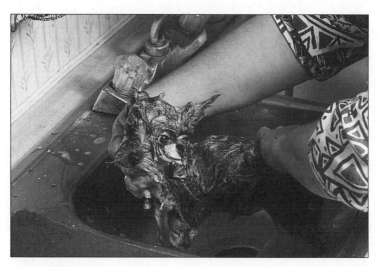

©Isabelle Francais

Figure 10-1: Gently work the shampoo through your Yorkie's hair to avoid creating more snarls.

Brushing basics

Whether you're brushing a dog you just bathed or simply doing the daily 100 strokes, make sure that the hair is at least a little damp. Brushing a completely dry coat can cause breakage. If your dog hasn't just come out of the tub, spray her lightly with a mixture of conditioner and water (3 parts water to 1 part conditioner).

To brush your Yorkie's coat, gather your pin brush and your comb (see Chapter 5 for a list and description of the necessary supplies) and then follow these directions:

1. **Using the pin brush, brush through the entire coat thoroughly.**

   Just as you would brush long human hair, begin at the ends and work your way to the skin to avoid turning a little snarl into a painful tangle.

2. **As you come across mats, pick as much apart with your fingers as you can and, using your comb, carefully comb through them.**

   If your Yorkie tends to get a lot of mats, consider buying a mat rake, which is essentially what it sounds like: a wide-toothed comb designed to rake through most snarls. Also keep in mind that if, despite your regular grooming, your Yorkie still has problems with matting, it may be because your Yorkie doesn't have the proper silky single coat, but a much softer double coat. If this is the case, consider buying a soft slicker brush to work out the mats before you bathe him.

   If you come across a particularly stubborn mat that won't let go, cut it out with a pair of scissors. And then promise yourself that you'll brush more regularly to avoid that problem in the future.

3. **End by using your fine-toothed comb to comb through the hair one last time.**

   Don't forget this last step. You'll be surprised at the little snags and knots that remain in the coat, and this final comb-through gets them out (see Figure 10-2).

If you're gentle and brush your Yorkshire Terrier regularly enough so that mats don't form, your dog will love having her coat brushed and combed — which makes your job easier and more enjoyable.

©Isabelle Francais

Figure 10-2: Finish any brushing session with a fine-toothed comb to get out any remaining snarls.

Blow drying

You don't have to blow dry your Yorkie's coat (you can let her air dry, if you want), but here are reasons why you may want to:

✔ If you're trying to create the sleek, smooth look of the traditional Yorkie coat, blow drying helps straighten any wayward waves.

✔ When the weather's cold or if your house is drafty, blow drying reduces the chance that your Yorkie will become chilled.

✔ If you don't have time to wait for her to air dry — for example, you're leaving and don't want a wet dog on the furniture or you're planning to take her outside — you'll need to blow dry her.

✔ If you get your dog professionally groomed, you can bet the groomer will use a blow dryer. By blow drying at home, you help her get accustomed to the noise and sensation of air blowing over her (see Chapter 8 for tips on helping your Yorkie make friends with your blow dryer).

The supply list for blow drying is pretty short: a blow dryer and a towel or rubber mat for your dog to stand on so she doesn't slip around. You can use a blow dryer made for humans or one made especially for grooming dogs (some models come with a stand so that both your hands are free; look in pet-supply stores for various models). If you use a human blow dryer, be sure it has multiple heat and power settings that let you control how much and how hot the air is. To blow dry, follow these steps:

1. **Towel dry your dog's coat and brush it thoroughly, being sure to remove all snarls and mats.**

   See the preceding section "Brushing basics" for instructions on how to brush your dog's coat and get rid of snarls and mats.

2. **Set the dryer's heat setting on low or medium and the power setting on medium.**

   If this is your dog's first time under the blower, set the heat and power switches on low. Remember to take it slow and easy, and resign yourself to the fact that you may not be able to dry her whole coat.

3. **Begin drying the back area first and work your way to the front, gently combing through the hair with your fingers as you go.**

   To avoid burning your dog, move the dryer in small circular motions over the area you're drying rather than blast straight away at one spot. Combing through the coat with your fingers separates the hair, makes it dry a little faster, and also lets you feel how warm the heat is.

4. **Switch the power to low and dry the hair on the head and muzzle.**

   Be sure to get the hair behind her ears.

5. **Turn the power back up to medium and dry under the tail and on the crest, or chest.**

   You have to lift her tail to dry her tail area, and you may have to lift her chin to get a good shot at the crest.

6. **Hold on to your dog's front legs with your free hand and lift her to standing position; dry her tummy.**

   Pay particular attention to the upper part of her inner thighs and her "arm pits," which tend to get neglected.

7. **When she's dry, brush her coat thoroughly again.**

Voila! A Yorkie with that "fresh from the salon" look.

Simple trimming tasks

You trim your Yorkie's coat for a couple of reasons: one, to give her a particular style and to neaten her up. Two, to get rid of hair that can lead to problems, such as the hair around the anus or on the pads of the feet. Tasks that fall into the former category require practice, patience, and skill. If you lack these qualities or the desire to acquire them, rely on professional groomers. Tasks that fall into the latter category, however, are ones that any Yorkie owner can perform with confidence — after a little practice. In the following sections, I tell you what you need to know to do routine maintenance trimming.

Trimming can be as simple as clipping the hair around the feet to make them look neater or as extensive as cutting a long coat into one of the more sculpted shorter styles (such as the modified Schnauzer cut). Perform the tasks you feel comfortable with, and have a professional do the rest.

To groom your Yorkie, you need these necessary items:

- Standard hair-cutting scissors with rounded tips
- Hair clippers

Be very careful when you use scissors or clippers on your Yorkie, especially if you've never performed these tasks before. Combine your inexperience with a dog who isn't used to standing stoically for grooming, and you can end up hurting your dog or suffering a bite wound yourself. If the whole idea makes you nervous, rely on a professional groomer.

Trimming around the feet

One trimming task you should feel comfortable doing is trimming the hair around and under the pads of your dog's feet. This hair grows long enough to drag on the ground and cause all sorts of problems. Not only does it pick up dirt and burrs, but it also impedes your dog's traction. At least once a month, inspect your Yorkie's feet and cut away the excess hair using standard hair-cutting scissors with rounded tips that you can find in any drug or beauty-supply store.

Follow these steps:

1. **Hold your dog's leg firmly in one hand and carefully cut the excess hair in between the pads of his feet.**

   Sometimes this hair grows pretty thick. Rather than trying to cut through a whole clump at a time, take little snipping cuts.

2. **Hold the paw, pad down, and trim the hair in a half-circle around the front of the foot.**

   You don't need to cut the hair on top of the foot or up the leg. Simply trimming the hair around the foot is enough to neaten it up and keep it from dragging on the ground.

3. **Repeat steps with the three remaining feet.**

Trimming around the ears

You need to keep the hair around adult Yorkies' ears trimmed to accentuate their upright point. On puppies, you trim the hair around the ears to help the ears stand erect (although sometimes, when a puppy teethes, his ears droop temporarily; in this case, trimming doesn't help). To trim the hair around your Yorkie's ears, use clippers with a #40 blade (see Figure 10-3).

Follow these steps:

1. **With your Yorkie secure, trim the hair on the front of the ear about half the way down.**

   Figure 10-4 shows how far down on the ear you need to trim. To more easily apply the little bit of pressure you need to trim, put a finger behind the ear to hold it upright when you're clipping.

2. **Trim the hair on the back of the ear, again about half way down.**

3. **If necessary, use scissors or your clippers to neaten the hair on the sides of the ears to form a V-shape.**

   You don't want to cut into the ear skin, so make this final trim in bright light when you can see and follow the contour of the ear.

©Isabelle Francais

Figure 10-3: Use clippers with a #40 blade to trim the hair around the ears.

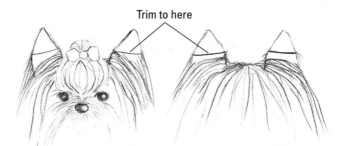

Figure 10-4: Trim the hair about halfway down on both the fronts and backs of the ears to keep them neat and trim.

Trimming around the anus

Long-haired breeds are notoriously difficult to keep clean around the rectal area. All that hair in the one place where you want a clear shot . . . well, suffice it to say that you have to help eliminate the problem. To do that, keep the hair around the anus short.

Use a pair of scissors, or preferably a clipper, and simply cut the hair short in a circle about an inch in diameter around the anal area. Do this at least every month.

The piece de resistance: Adding the bow

A little bow-ribbon is one of the immediately identifiable features of the Yorkshire Terrier breed. Sure it's cute, and you can spend quite a bit of time perusing the different patterns and styles and trying to figure out whether a rhinestone center looks chic or trashy, but the bow actually serves a practical purpose. It keeps all that hair out of your dog's eyes.

Putting in the bow, called *banding,* isn't difficult, but you do have to practice. You need a comb, three small latex bands (you can buy these items in the beauty section of most drug or grocery stores), and a bow, which you can get from a pet-supply store. Then follow these steps to put the bow in your Yorkie's hair:

1. **Using the comb, part the hair across the top of the skull, from ear to ear.**

   To put in two bows, create a center part and work one side at a time.

2. **Part the hair from the outer corner of each eye up to just above the ear.**

   Now you have the hair you're going to band.

3. **Put the first latex band on the hair and work it to the center, between the ears.**

   Don't use rubber bands, which tear and pull at the hair. Latex bands hold nicely and slide out easily without breaking the hair. Also, don't pull the hair very tight when securing the band, which can damage the skin and lead to (sometimes permanent) hair loss. And then what would you do with all your pretty bows?

4. **Pull a couple of strands of hair loose (but not out) to create a little poof over your dog's brow.**

5. **Put the second latex band in about an inch above the first one in the same tail of hair.**

   Although some people forgo the second band, the second band makes creating a nice little top knot that much easier.

6. **Put the second band behind the first band (this forms the top knot) and put the third band around both, to secure the top knot in place.**

7. **Finish with your bow.**

8. **Practice until you get the look you want.**

   If your first effort looks a little wobber-jawed, pull it out and try again. Of course, depending on how amenable your Yorkie is to your attempts, you may get only one practice session a day. But take heart. Before you know it, you'll be banding with the best of them.

If you have a puppy or a Yorkie with a short cut, you may still be able to put a bow in, although you may not have enough hair to create the flounce at the top (Steps 5 and 6). If that's the case, just let the hair stay loose above the band and add the bow.

Wrapping it up

Wrapping is a task for those owners who are serious about creating a show-quality coat. To wrap, you need latex bands, wax-paper squares (or some other appropriate paper, like rice paper or bakery tissue), and a comb.

To wrap your Yorkie's hair, make sure that the coat is clean and thoroughly brushed; then follow these steps:

1. **Fold wraps in a tri-fold (as you would a letter).**

   When you wrap the hair, it will lay in the middle section of the folded paper.

2. **Part the dog's hair into sections; put a latex band around each section to hold it in place, being sure to leave some space between the roots and band for comfort (think of a loose ponytail).**

   As you part your Yorkie's hair, keep in mind how his body moves. For example, the crest would be one section; the hair over each shoulder and flank would be other sections (to enable him to move freely).

3. **Take the first section of hair and place the end of the hair in the center of the tri-fold paper.**

4. **Fold the wrap in half, from bottom to top, with the hair inside.**

   This step clinches the hair so that it's less likely to come out while you're rolling the wrap up.

5. **Fold or roll the wrap up (as you would a hair curler) until it's about 2 to 3 inches from the dog's body; then fold the end sections of the tri-fold over the hair.**

6. **Secure the wrap with a latex band.**

7. **Repeat Steps 3 through 6 for the remaining sections.**

Now stand back and admire your handiwork.

Don't wrap a soft coat. Doing so can break your Yorkie's hair, which isn't a good thing if your objective is a long coat (and presumably it is if you're taking the time and effort to wrap it).

Tackling Other Grooming Tasks

In addition to grooming your Yorkie's coat, you also have other areas — such as her eyes, ears, nails, and teeth — that you need to attend to.

Clipping nails

Untrimmed nails can cause a variety of problems for your dog. They're more prone to cracking and bleeding, can get caught on things, and can impede his balance on hard surfaces. In addition, some nails curl and, if left alone, grow back up into the soft tissue of your dog's paw. An easy way to prevent any of these problems is to regularly clip your dog's nails.

The best time to clip your Yorkie's nails is right after a bath, when the nail is softer and easier to cut. So after every bath, check your Yorkie's nails to see whether they're due for a clipping. The other good time to trim nails is whenever your dog needs it. An obvious sign that your dog needs a trim? The clitter-clatter of nails over hard surfaces.

The key to trimming nails is to *not* cut into the *quick* — the nail bed that runs down the middle of your dog's nail and grows as the nail grows. The quick is full of nerve endings and blood vessels, which means that it hurts like the dickens and bleeds like a fountain if cut.

Yorkies' nails are challenging to clip because their nails are black, and you can't see the quick. So, when you cut the nails, you're cutting blind. (In Figure 10-5 I reverse the colors, so you can visualize where the quick is located.) If this task is too stressful for you, leave the job to your groomer or vet.

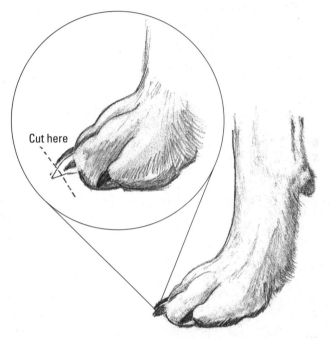

Cut here

Figure 10-5: Although you can't see the quick, it extends into your Yorkie's nail, and you must avoid it when you clip.

To trim nails, you need a pair of sharp nail clippers designed for use on dogs and some styptic powder (which hopefully you won't have to use). Then follow these directions:

1. **Hold your Yorkie in your lap and with your free hand lift one paw, using your thumb and fingers to work the hair away from the nail and apply enough pressure to the toes to extend the nail slightly.**

2. **Clip several small slivers of the nail off at a 45-degree angle, looking carefully at the nail after each snip.**

   You're looking for a small black dot underneath the center of the nail, which is the beginning of the quick.

3. When you see the quick, stop.

If you happen to cut into the quick, use the styptic powder to stop the bleeding, prostrate yourself in front of the dog and beg his forgiveness, and then give him praise and a treat.

4. Repeat these steps for each nail.

Only clip as many nails in one sitting as your dog can comfortably tolerate. If you get only one paw done, fine. Do another paw later, and another after that one until you can cross this task off your list.

Cleaning and examining the ears

At every grooming session, make a quick check of the ears. You're looking for dirt or wax, any signs of infection or problem, and hair blocking the ear canal.

To keep your dog's ears in tip-top shape, you need a cotton ball or cotton swab, ear-cleaning solution (you can find this solution at pet-supply stores or at your vet's office), and scissors or tweezers. Then, follow these steps:

1. Remove any excess hair blocking the ear canal.

You can clip it with scissors, tweeze it out, or pluck it with your fingers.

2. Dab the ear cleaning solution on a cotton swab or cotton ball and gently wipe out the inside of the ear.

The part of the ear you can see is called the *ear pinna*. This part is the area that you clean. Don't stick the cotton swab down the ear canal because you can puncture the ear drum.

If you notice signs of infection — redness, swelling, sensitivity to touch, or a foul odor — take your dog to the vet immediately.

Checking and cleaning teeth

You brush your dog's teeth for the same reason that you brush your own: to forestall gum disease and infection, get rid of plaque, avoid bad breath, and brighten your smile (see Figure 10-6). Of course, dogs don't smile, but you can bet that a healthy mouth makes for a happier dog.

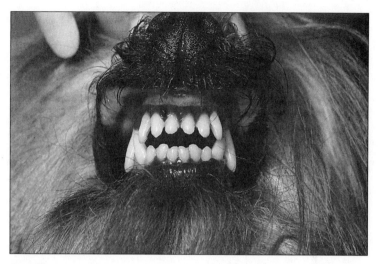

©Isabelle Francais

Figure 10-6: Regularly brushing your Yorkie's teeth keeps them clean and gives you the opportunity to check for sores or infection.

Although dogs don't get cavities, they do suffer from gum disease, which, if left untreated, can become very painful and lead to tooth loss.

When you're ready to brush your dog's teeth, gather your supplies (pet toothpaste and your dog's toothbrush) and do the following:

1. **Squeeze a small amount of toothpaste onto the toothbrush; work the toothpaste into the bristles.**

2. **Place the bristles at your dog's gumline (where the teeth and gums meet), and using a gentle rotating motion, brush the teeth in that area.**

   Be sure to get around the base of the tooth and between the teeth.

3. **Move to a new section and repeat Step 2.**

   Spend most of your effort on the outside of the upper teeth, where the bulk of the plaque builds up.

4. **Repeat these steps until all the teeth are cleaned.**

5. **Rinse and spit.**

   Just kidding.

Chapter 11

Keeping Your Yorkie Hale and Hardy

*F*eeding your Yorkie the right food, making sure that she stays active, and grooming her regularly (the topics of the preceding two chapters) go a long way toward ensuring your little dog's health and well-being. But this list is incomplete. Routine healthcare — in other words, veterinary care — is the other vital component. Your dog requires different medical care for the different stages of her life — puppyhood, adulthood, and seniorhood. In this chapter, I explain what you can expect during routine visits (health-checks and vaccinations) and how to care for an older Yorkie.

Spaying or neutering is another routine procedure that can make your Yorkie happier, more pleasant to live with, and less suscepti- ble to certain serious health conditions. And to increase your chances of being reunited with your Yorkie if she wanders (or is lured) away, make sure that the person who found her can identify her as yours through some sort of permanent ID. In this chapter, I cover those issues, too.

Hi Ho, Hi Ho, to the Vet We Go

Besides you, your vet is probably the most important person in your Yorkie's life (see Figure 11-1). He's the expert you can count on to provide trustworthy nutrition information, preventive and emergency healthcare, and solutions or suggestions for problems your Yorkie may be having.

©Isabelle Francais

Figure 11-1: A good vet is a pal to your Yorkie and a trusted resource for you.

Of course, your vet can't do any of these things unless you actually involve him in your dog's life — which means scheduling regular appointments. How regularly you schedule appointments with your vet depends on your Yorkie's age and medical needs. Pups need a few initial visits to track their growth and provide necessary vaccinations; healthy adult dogs usually need an annual check and booster shots. The following sections explain what you can expect at these routine vet appointments; head to Chapter 12 for information on emergencies that require veterinary attention.

Puppy visits

If you adopt a puppy, you're going to spend a bit of time at the vet's office because puppies need an initial checkup and however many additional appointments necessary to provide the series of vaccines.

The very first visit

If you adopt a puppy, your first visit to the vet should fall within the first few days that your puppy's home. For this vet visit, take the following:

- ✔ Any health information you received from the breeder
- ✔ Any medications your puppy is on
- ✔ A stool sample (that is, a sample of her feces)

Be sure to check your breeder contract (refer to Chapter 6). If it stipulates when this initial vet appointment must occur, schedule your appointment within that time frame (usually a couple of days to a week following the adoption of the puppy). If you don't, you risk voiding the contract's health guarantee.

During this visit, expect the vet to assess your puppy's general health and temperament and to give you advice on any health issues you need to be aware of. Although this check often turns up nothing (or nothing serious, anyway), it's vitally important if you bought your Yorkie from a pet store or an agent, where you had no opportunity to see the conditions under which she was born and raised. A puppy whose early environment was crowded and unclean, for example, may have internal parasites that the seller is unaware of but that, if not treated, can impair her growth and development.

Depending on the timing of this initial visit, your Yorkie may also get the first or another of the series of vaccinations she needs. See the section "Ouch! Vaccine Facts" later in this chapter for a rundown of the vaccination schedule for puppies.

At the end of this first visit, your vet tells you when you need to return and what you need to bring. If, for example, your Yorkie tested positive for an internal parasite, the vet will want to check another stool sample. (Many vets, in fact, keep checking your Yorkie's feces until two stool samples come back negative.)

Subsequent puppy visits

After the first visit, you may have other visits to look forward to. Depending on your puppy's age and whether he received any immunizations prior to being adopted, you may visit every three or four weeks until he receives all his vaccinations. Plus, you may have another visit for his rabies vaccination (if your puppy wasn't old enough for this vaccine when the rest of the series was completed; see the later section "Common vaccines" for more on rabies).

In addition, some vets recommend bringing your pup in for regular weighings, just to make sure that he's growing properly. Your vet will let you know whether these checks are necessary.

After your puppy receives the necessary puppy vaccinations, you can begin the adult schedule of annual checkups (see the next section "Regular checkups for your adult dog"). Of course, if your pup has a health condition, your visits may be more frequent. Again, your vet will let you know.

 If you have questions or concerns about your puppy or want advice on training, nutrition, and behavior, ask your vet. He can give you the information you need, recommend techniques you can try, or give you the names of other resources in your area.

Regular checkups for your adult dog

Healthy adult dogs need an annual checkup. At these checkups, your vet

- ✔ **Weighs your Yorkie:** Your vet wants to make sure your Yorkie is at a healthy weight, given her size and activity level. He also uses this information to track your Yorkie's weight since her last checkup. Excessive weight loss or gain can indicate a more serious health concern than not being able to say "no" to leftovers.

- ✔ **Checks her stool sample:** The stool sample reveals the presence of intestinal parasites.

- ✔ **Checks her heart rate and respiration:** Your vet listens for a strong, regular heart beat and clear breathing. Other sounds, such as a murmur, can indicate a more serious heart condition.

- ✔ **Examines her eyes, ears, and nose:** Your vet looks for signs (dullness, discharge, odor, and so on) that can indicate a medical condition like jaundice, ear mites, and so on.

- ✔ **Inspects her mouth:** Yorkies have notoriously small mouths and the problems, like overcrowded teeth, that come with them. For this reason, dental hygiene is particularly important for Yorkshire Terriers. As your vet looks for early signs of gum disease and tartar, be prepared for a lecture on brushing your dog's teeth more frequently.

- ✔ **Feels her major organs:** To feel your dog's organs, the vet simply presses gently in the right places. He's looking for signs of enlargement or tumors.

✔ **Checks her skin and coat:** He checks your Yorkie's overall skin and coat quality for dryness, rashes, signs of irritation (which can indicate a parasite or ringworm), sores, and so on.

✔ **Checks her fore and hind legs:** Your vet looks for any skeletal problems, such as a *luxating patella* (dislocating kneecap), a condition common to Yorkshire Terriers. You can read more about this condition in Chapter 12.

✔ **Gives the necessary booster vaccines:** As an adult, your dog may require booster shots, which your vet gives during these yearly appointments.

✔ **Discusses any healthcare concerns you have:** If something's bothering or worrying you about your Yorkie — she's limping, coughing a lot, or doing something else out of the ordinary — let your vet know so you can resolve the issue.

Healthy adults need to go to the vet once a year. Senior Yorkies and Yorkies with health conditions (see Chapter 12) may require more frequent visits. If this is the case with your Yorkie, your vet will work out an adjusted schedule with you and let you know what to expect during these visits.

Ouch! Vaccine Facts

To keep your dog healthy, make sure that he gets the necessary vaccines and that he gets them within the appropriate time frame. The following sections tell you what you need to know.

Puppy protection

Most puppies have a natural immunity that they get from their mothers. This immunity lasts until they're about 8 weeks old. Vets usually recommend that puppies get the first of a series of three or four shots around the time that their natural immunity begins to wear off, which is around 6 to 8 weeks old. Puppies receive subsequent shots at three- to four-week intervals, which means that they get the last vaccine when they're about 15 or 16 weeks old.

These vaccines routinely include parvovirus and distemper, among others (for more info, see the section "Common vaccines" later in this chapter). Ask your vet specifically what diseases these vaccines protect your puppy against.

Turf wars: How a vaccination works

To oversimplify a very interesting biological sleight of hand, vaccines train the immune system to recognize and respond to threats. Here's how they work: Vaccines contain a dead or weakened form of the disease. When the vaccine enters your dog, it stimulates your dog's immune system. The immune system recognizes the disease agents as foreign, kicks into defense mode, and starts churning out antibodies to destroy the infectious agents.

The fight is rigged to favor the immune system, but that fact doesn't matter. What matters is that the immune system, having already whipped the enemy, is now hepped up, rarin' to go, and determined to protect its turf. If that particular invader reappears in the future, the immune system responds more quickly — this time knocking out *real* disease agents before they cause any harm. And to keep the immune system in fighting form (just in case the lack of activity has made it fat and lazy), your vet gives periodic booster shots.

Be sure to inform your vet of the type of vaccine, if any, that the puppy received before coming to your home. That way, your vet can use the same type of vaccine for the later shots.

Between 3 to 6 months old, your Yorkie needs a rabies vaccine. Your vet may schedule this shot to coincide with the last parvo/distemper vaccine, or he may decide to wait.

Hang around the vet's office for about 20 minutes after your dog gets his rabies vaccine just in case your Yorkie (like many other Toy dogs) has a reaction.

Until puppies are fully immunized, they're vulnerable to all sorts of nasty stuff. For this reason, avoid exposing your pup to areas where unvaccinated dogs may have been, like dog parks and pet stores.

Adult immunizations

During their annual checkups, adult dogs get a physical exam and any necessary annual booster vaccines. Discuss with your vet what booster shots are necessary for your dog. Some vaccines, like the rabies vaccine, for example, last for three years, but many state laws still mandate an annual shot. Other states accept a rabies booster every two or three years instead. Your vet can advise you on how frequently your dog needs booster vaccines.

Every dog's needs are different. Not all dogs need all available vaccines. Most Yorkies are indoors except when they have to go to the bathroom. If this describes your Yorkie's lifestyle, he'll do just fine with a rabies vaccine (according to state law), a distemper-parvo vaccine every three years after the initial booster at one year, and an annual bordetella vaccine. If you live in an area where Lyme Disease is prevalent, vets recommend that your dog get an annual Lyme vaccine. Coronavirus and giardia vaccines aren't recommended for all adult dogs. If your vet thinks your dog needs these, he'll inform you.

Health insurance for your dog

In the last few years, health insurance for pets has become available. Like insurance for humans, the premise and procedure is pretty much the same. You pay an annual or monthly premium and, if your pet needs medical treatment that's accepted by your policy, the insurance pays a percentage (around 80 percent is fairly common) of the costs.

Certainly, having pet health insurance can eliminate the sticker shock and give you more options if your pet requires intensive treatments. Some insurance companies even provide wellness plans that cover routine vet visits, vaccinations, and so on. If you decide to purchase healthcare insurance for your Yorkie, be sure to find out the following info before you settle on any one plan:

✔ **What medical care the policy covers:** If you're buying only emergency care, for example, make sure you understand what conditions qualify as an emergency under your coverage. Although you may consider sudden, uncontrolled vomiting an emergency, you don't want to find out after the fact that your policy considers it an uncovered illness.

✔ **How to make claims:** Most insurance companies expect you to pay the veterinary bill in full and then submit the receipt along with the necessary paperwork yourself, and the insurance company reimburses you directly. Others (very few, actually) expect you to pay nothing, and the vet's office files the claim and is reimbursed.

✔ **How much of the bill is covered:** Most pet healthcare plans pay for a percentage of the final cost. Be sure you know what percentage your plan pays.

✔ **Whether a multi-pet discount is available:** If you insure more than one pet, many companies give you a discount.

If you're interested in finding out more about health insurance for your Yorkie, talk to your vet or go online. Simply enter "pet health insurance" in your search engine to access a whole slew of sites selling coverage.

Although most veterinary offices keep records of your Yorkie's visits and the vaccines he received and send you reminders when the time comes for a booster and an annual checkup, don't rely solely on their bookkeeping. Keep your own records — the receipts and notes from the visit usually suffice — in a file at home. Maintaining your dog's medical information not only keeps your records up-to-date, but it also allows you to have immunization information on hand if something happens or if you need to board him unexpectedly. (All reputable kennels require proof of immunization for any pet they board.)

Common vaccines

Gone are the days when your Yorkie was vulnerable to any canine pathogen that she came across. Today you can vaccinate her against several diseases. Which of these diseases you vaccinate your dog for depends on a number of factors:

- ✔ **The prevalence of the disease in your area:** Lyme Disease, for example, isn't a problem everywhere, and dogs who live in regions where few or no cases of Lyme Disease are reported don't need to routinely have vaccinations against it. Be sure to discuss the special disease risks in your area with your vet. And, if you're traveling with your Yorkie, discuss your plans with your vet, who can let you know whether your dog needs other vaccines.

- ✔ **Your individual dog's needs:** Some vaccines, such as Bordetella, are necessary only if you plan to board or groom your dog while you travel or take your dog to places, such as dog shows, where she'll be in contact with several other dogs.

- ✔ **State law:** Most, if not all, states have laws regarding rabies vaccines (in fact, the rabies vaccine is the only legally mandated vaccine). These laws stipulate how frequently (annually, biannually, and so forth) dogs must be vaccinated against this disease.

In addition to the rabies vaccine, which is mandated by state law, most vets also routinely vaccinate against distemper and parvo. I discuss these vaccines, as well as others that are fairly common, in the following sections.

Rabies

Rabies is no joke. It's a virus that attacks the brain, is transmitted primarily through the bite or saliva of an infected animal, and is almost always fatal once the symptoms begin to appear.

Because rabies is one of the few diseases that dogs can pass to humans, every state mandates that dogs be vaccinated against rabies. Puppies receive their first rabies vaccine when they're 3 to 6 months old, their second vaccine a year later, and subsequent vaccines according to the laws in your state.

Although most rabies vaccines offer complete protection for three years, some state laws haven't kept up with the medical advances and still require an annual rabies booster. Your vet can tell you how frequently your Yorkie needs to be vaccinated.

Canine distemper

Canine distemper is about as ugly as rabies. It's a highly contagious and often incurable virus that attacks your dog's respiratory system, gastrointestinal system, and central nervous system. Despite its name, canine distemper doesn't affect only dogs. It affects other animals too, such as foxes, raccoons, and skunks, and this virus is pretty common in the wild. Symptoms include fever, diarrhea, vomiting, pneumonia, discharge from the eyes and nose, paralysis, and seizures.

Although a dog can become infected by coming in contact with body fluids of an infected animal, most dogs are infected by simply breathing air that has the viral particles in it. In other words, distemper is an airborne disease. So even if you can keep your dog away from other animals, you can't stop him from breathing any more than you can check the air for the disease.

Canine parvovirus

Canine parvovirus is another highly contagious viral infection that attacks the gastrointestinal tract of dogs. Symptoms include loss of appetite, lethargy, bloody diarrhea, and vomiting. Dogs can contract the disease by coming into contact with feces from an infected animal. Puppies are especially vulnerable because of their under-developed immune systems.

Canine parvovirus is a relative newcomer in the world of dog diseases. The original canine parvovirus, which was relatively harmless except to newborn pups, was first identified in 1967. By 1978, a new, more virulent strain appeared. Researchers believe this new strain was a mutation of the *feline parvovirus* (also known as feline distemper). In 1979, another mutation appeared that was even more aggressive than the 1978 variety.

Canine adenovirus

There are two types of canine adenovirus: type 1 and type 2. Type 1 causes infectious canine hepatitis and can result in severe liver and kidney damage. Type 2 causes a respiratory infection that can lead to kennel cough. Many distemper vaccines include a vaccine for canine adenovirus.

Bordetella

Bordetella is a very contagious respiratory disease. Outbreaks are most common in the summer months when dogs are kenneled while their families are on vacation. In the kennel, dogs come in contact with the bacteria and then bring it home to share with their canine friends in the neighborhood. The primary symptoms are coughing and various degrees of breathing difficulty. In the most severe cases, bordetella can become bronchopneumonia (basically pneumonia) with complications and can lead to death.

Lyme Disease

You may have heard about Lyme Disease as it relates to humans, but dogs are also susceptible. Lyme Disease, which is spread by deer ticks, attacks the joints, heart, and nerve tissue. Some dogs also develop lesions on their kidneys. Symptoms of Lyme Disease include fever, loss of appetite, sore joints, and limping, which can progress to complete lameness because of the joint pain.

Keep in mind that some controversy surrounds the effectiveness of the Lyme vaccine. Some vets believe that the vaccine provides adequate protection; others believe that it actually causes a more severe reaction in particularly susceptible dogs who contract the disease.

Discuss the issue with your veterinarian. Although the disease has been found in dogs in every state, some regions pose more of a problem for your dog. In the end, you have to weigh the risks of the disease against the potential risks of the vaccine.

A few more

Following are four other diseases that your vet may routinely vaccinate against. In many cases, the vaccines for these diseases are automatically included in the vaccine combo your vet gives:

- ✔ **Infectious Canine Hepatitis (which isn't related to human hepatitis):** This disease is highly contagious and affects the liver and other organs. Symptoms include nausea, vomiting, a distended stomach, loss of appetite, light-colored stool, and jaundice.

- ✔ **Parainfluenza:** This disease is a frequent cause of a mild respiratory infection that often plays a part in kennel cough.

✔ **Leptospirosis:** This condition is a bacterial infection that may lead to permanent kidney damage.

✔ **Coronavirus:** This disease is the second leading viral cause of diarrhea in puppies (canine parvovirus is the first). Vaccinating adult dogs for coronavirus isn't necessary.

Watching for reactions

Some dogs have reactions to their vaccines. Reactions in young dogs and Toy breeds — yes, that means your Yorkie — are most common. Usually, the reaction is mild: Your dog may eat less and sleep more for the next 24 hours. Some dogs may have a little stiffness or tenderness in the area where the vaccine was given. Occasionally, the reaction is more severe and can include vomiting or swelling.

If your Yorkie has an adverse reaction to a vaccine, be sure to discuss the situation with your vet. He can let you know whether the reaction is severe enough to warrant medical attention (it usually isn't) and can take precautions (giving an antihistamine prior to the vaccine or giving a vaccine that doesn't include leptospirosis, which often causes the most severe reactions) the next time your dog is due for a booster.

Let the Good Times Roll: Neutering and Spaying

If you don't neuter your male Yorkie or spay your female, here's what you can expect:

For the girls: At around 6 months, your female is going to go into her first heat, also called her *season*. Her season begins with a bloody discharge that can last for up to 15 days. Following the discharge, she's at her most fertile. Feeling saucy and cute, she'll flirt with other dogs, giving them that come-hither signal (lifting her tail and twitching her rump). She may seem hyperactive, stressed, and, if her wiles haven't secured her a date, may spend a lot of time whining and fussing. This business can last up to 30 days, and it happens about twice a year.

For the boys: The boys mature sexually around 6 months of age, too. However, males don't have seasons: They're in the mood whenever they come across or sniff a female in heat. Which means that, boys being boys, they spend nearly all their time looking for females in heat. And just in case one is near, they lift their legs to spray their scent (read urine) anywhere they think she's likely to notice and be duly impressed. They don't care where they spray: The target can be your prize rose bush, the fence post, or the chintz sofa your grandmother left you. They also become highly obnoxious if their true love (or any available female) isn't near and will look for substitutes: pillows, cushions, legs, your daughter's favorite stuffed animal.

If you're not breeding (and you probably shouldn't be) and you don't spay/neuter your Yorkie, you're subjecting her to misery every time she goes into season and him to misery all the time. So spay/neuter your dog. Not only does it make her and his life (and your life) more pleasant, but it also protects your dog from potentially life-threatening diseases: for her, uterine infections and uterine cancers; for him, prostate disease and testicular cancer.

Here's the optimum time to have your Yorkie fixed and a very short explanation of what parts are removed:

- ✔ **Spaying:** Spay your female when she's between 4 and 6 months old. During the procedure, the vet removes her ovaries, uterus, and fallopian tubes.

- ✔ **Neutering:** Neuter your male before he reaches sexual maturity at 6 months old. When your vet neuters your dog, he removes your dog's testicles.

In both procedures, your dog is put under general anesthesia. After waking up, your Yorkie will feel some pain or discomfort (talk to your vet about pain medication because dogs feel pain just as much as we humans do), but will be up and about by the second day.

Many vets recommend waiting until your Yorkie is around 6 months old before spaying or neutering. Why? To give your Yorkie's baby teeth a chance to come out on their own; if they're not gone by six months, they're probably not going to pop out by themselves (a common problem with small dogs, including Yorkies). So, what's the connection between baby teeth and the reproduction organs? There isn't any. Your vet just wants to take care of two birds with one stone: When he spays or neuters your Yorkie, he can also remove any remaining baby teeth, which saves your dog from undergoing another procedure that requires general anesthesia and saves you the expense and hassle.

The only reason not to neuter or spay your Yorkie is when you have a show-quality dog (refer to Chapter 4) who you intend to enter in conformation events or breed.

No more snip-snip?

A new technique for neutering doesn't require surgery at all. Instead, vets inject a medication into the testicles that retards the growth of the reproductive organs. The potential benefits of this procedure are that it doesn't require anesthesia, it has a short recovery time, it seems to provide permanent sterilization, and it's less expensive than traditional neutering. The downside is that the procedure is so new that vets haven't completely endorsed it yet. The procedure isn't approved for use in females. If you're interested, discuss this option with your vet.

ID-ing for Safety

One of the easiest ways to protect your Yorkie is to make sure that, if he gets lost or stolen, you have a way to identify him as yours. Your ID-ing options include the collar tag, a microchip, or a tattoo.

Using a collar tag

Collar tags are your first line of defense. If a well-meaning stranger finds your Yorkie, the first place he's probably going to look for identification is the tag hanging from your dog's collar. So make sure that whenever your dog isn't in the house, she's wearing her collar and tag. And make sure that the tag has your name and phone number on it. You also may want to include your veterinary clinic's name and number.

Don't expect the collar tag alone to protect your Yorkie. It can be easily lost or destroyed, so use another identification method as well.

Microchipping

To use *microchipping* as a form of identification, your vet implants a small microchip (about the size of a kernel of rice) just under your dog's skin, usually at the base of the neck between the shoulder blades. The microchip contains an ID number and links to a database where the corresponding identification information resides. If you lose your microchipped Yorkie, the person who finds him takes him to a veterinary clinic, an animal shelter, or a local humane society so that he can be scanned. Here are some facts about microchipping:

- ✔ Microchipping is a safe, permanent, and relatively inexpensive way to identify your dog.

- ✔ Implanting the microchip takes only a few seconds and doesn't require the use of an anesthetic — a good thing for dogs as small as Yorkies, who may have a negative reaction to anesthesia.

- ✔ Some implanted microchips can *migrate,* that is move to a different part of the body. Although a relocated microchip isn't necessarily harmful, if your dog is lost, finding it does take longer. Check with your vet to find out whether the microchip he uses will migrate.

- ✔ Microchips are invisible. If the person who finds your dog is unaware of the technology, he won't know to have her scanned.

- ✔ For the microchipping method to work, the dog has to be taken to a location that has scanning equipment. These places include veterinary clinics, animal shelters, humane society offices, and so on.

Tattooing

Tattooing your dog is one of the older methods of permanent identification. Like microchipping, tattooing uses an identification number that links to a registry containing your identification info. In order for tattooing to protect your dog, you also must register in a national tattoo database, such as Tattoo a Pet (`www.tattoo-a-pet.com`) or the National Dog Registry (`www.natldogregistry.com`). If you're interested in tattooing your Yorkie, keep these points in mind:

- ✔ You can take your dog to your vet or to a skilled tattooist (ask your vet for a recommendation) to be tattooed. You pay for the cost of getting the tattoo and the registration fee. Your vet or tattooist can give you more details on the specific charges.

- ✔ The procedure doesn't require general anesthetic, but the area that's getting tattooed is numbed with a local anesthetic. Although the procedure itself is painless (after the numbing, that is) most dogs don't like the buzzing sound of the tattoo needle, so you want to be on hand to help keep your dog calm and still.

✔ The two most common areas to put the tattoos are on the inside of the ear and on the inside of the thigh, near the groin. Always opt for the thigh tattoo, because an ear tattoo can be cut off.

✔ By law, no laboratory can use a dog who has a tattoo.

✔ The tattoo doesn't protect your dog unless you're also listed in a national database.

Caring for Your Older Yorkie

By the time your Yorkie reaches the ripe old age of 7, she's considered a senior citizen in the canine world. Of course, you're only as old as you feel. As your Yorkie gets older, the trick is to do what you can to make sure she continues feeling well. You need to

✔ **Pay special attention to her teeth.** Brush them regularly (see Chapter 10 for instructions), give her hard kibble to eat and Dentabones to chew on, and schedule regular cleanings with your vet at least every year or two.

Keeping your aging Yorkie's teeth clean is vital to her overall health. Yorkies are prone to having difficulties with their teeth because of their small mouths. Add gum disease or infection to the mix, and your previously healthy Yorkie won't eat what she should because it's too painful. In addition, bacteria in the mouth can affect her heart, kidneys, and immune system.

✔ **Keep an eye on her weight.** As she grows older, your Yorkie has a tendency to put on a few extra ounces or pounds. Carrying extra weight puts a strain on her joints and her heart. It also exacerbates other medical conditions that she may be predisposed to develop, like arthritis, high blood pressure, and diabetes. Follow this advice:

• **Make sure she gets enough exercise.** Play with her, go for walks, and continue doing what you've always done. She'll let you know when she's had enough.

• **Discuss her diet with your vet.** As long as she's active and not gaining weight, you may not need to switch to a senior-dog food formula, but when she slows down and becomes less active or begins putting on weight despite her activity level, you'll probably have to switch to a food especially formulated for senior dogs. Get your vet's opinion on the matter.

Some wonderful new medications are available to treat arthritis in dogs (a common ailment of the older set), but the best idea is to minimize her risk by keeping your Yorkie slender.

✔ **Groom her weekly.** During grooming sessions, your primary goal isn't to keep her looking good; it's to look for signs of potential medical concerns: lumps, lesions, dry skin, foul odor, and so on. If you find something out of the ordinary, call your vet.

Of course, at some point, your senior dog's going to begin feeling like a senior dog. You'll notice her slowing down and sleeping more, and you may notice that she's beginning to lose some sight and hearing. She may develop aches and pains in her joints. When these changes begin, you're entering a very special and poignant time. Your goal is to make her as comfortable as you can for as long as you can and to keep a watchful eye on her health:

✔ **Schedule a senior checkup with your vet.** Discuss any out-of-the-ordinary behaviors you notice (excessive coughing, odd body movements, failure to hear her name being called, and so on). In addition to performing a thorough exam, your vet can let you know which health issues you should be concerned about (and offer treatment suggestions) and which ones you can ignore.

✔ **Put comfy dog beds or pillows in the rooms your dog is often in.** Chances are, at some point, your Yorkie won't be able to jump up to her favorite spot on the couch. And when you're old and your joints hurt, having a soft place to rest your bones is a godsend (see Figure 11-2).

✔ **Help her navigate when she's having difficulty.** Climbing stairs can be hard on an older dog. Rather than trying to coax her up (or down), carry her. When she wants to go up on the bed or rest beside you on the couch, pick her up and settle her in. And remember that jumping down can be even more painful to sore joints, so help her down, too.

✔ **If she loses her hearing, don't let her out of your sight when you're outside.** She can easily become disoriented and lost. And how will you find her, other than luck, if she can't hear you calling her?

✔ **Enjoy these last years.** Both you and your Yorkie deserve it.

For detailed information on caring for your old pal, pick up a copy of *Senior Dogs For Dummies* by Susan McCullough (Wiley).

©Isabelle Francais

Figure 11-2: A quiet corner and a soft bed are musts for a senior dog.

Chapter 12

Critters, Crises, and Health Conditions Common to Yorkies

*P*art of being a responsible pet owner is dealing with and preparing for things you'd rather not have to even think about. Like what? you ask. Oh, those things that gross you out (like parasites), scare you (like emergencies), or worry you (like the health problems that are, unfortunately, common to the breed).

So raise your right hands and repeat after me: "I (state your name), do solemnly swear to be on the lookout for and deal absolutely mercilessly with any disgusting critters that try to claim a home in or on my Yorkie. I further avow to remain calm and collected during times of emergency and to memorize my vet's phone number or put it on my speed dial. And I promise to find out as much as I can about the health problems my little dog may experience so that I can get him the help he needs."

Okay. Now read on to find out what you can do to help your Yorkie overcome any health challenges that the world (or genetics) throws his way.

Eeew! Parasites

All dogs, bless their furry little hearts, are vulnerable to fleas, ticks, worms, and other lovely parasites. And Yorkies are no different. Not only are these parasites disgusting (have you ever seen a picture of a well-fed tick?), but they also pose a real health threat to your dog. Fortunately, you can take steps to protect your dog from these unwelcome guests. The following sections outline the most common parasites and tell you what to look for and how to get rid of them.

External parasites

The *external parasites* — those buggers that live and feed on the outside of your Yorkie — are often the easiest to see and get rid of. Either the critter itself is visible or the signs of its existence are apparent. You just need to know what signs to look for and how to get rid of these critters.

The best way you can guard against external parasites is to keep an eye out for them. At every grooming session, look for these critters and the signs they can leave behind.

Fleas

Everyone knows a little about fleas. They're the hopping, biting, annoying bugs that reproduce like mad (a single female can lay up to 2,000 eggs), drive your dog crazy, and can infest your home if you don't take action. Too many fleas can also make your Yorkie sick: Fleas carry diseases, frequently cause an allergic reaction that leads to dermatitis (an oozing, crusting, skin inflammation), and can give your dog tapeworms.

Fleas are relatively easy to spot. The first tell-tale sign is a dog who scratches like a maniac or bites at herself. If you take a closer look (pay particular attention to the areas around her tail and groin, and in the warm, dark areas between the legs and body), you may very well see a few fleas poking through your dog's fur.

Another sign of fleas is the stuff (read excrement, but also called *flea dirt*) that they leave behind. Because seeing these brown or black specks in a Yorkie's coat is nearly impossible, the best way to find them is to dampen a paper towel, stand your Yorkie over it, and ruffle her hair. If your dog has fleas, the excrement will fall to the paper towel and turn into little blood spots (that is, after all, what flea excrement is made of — your Yorkie's blood).

The best defense against fleas is prevention. And the safest prevention is using a flea-control solution or medication that your vet prescribes. Topical solutions, such as Advantage, spread through your dog's skin to kill fleas on contact, and the solutions last for a specified period of time (Advantage protects your dog from fleas for a month, for example). An alternative is to give your dog a heartworm preventive, such as Sentinel, that includes flea control; the benefit of this medication is that you're killing two critters with one stone, so to speak.

Before you use any over-the-counter flea preventive or powder on your Yorkie, talk to your vet about the safety of the product. If you're already dealing with an infestation, this discussion is even more vital because you have to use what are essentially insecticides to rid your dog (and house) of the unwanted critters.

Ticks

Ticks are small, eight-legged creatures that hang out in wooded areas, grasslands, and weedy patches. They have no sense of portion control, feeding on the blood of their hosts until they become engorged and bloated to several times their pre-dinner size.

Your Yorkie can become a host for a tick just by walking near or brushing against a bush, limb, or blade of grass that has a tick on it. Unfortunately, unless you go looking for a tick on your dog, you probably won't know she has one (or several) because there are few, if any, initial signs. Despite the fact that signs are scarce when a tick first pulls its chair up to the Yorkie dinner table, ticks do pose a real health threat to your dog. For instance:

- ✔ Several ticks feasting on your dog can cause anemia, fever, and sometimes paralysis.
- ✔ Some ticks carry Lyme Disease (see Chapter 11 for info on this disease).

After every walk through an area that may have ticks, be sure to inspect your dog. Part her hair a small section at a time, paying particular attention to her head, neck, feet, and the places where her legs meet her body. If you find a tick, follow these steps:

1. **Using a pair of tweezers, grasp the tick as close to the skin as you can.**

   Don't use your fingers. First, you can't get a good enough grip on the little bloodsucker. Second, if the tick is carrying some disease, its saliva can affect you, too. Third, who in their right mind wants to touch a tick?

2. ***Slowly* pull the tick out.**

   The goal is to keep the head (the part that's burrowed in the skin) and body intact. If you can't get the tick off your dog or if the head breaks off while you're trying to remove it, call your vet.

Don't try to burn the tick off. You're more likely to scare and hurt your Yorkie than you are to get the tick out.

3. **Flush the sucker down the toilet, wash the area on your Yorkie with an antiseptic, wash your own hands with soap and water, and keep an eye on your Yorkie for the next week or so for signs of illness.**

If you frequent areas where ticks congregate, talk with your vet about tick preventives for your Yorkie.

Mites (ear and skin)

If your Yorkie is scratching like crazy but you haven't seen any evidence of fleas (refer to the section "Fleas" earlier in this chapter), he may have skin mites. *Skin mites* are microscopic critters that your dog can contract by coming in contact with a dog who has them or an area where a contaminated dog has been. The only way to confirm whether your dog has mites is to have your vet take a skin scraping and look at it under the microscope.

Beyond scratching like a demon, a dog with skin mites develops mange. *Mange* is when the irritated skin swells, can form puss-filled scabs, and may lose its hair. Mange is extremely uncomfortable and unsightly, too. Some dogs need regular dips in veterinarian-approved insecticide and a medication to help alleviate some of the discomfort and itch. Others can be treated with injections or oral medications.

Ear mites are parasites that feed on earwax and other things (like dirt, flaking skins, and so on) in your Yorkie's ear canal. Signs that your dog has ear mites include head shaking, smelly ears, and excessive ear scratching. Your vet can recommend what product to use to get rid of them. Keep in mind, however, that because ear mites are so contagious, if one dog has them, chances are, any other dog in your house has them, too. So have your vet check all your dogs.

Ringworm

Okay, ringworm isn't really a parasite. It's a highly contagious fungus that often appears as a swollen red ring surrounded by a bald spot. Your vet can confirm whether your dog has ringworm by taking a skin scraping. Treatment typically involves special baths with medicated shampoo. Your vet may also prescribe an anti-fungal drug.

Ringworm spreads easily to people and animals. Small children and other pets are especially vulnerable, simply because they don't know not to touch the infected areas.

Internal parasites

As disgusting as the external parasites are, they don't really hold a candle to the *internal parasites* — those that live and feed on the inside of your Yorkie. Although you may see signs of their existence, you're probably not going to actually see the parasite itself (consider yourself lucky in this regard). Often, the only way to really identify what ails your dog is to have your vet run a blood test or check your dog's stool. The following sections, arranged from most to least serious, tell you what you need to know about internal freeloaders that can wreak havoc on your dog's health.

Heartworms

Heartworms are the deadliest of all the internal parasites your dog can get. Transmitted through mosquito bites, *heartworms* travel through the dog's tissues (or body) to his heart, where they develop and reproduce. Mature heartworms can be up to a foot long, and they block the blood flow from your dog's heart to his lungs.

Unfortunately, very few signs let you know when your dog has heartworm. In some cases, you may not realize how sick your guy is until he collapses or dies. If your dog has heartworm, his chances of survival depend on how advanced his condition is. If caught early (through a blood test), your Yorkie has a 90 percent chance of making a full recovery; the percentage declines as the condition progresses. Left untreated, heartworm is always fatal, and for dogs as small as Yorkies, as few as two heartworms can be deadly.

For all these reasons, having your dog checked during his annual vet visit and protecting him by giving him a monthly heartworm preventive are absolutely vital. If you stop giving the preventive for any reason, your vet needs to recheck your dog's blood for heartworms before you can resume giving him the preventive.

Hookworms

Hookworms are, as their name implies, hook-shaped worms that puppies can get from their mothers and that older dogs can get from contaminated ground. (Hookworm larvae live in moist soil. When it's moist and warm, they live near the surface of the ground. When it's dry, they go down with the water table.) These worms hook themselves into the pads of the dog's feet and burrow into her body, eventually traveling to her intestines where they set up house, feeding off your Yorkie's blood supply, and reproducing. The eggs come out in your dog's bowel movement.

Both puppies and older dogs with hookworms develop anemia and have black or bloody diarrhea. Older dogs may also vomit and lose weight. Although hookworms aren't usually fatal to adult dogs, the diarrhea and anemia alone can be fatal to puppies.

Your vet can confirm whether your dog has hookworms by checking a stool sample. If the sample is positive, he'll prescribe medication to get rid of the worms.

Coccidia

Coccidia is a microscopic parasite that lives in a dog's intestinal tract. It spreads through contact with contaminated feces and causes bloody and mucousy stools. Puppies born and raised in crowded and unclean conditions are most susceptible. They are also most vulnerable to the weight loss, weakness, and dehydration that coccidia can cause.

To confirm coccidia, your vet checks a stool sample. Treating coccidia involves a vet-prescribed medication, retesting the dog's stool until it comes back clean, and a thorough cleaning of the dog's home environment. So get out the broom, mop, scrub brush, and bleach.

Roundworms

Roundworms are long, spaghetti-shaped worms that appear in your dog's stool. Your puppy can get roundworms from his mother, if she had them while pregnant, or he can pick them up by walking through contaminated areas. Roundworms can make puppies very ill. And although they may not harm adult dogs, severe infestations can make adult dogs very sick too, causing vomiting and diarrhea.

Symptoms of roundworms include swollen stomach in contrast to other body parts, vomiting, a dull coat, and diarrhea. Your vet can determine whether your dog has roundworms through a stool sample, and he can prescribe a worming medication to get rid of them.

Roundworms' eggs live seven to ten years on the ground. If a child touches a microscopic egg, the larvum goes into the child and can cause liver damage or blindness (due to damaged retinas). Roundworms are the number-one cause of juvenile blindness in the southeastern United States. The Centers for Disease Control (CDC) considers worming dogs on a routine basis a must in order to protect children.

Giardia

Giardia, like coccidia, is an intestinal parasite. Your Yorkie can ingest giardia by drinking from stagnant, feces-contaminated water supplies, such as creeks, drainage ditches, and ponds — even puddles after a rainfall. Giardia causes intestinal upset and diarrhea. Your vet uses a stool sample to test for giardia and, if found, can prescribe medication to get rid of it.

To prevent your Yorkie from getting giardia, let her drink only water you provide or, if you're camping and want to use the natural water supplies, boil the water first or treat it with a chemical designed to kill giardia. Take this step for your health, as well. Humans can contract giardia, too.

Tapeworms

Tapeworms are flat worms that can be anywhere from an inch to several feet long. Dogs typically get tapeworms from fleas or rodents carrying tapeworm eggs. Tapeworms don't pose serious health concerns for your dog, but they do cause diarrhea, loss of appetite, and a dull coat. Another sign that your dog has tapeworms is if you see what resembles rice stuck in the hair around your dog's rectum. What you're really looking at are dead, dried-up tapeworms. Of course if you see any worm — dead or alive — hanging out around that area, get thee, a stool sample, and the worm, if you still have it, to your vet. Your vet can check the sample and prescribe a deworming medication.

Emergency! When to Call Your Vet

Yorkies, overall, are healthy little dogs. But even healthy little dogs periodically feel under the weather. Sometimes the culprit is nothing more serious than indigestion caused by eating too much or eating foods (like table scraps) that are too rich. Other times, the culprit is more serious — an underlying condition, for example — or more frightening because you don't know what's going on.

If the symptoms are sporadic or short-lived and your dog's otherwise acting normally, you can usually take a wait-and-see approach. But when the symptoms are severe or long-lasting and your Yorkie's overall behavior concerns you, the safest course of action is to contact your vet. He can advise you about what you should do.

Because Yorkies are such small dogs, you need to be extra vigilant when your little guy's not feeling well. They don't have much spare weight to lose, they can become easily dehydrated, and their blood-sugar levels can get all out of whack — all of which can complicate whatever health issue is making them ill in the first place.

Accidents and injury

If your Yorkie is involved in an accident, your first reaction may be panic — especially if you see signs of injury. Signs that your dog is hurt include blood, limping or favoring a leg, yelping, crying, or biting when you touch a certain area.

First, you need to settle down. An injured dog is already frightened and in pain, and your distress only makes matters worse. Then, as calmly as you can, try to figure out where the injury is (not always an easy task with a long-haired dog like a Yorkie) and how bad it is.

If the injury is minor (such as a scrape that's no longer bleeding), clean the wound and apply antiseptic. If the injury is more serious, such as the following, call your vet immediately:

- ✔ She limps or refuses to use a limb or yelps when bumped or jarred.
- ✔ She can't move, is reluctant to move, or collapses when she tries to move.
- ✔ The wound is bleeding profusely or is a puncture wound.
- ✔ She shows signs of shock (rapid heart beat, rapid breathing, extreme lethargy or unconsciousness, and low body temperature), even if you see no evidence of an injury.

In these situations, your vet needs to examine your Yorkie, and in the last two cases, immediately. To transport your Yorkie to the vet, place her on a pillow (so that you can pick the pillow up rather than the dog) and take her in.

As loving as your Yorkie is, if she's in pain, she may very well bite or snap at you, the vet, or the vet's assistants when you move her or touch her. To protect yourself and get your dog the care she needs, fashion a temporary muzzle: Drape a long strip of soft cloth over the bridge of her nose, cross the ends underneath her chin, and then tie the ends securely, but not too tightly, behind her ears. Keep a pair of scissors nearby to cut the muzzle away if she begins to choke.

Heatstroke and hypothermia

For a long-coated breed, Yorkies don't tolerate cold particularly well because they're *singled-coated* dogs. Single-coated means they don't have an *undercoat,* the soft, downy fur that keeps double-coated dogs warm. In fact, their coat offers them about as much protection from the cold as your hair offers you — in other words, not much. You may then assume that, because the Yorkie coat isn't heavy enough to keep them warm in winter, it therefore isn't heavy enough to cause overheating during the hot summer months. Well, you'd be wrong there, too.

The best way to avoid heatstroke or hypothermia is to protect your Yorkie during extreme temperatures: Don't keep him out in the cold for prolonged periods of time and, when he is out, dress him in a dog coat for added warmth. In the summer, make sure he has ample shade and plenty of fresh water, and *never* leave him unattended in a warm car. If, despite your efforts, you notice the following signs of hypothermia or heatstroke, call the vet immediately:

- **Hypothermia:** Pale gums, shivering, low body temperature
- **Heatstroke:** Excessive panting, drooling, rapid pulse, glazed expression

Excessive vomiting

All dogs spit up occasionally. If she drinks too quickly, if you change her diet, or if she's feeling under the weather can all lead to relatively harmless episodes of vomiting. Just keep an eye on her and keep her diet bland (boiled rice and chicken, for example) for a couple of days, and she should be back to her normal self. In the following circumstances, however, you need to call your vet immediately:

- **When the vomiting is excessive, that is, explosive, frequent, or ongoing:** Excessive vomiting can be a sign of a much more serious medical problem, including an obstruction in the stomach or bowel, kidney failure, cancer, or poisoning.

- **If your vomiting dog is a puppy (under a year old) or a senior (older than 7 or 8):** Young and old dogs, like babies and elderly humans, are at higher risk for complications when they contract an illness.

- **If she has stomach pain or her vomiting is unproductive (meaning she's still vomiting but nothing much is coming up):** Like excessive vomiting, these symptoms can be a sign of serious medical conditions that need immediate treatment.

- **She has diarrhea, too:** Vomiting and diarrhea together are a double threat because dogs as small as Yorkies become dehydrated very easily. See the next section for additional info on when diarrhea is a problem that requires medical attention.

Strange stools

Again, all dogs occasionally experience bouts of diarrhea, for many of the same reasons they occasionally vomit (see the preceding section). But, like vomiting, diarrhea can indicate a problem that's more serious than an upset stomach. If your Yorkie experiences the following, call your vet:

- ✔ **Diarrhea for more than a day:** Especially when the diarrhea is combined with any other symptom, such as vomiting, lethargy, loss of appetite, and so on.

- ✔ **Bloody or black stool:** Stool that has blood in it or that is black (a sign of internal bleeding).

- ✔ **Mucousy or pale stool:** Again, this stool can be a sign of an internal parasite. Your vet needs to determine what kind of parasite is causing the problem so that he can prescribe the necessary medication.

In some cases, you may notice that your Yorkie is having a hard time having a bowel movement at all. If he's straining and nothing comes of it, first check to make sure the hair isn't matted around his rectum (a very common occurrence during the puppy stage). If it is, it's bath and trimming time (see Chapter 10). If the area is clear and your Yorkie still has difficulty or, after much straining, can produce only a very loose or liquidy stool, call your vet to have him checked out.

Seizures

Seizures are scary — especially if your dog hasn't had one before and you haven't had a reason to suspect that she ever would. The causes of seizures can be pretty scary themselves: epilepsy, hypoglycemia, poisoning, organ failure, and more.

During a seizure, your Yorkie may shake and jerk, be unresponsive to verbal commands, lose bladder or bowel control, and collapse. An episode can last from a few seconds to several minutes, and the only thing you can do is stay near and make sure your dog doesn't hurt herself by falling into hard objects, for example, or by falling off a couch or down the stairs, if that's where she is when the episode starts. When the seizure ends, your dog will be slightly weakened, but other than that, she'll be back to normal.

If this is the first time your dog has had a seizure, time the seizure and call your vet immediately after the episode ends. Something caused the seizure, and you need to find out what it is. If, however, you know why your dog had the seizure (she has epilepsy, for example) and you've discussed how to handle these situations with your vet, then do whatever your vet has instructed you to do when the seizure ends.

Do not put your fingers near your dog's mouth when she's having a seizure; you can suffer a serious dog bite. In addition, don't try to put anything in her mouth. Your Yorkie won't swallow her tongue, and anything you put in there can break or injure her if her jaws clench during the seizure.

Other things to share with the vet

Basically, you should feel free to call your vet for advice and help whenever you're concerned about your dog's health. The following situations may prompt such a call:

- ✔ **Shortness of breath:** If your dog has a hard time breathing or can't seem to catch his breath for no apparent reason, call the vet.

- ✔ **Poor appetite or sudden weight loss:** Yorkies, being, on average, between 4 and 7 pounds, don't have much excess weight to play with. If your dog isn't eating and is beginning to thin out, share this info with your vet.

- ✔ **Excessive drinking:** Obviously, your Yorkie should drink whenever he's thirsty. But if you find that he's drinking all the time and still can't seem to quench his thirst, call the vet.

- ✔ **Lumps:** Anytime you feel a lump, especially if the lump is changing in any way or bleeding, call the vet.

- ✔ **Poisoning:** If your dog ingests any potentially poisonous chemical or food (see Chapter 5 for substances dangerous to your Yorkie and Chapter 9 for a list of foods that cause problems), call the vet.

Conditions and Diseases Common to Yorkies

As a breed, Yorkshire Terriers are predisposed to certain conditions. The following sections explain these conditions. As you read, keep the following points in mind:

✔ Although some of these conditions are life-threatening, many are not. Even in many of the more serious conditions, treatment options are available, and most of the chronic conditions can be controlled through diet or medication.

✔ Just because these conditions are common to the breed doesn't mean that every Yorkshire Terrier is afflicted by them. In fact, most Yorkshire Terriers aren't.

✔ Your best chance of avoiding these conditions is to buy your Yorkie through a reputable breeder who breeds only dogs who are free from these conditions and therefore are less likely to pass them on to their offspring. Head to Chapter 3 to find out how to find one.

Portosystemic (liver) shunt: Blood bypassing the liver

Portosystemic (or liver) shunt is a congenital condition, meaning that the Yorkie is born with it. In a healthy Yorkie, the blood travels through the liver where the toxins are removed. In a Yorkie with portosystemic shunt (or liver shunt), the blood travels through a *shunt* (a wayward blood vessel) that bypasses the liver. As a result, the toxins don't get cleaned out, and the contaminated blood continues circulating through the Yorkie's body. This condition is usually diagnosed by the time the Yorkie is a year old. Although it's always serious, the condition can range from mild to severe. The symptoms of liver shunt include

✔ **Small size and extreme slenderness:** Dogs with liver shunt are usually small for their age and have poor weight gain.

✔ **Digestive system problems:** Your Yorkie may have a poor appetite, diarrhea, drooling, vomiting, or may eat odd things, like paper.

✔ **Urinary system problems:** Some Yorkies with liver shunt have increased thirst and urination, and early onset of bladder stones or crystals in the urinary tract (for more on bladder stones, see the section "Other conditions" later in this chapter).

✔ **Depression, listlessness, uncoordinated movements, or seizures that usually appear shortly after eating:** Your dog may also have convulsions or fall into a coma. The cause is ammonia (a by-product of digestion) that doesn't get cleaned out by the liver and reaches the brain.

To diagnose liver shunt, your vet runs a series of tests, beginning with blood and urine tests. If these samples suggest that a shunt is a possibility, he runs other tests to determine how your dog's liver is functioning and where and how extensive the shunt is.

Treatment options depend on where the shunt is and its severity. If a dog has only a single shunt that's on the outside of the liver (fortunately, the kind of liver shunt most common among Yorkies) — and the diagnosis is made early — surgery is an option. If the shunt is on the inside of the liver, surgery isn't an option, but the condition can be treated with diet and medication. Left untreated, all liver shunts are fatal because of the increasing amount of toxins in the blood.

If your Yorkie needs an anesthetic, ask your vet whether he uses seroflurane or isoflurane. These anesthetics are the safest and most often used for Toy breeds.

Legg-Perthes Disease: Degeneration of the hip joint

Legg-Perthes Disease (or if you'd rather wrap your tongue around its medical name, *avascular necrosis of the femoral head and neck*) is a degeneration of the dog's hip joint. The symptoms of the disease usually begin appearing when the dog is between 4 and 11 months old, and they include

- ✔ Lameness in the affected leg
- ✔ Pain, ranging from mild to severe
- ✔ Wasting away of the muscle

To diagnose Legg-Perthes Disease, your vet may need to take a series of X-rays of your Yorkie's leg over the course of a few weeks in order to see the degeneration. Mild forms of this condition require less intensive treatment; forced rest or immobilization of the limb can let the damaged areas heal. More severe forms may require surgery to remove the dead parts of the bone and relieve pain.

Luxating patellas: Trick knees

Luxating patella is a fancy way of saying *trick knee* (*luxating* means slipping and *patella* means kneecap). In plain English, dogs with this condition have kneecaps that slip out of place. Like most conditions, this one can vary in severity, with Grade I being the least severe and Grade IV being the most severe:

- ✔ **Grade I:** The kneecap slips out of place only when the vet manipulates it.

- ✔ **Grade II:** The kneecap slips out of place when your Yorkie is walking or running (you may hear her yelp or see her hold the leg still for a few steps) and usually slides back into place as she continues moving.

- ✔ **Grade III:** The kneecap slips out of place frequently enough to cause lameness.

- ✔ **Grade IV:** The kneecap slips and stays out of place, making it difficult and painful for your dog to bend her leg.

Your vet can diagnose a luxating patella by feeling the knee joint and taking X-rays. Treatment depends on the severity. Grade I, for instance, doesn't pose enough of a problem to warrant extensive treatment. Grade II, depending on how frequently the kneecap slips and how impaired your Yorkie is may require anything from enforced rest (to let the ligaments heal) to surgery. Grades III and IV require corrective surgery.

Hypoglycemia: Low blood sugar

Yorkie puppies are especially vulnerable to *hypoglycemia,* or low blood sugar. Quick physiology lesson: Similar to your body, your Yorkie's body uses sugar as energy. This sugar (called *glucose*) fuels the functioning of all the systems in his body. Without this fuel source, his body shuts down. When your Yorkie's blood-sugar level drops to dangerously low levels, you may notice signs such as confusion or disorientation, shivering or a staggering gait, and drowsiness. In the worst case, he may have a seizure, fall into a coma, or even die.

Your puppy can have a hypoglycemic episode if he doesn't eat regularly, is stressed, has engaged in strenuous activity, or is overly tired. Vomiting, diarrhea, and intestinal parasites can also trigger hypoglycemic episodes.

If your puppy has a hypoglycemic episode, your first order of business is to boost his blood-sugar level. You can do that by rubbing a dab of Karo syrup or honey on his gums. Alternatively, you can mix a few drops of the syrup or honey with water and place it on his tongue. Then call the vet who can suggest alternative treatments (such as electrolyte fluids) for use in the future. If the episode is severe, however, and your Yorkie falls into a coma or has a seizure, call the vet immediately.

Collapsing trachea: Closed windpipe

A *trachea* is simply a windpipe, so a collapsing trachea is a windpipe that periodically closes on itself. Yorkies who suffer from this condition have shortness of breath, honking coughing fits (attempts to re-open the trachea), and, because of the restricted air flow, fatigue.

The condition typically appears as your dog gets older. You may not notice any symptoms at all until your Yorkie's several years old, and then the symptoms may initially appear only after she's been active. To confirm the condition, your vet may put very light pressure on the trachea, take an X-ray, or use an instrument to look at the trachea while your Yorkie's breathing.

Treatment options vary and include anti-inflammatory drugs, cough suppressants, medication to keep the bronchial tubes open, and surgery. Your vet can guide you in getting the most appropriate treatment for your dog.

PRA (Progressive Retinal Atrophy): Degenerating retina

Progressive retinal atrophy (PRA) is a degenerative disease of the retina. The condition is inherited and incurable. The first symptom is night blindness, followed by a gradual loss of daytime vision, and then total blindness.

Although PRA isn't widespread among Yorkies, it has occurred in the breed often enough to spur the Yorkshire Terrier Club of America (YTCA) to investigate the possibility of requiring PRA screenings at regional dog shows — the purpose being to evaluate the breeding stock. If you're concerned about PRA, make sure to have your dog's eyes tested during routine veterinary visits. If your vet suspects PRA, he may direct you to a canine ophthalmologist, who has the equipment to perform the necessary tests (she'll look for thinning of the retina and reduction of blood vessels in the eye).

Other conditions

A few other conditions that can afflict Yorkies are

- ✔ **Retained primary teeth:** Yorkie's are known for having trouble with their mouths, which often are too small for all their teeth to fit nicely. Making this matter worse is that many Yorkies don't lose their baby teeth as they should. When your Yorkie's around 6 or 7 months old, have your vet check to make sure all her baby teeth are gone. If they're not, they need to be pulled.

- ✔ **Underactive thyroid:** If your Yorkie's thyroid isn't functioning properly, you may notice a dull coat, hair loss, lethargy, extreme intolerance for cold weather, weight gain, and chronic skin disorders. Your vet can test for an underactive thyroid, or *canine hypothyroidism,* through a series of blood tests. Treatment usually involves a daily dose of a synthetic thyroid hormone.

- ✔ **Heart disease:** Yorkies, like other small breeds, are prone to heart trouble and tend to develop problems with the *heart valves* (the membranes that open and shut to allow blood to circulate through the chambers of the heart). If the valve fails to close properly, the blood flows back into the chambers, possibly causing the chamber to enlarge, which itself leads to other problems (such as constricting the windpipe, flowing back into the lungs, or causing an irregular heartbeat). Your vet can diagnose heart disease, also called *cardiomyopathy,* in your Yorkie through X-rays, ECGs (electrocardioagrams), and ultra-sounds. He can also discuss your dog's treatment options with you.

- ✔ **Bladder stones:** Middle-aged Yorkies tend to get "stones" (technically, *calcium oxalate urolithiosis*) that form in the uri-nary tract or bladder. Signs are difficulty going to the bathroom or blood in the urine. Your vet can confirm whether your dog has bladder stones through an X-ray and urine test. Treatment options vary, including flushing the stones out of the urinary tract, surgically removing them, or breaking them up with shock waves so that they can exit the body on their own.

- ✔ **Undescended testicle(s):** *Cryptorchidism* is a long word for this simple problem affecting some male Yorkies. Sometimes, one or both your of Yorkie's testicles hasn't "dropped " — or, descended into the scrotum. If your dog has this problem, you need to have him neutered. Your vet can give you details.

Part IV
Training with TLC

The 5th Wave   By Rich Tennant

"We're still working on the basic commands.
'sit', 'stay', 'stop flushing daddy's neckties
down the toilet'..."

In this part . . .

Don't assume that because a Yorkshire Terrier is such a cute little dog that training doesn't matter. It does matter, for a number of reasons. First, training keeps your dog safe. If you teach her to respond to her name every time you say it, come whenever you command it, and release objects when you direct her to, you can control her in potentially deadly situations. Second, training keeps her happy. A key component of training is getting your Yorkie to look to you as the leader of the pack. If you're not the boss, then to her canine mind, that job falls to her. And leading a pack — especially a pack of unpredictable and sometimes difficult-to-read humans — is a very stressful, anxiety-producing, thankless job. Third, training your Yorkie keeps you happy, partly because *you* can relax when you don't have to keep an ever-watchful eye on your dog, but mostly because a well-behaved dog just makes you feel good all over. So let the love flow: Teach your Yorkie well.

Chapter 13

Rules to Train By

*Y*ou can train your dog using all sorts of approaches, but in this chapter and the following two chapters, I present the method I think is most effective and humane: the positive dog training method. This method is based on the premise that you don't have to force dogs or punish them into submission in order to make them behave. Instead, you use rewards (giving and taking away) to teach dogs appropriate behavior. Of course, for any training method to work, you need to know your dog and the traits he has that can help (or hinder) you in your training efforts. You also need to know how *your* actions can impact, for better or worse, how your dog learns.

Positively Marvelous: The Positive Training Method

Punishment-based training methods have been around for a long time. Using these methods, you teach your dog that he can avoid punishment (pain or intimidation, for example) by doing what he's supposed to. In punishment-based training, dog owners use force — collar jerks, ear pinches, intimidation, and so on — to teach their dogs appropriate behavior. These methods certainly work, and you can find many trainers who swear by them.

The training instructions in this book, however, are based on the principles of *positive dog training* (also called *positive motivation dog training*). In this training method, you teach your dog that when he does good things (that is, what he's supposed to do), good things (praise, treats, rewards, and so on) happen; when he does bad things, the good things go away.

How the method works

Like any dog-training technique, positive dog training requires that you be consistent and vigilant. Unlike traditional methods, however, it requires a shift in what you look for. Traditional methods rely on fear and submission; for these methods to work, you have to catch your dog being bad so that you can teach him the lesson: Don't do that again. Positive dog training requires that you catch your dog being good because the lesson here is: Do that again! Here's how positive dog training works:

- ✔ **You reward your Yorkie for behaving the way you want her to; because she's always on the lookout for rewards, she'll continue to repeat the desired behavior.** Then you associate the behavior with a *cue* (a movement or phrase) so that you can elicit the behavior on command. Eventually, when the behavior is ingrained in your dog, reduce the amount of rewards you give until you give them only occasionally. (After all, don't *you* like a periodic bonus for a job well done?)

- ✔ **You interrupt and redirect unwanted behaviors.** If your Yorkie is chewing away happily on a sofa leg, interrupt that behavior by saying "no" in a quiet, low voice, and then making a sudden noise that startles her enough to look up at you. In that brief second when you have her attention, say "Good girl" (that's the praise you give her for stopping her attack on the sofa leg) and give her an alternative — her favorite chew toy, for example. If she caught you off guard and you don't have an immediate alternative, keep her attention by making kissing noises and then redirect her to something more appropriate.

In an emergency, you must manage your dog's behavior to keep her safe. If your dog's doing something that can get her hurt or put her in danger — running toward the street, for example, or getting into a fight — immediately stop her, even if you have to jerk on the leash or pull her back by the collar. But consider this crisis management, not training. You're trying to prevent an injury or a catastrophe; you're not teaching your dog any sort of lesson.

- ✔ **You withhold attention and rewards when your Yorkie's doing something she's not supposed to.** Remember, dogs repeat whatever behavior gets them attention. If your Yorkie starts pawing and whining for you to let her in your lap, for example, look away with your chin up (this action is a dismissal thing) and ignore her until she settles down. *Then* you can stroke her (she's doing what you want — she stopped nagging) or put her in your lap.

The skinny on B.F. Skinner

Positive dog training is based on *positive reinforcement* and *negative punishment*. These ideas come from the theory of operant conditioning (which forms an association between a response and a consequence), based on behavioral scientist B.F. Skinner's work in the 1930s.

Don't let the term *negative punishment* throw you. Although it sounds really, really bad (if punishment brings to mind community service, negative punishment can't mean anything other than chain gang work in *Cool Hand Luke*), these words mean different things to behaviorists. To understand, you have to think like a scientist and suck all the emotion and metaphorical images from your brain: *Negative* means something (either good or bad) is taken away, and *punishment* means something that reduces the likelihood of a behavior being repeated. Hence, in dog-training terms, negative punishment means that the dog's misbehavior makes something good — like attention, a treat, or a reward — go away. Similarly, positive reinforcement means that the dog's behavior makes something good happen — like praise or a treat.

Some benefits of staying positive

People who subscribe to positive dog training believe that not only is it as effective as punishment-based training, but it also creates a better human-canine bond because the method isn't based on fear. So suppress whatever Machiavellian spirit you have (Machiavelli was a late 15th-century Italian statesman who argued that an effective ruler must be feared by his subjects) and keep reading to discover the benefits of positive training:

- ✔ Instead of relying on pain, intimidation, or coercion to shape or correct your Yorkie's behavior, positive dog training uses praise and rewards — or the withdrawal of them — to shape your dog's behavior.

- ✔ With positive dog training, you focus on your Yorkie when he behaves appropriately rather than the times when he breaks the rules. A hallmark of the training plan is to catch your dog being good so that you can reinforce the behavior you want and thus increase the likelihood that your dog will repeat it.

- ✔ For dogs who tend to be shy or timid, as some Yorkies are, punishment-based training only makes those tendencies worse. Intimidating or using pain to train a timid dog just makes him more so — even though the pain and intimidation may also stop him from engaging in the misbehavior. And a timid dog on the defense is more likely to snap and bite out of fear. A more aggressive dog is more likely to defend himself — aggressively.

✓ Positive training is just a heck of a lot more fun — and more effective. If positive and punishment training methods can yield the same results (and many would argue that the results you get from positive training are better because you take fear out of the equation), why wouldn't you go with the method that gives both you and your dog warm fuzzies instead of cold chills? (I refuse to believe that any dog lover enjoys some of the punishment techniques — like the alpha roll, where you grab your dog by the scruff of his neck, throw him to the ground on his back, and then stand over him and growl menacingly in his face; punishment-based training insists this technique is necessary.)

Knowing How Your Yorkie Operates

The first rule of training: Know your dog. Certain breed characteristics — such as the Yorkie's independent spirit and innate intelligence level — impact how agreeable a dog is to training.

But to train effectively, you have to know more than a general description of the breed characteristics. You also need to know *your* little Yorkie in particular. Just as children respond individually to praise and direction, depending on their personalities, dogs do, too. By understanding how your dog's personality can shape her response to your training efforts, you can modify your techniques to get the best from your dog.

Traits that work in your favor

When you train a Yorkshire Terrier, you have a couple of very important factors going for you, simply based on the breed's characteristics:

✓ **They're smart.** Beauty-queen looks aside, Yorkies are pretty intelligent little dogs. They may not be in the Mensa crowd with Border Collies and Poodles (generally regarded as the smartest of the smart), but they certainly hold their own on dog-intelligence lists, usually falling slightly above average.

Yorkies may not learn the command the first five or ten times you introduce it, but they can learn it, usually by the 20th or 25th time (according to Stanley Coren, author of *The Intelligence of Dogs*). The significance of this bit of info? The key to training your Yorkie is to not give up. And you can take solace in the fact that you don't have to be as patient and persistent as someone who owns a Pekingese or Shih Tzu.

✔ **They're eager to please.** Nearly all dogs hold their humans' esteem in high regard. They're happy when we're happy — or so we like to think. More likely, they're happy because our happiness means more good stuff — treats, praise, affection, and attention — for them. Yorkshire Terriers, however, were bred to work closely with man, so they instinctively look to you for rewards and praise — a big advantage, if you know how to use it.

Traits you have to work around

On a scale of 1 to 10, with 1 being the most difficult to train and 10 being the easiest, Yorkies fortunately claim a place around a 7. Not an 8 or 9? you ask. Well, they do have a couple of traits that may present a challenge to your training efforts:

✔ **Yorkies can be stubborn — or determined, depending on what kind of spin you want to put on it.** For this reason, *your* consistency and diligence are absolutely vital. Throw up your hands in resignation when your Yorkie continues doing something that you told her time and time again not to do, and you teach her a very important lesson: If she can hold out longer than you, she gets her way.

✔ **They're independent.** Animals who were bred to hunt, chase, and kill vermin have to be self-directed. That rat would be long gone if a Yorkie waited for the go-ahead from the boss to catch it. In training, this trait appears when your Yorkie behaves as though what you want her to do doesn't quite have the same urgency as what she wants to do. To overcome this power struggle, you have to make your Yorkie eager to perform the task you're training. And that means keeping things fun and interesting.

Thinking Like a Dog

To get the most bang for your buck, you need to see the world from a dog's perspective. In the wild, dog packs have a hierarchy. The dominant dog (or alpha dog) has the highest status and power. He's the leader of the pack, the one who gets the choicest food, the comfiest sleeping position, and the obedience of the more subservient pack members.

Don't think a 7-pound cutie could ever dominate you? Ask yourself these questions: Do you pet him whenever he cuddles close and nudges your hand? Do you feed him whenever he demands it (by begging, whining, or any other behavior that you know means "Feed me NOW!")? Do you let him sit on the back of the couch and rest his sleepy little head on your shoulder? Do you end up with the corner of your pillow because your Yorkie claims the bulk of it for himself? HAH! You're already puppy-whipped, and you don't even know it because you aren't thinking like a dog. Consider these factors:

- ✔ **Interactions:** The lead dog is the one who determines the timing and length of interactions with other pack members (that'd be you and anyone else in your family). If your Yorkie can force you to pet him whenever he wants and for however long he wants, he's the one controlling those interactions. Not you.

- ✔ **Space issues:** Alpha dogs also control the space that they're in. They don't move for anyone — unless they want to. If you need to get through a doorway that your Yorkie is blocking and you walk around him, you think you're being nice by not disturbing him; he thinks you're giving him his due. Another space issue is height. Subordinate dogs keep their heads lower than the dominant dog's head. You may think that your Yorkie climbing up to your shoulder and resting his head on yours is s-o-o-o-o cute (you may have even gotten a picture of it), but your Yorkie is thinking, "It's good to be king."

- ✔ **Food:** For a dog, food is power, and dining order translates to status. In the wild, after hunting and killing their prey (or scavenging it, as the case may be), the dog who's highest in the hierarchy eats first, followed by the next highest, and so on. Although your Yorkie has to rely on you to actually provide the food, when he brow-beats you into handing over the kibble, opening the treat box, or relinquishing a hunk of pork from the table, who do *you* think really controls the resources?

Fortunately, you can use all these things to your advantage when you're training your Yorkie. By benevolently controlling the interactions, the space, and the food yourself, you send the message that you're the leader of the pack, the one your Yorkie has to follow and please. See the next section for information on how to become the wise and benevolent leader that your dog needs.

Basic Training Tips

Although some dogs take less time to train than others, all dogs are trainable. Of course, how you go about training has a huge impact on how smoothly the training goes and how enjoyable the sessions are for both you and your dog.

In the following sections, I offer basic training tips and advice that you can use when housetraining (see Chapter 14) and teaching basic commands (see Chapter 15) to make your training more pleasant and much more effective.

Be the leader of the pack

As a conscientious dog owner, you probably willingly give your Yorkie whatever she needs. Well, the first thing she needs is a leader — someone to count on, look to for reassurance or protection, and to take care of things. That person should be you. Even if your Yorkie isn't a status seeker, you still need to make your own alpha status apparent. Why? Because doing so makes her life easier. With you clearly in charge, she doesn't have to worry about who's minding the farm. To claim (or reinforce) your alpha status and bring peace to your kingdom (you can find instructions on the specific commands in Chapter 14), do the following:

- ✔ **Lead — literally:** Be first through doorways, first up and down stairs, and first on the couch. To accomplish this task, you need to teach your Yorkie a little patience so that she can wait those few seconds for you to go first. You do that by using the Wait command.

  A good way to teach puppies that you're the one to follow is to use a *tether* (a leash with clasps at both ends) to keep her with you while you're at home (see Figure 13-1). See Chapter 8 for how this technique works.

- ✔ **Make your Yorkie earn her food:** Only love is free (except on reality TV shows); food isn't. No handing over the goods until your Yorkie is calm or sitting down. So use the Sit or Settle command, and as soon as your Yorkie complies (even if you have to help her), give her her food dish or the treat she's looking forward to.

- ✔ **Avoid looking at your dog in stressful situations:** Followers look to their leaders in times of trouble. So how does your dog interpret your anxious glance toward her when you hear the car door shut and know that the pizza man is just a few steps from your door? She goes on immediate alert, and when the doorbell rings, her vigilance is rewarded because now she has an intruder to announce or scare away. Bottom line: If you glance at your dog when you expect a reaction from her, you'll get the very reaction you were probably hoping to avoid.

REMEMBER

Dogs live for attention, whether it's praise, touch, or a glance. Any attention they get typically reinforces whatever behavior — good or bad — that warranted your attention in the first place.

✔ **Pet your dog when you choose to, not when she demands it:** Of course you love petting your dog as much as, if not more than, your dog loves being petted. As head dog, you — not your Yorkie — determine when and how long these sessions last. When you want to stop petting her, stop. And if your Yorkie nudges you, paws at you, or stares at you pathetically to get you to keep it up, use the Enough command. You can also use your body (turning away, crossing your arms and looking away, and so on; see the upcoming section "Talk to the hand: Connect words and movements") to signal the end of the interaction.

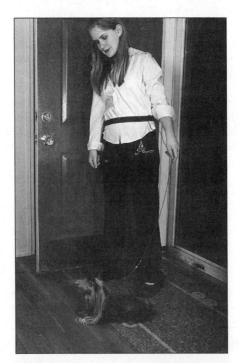

©Isabelle Francais

Figure 13-1: By keeping your puppy near, you teach her that you're the one to follow.

Talk to the hand: Connect words and movements

We are so close to our dogs that we sometimes forget we're different species with different ways of perceiving and interacting with the world. Take communication for example. We humans are a chatty bunch. Despite the fact that researchers assert that more than half our meaning is conveyed through our body language, we consider our ability to turn a phrase our most efficient and effective communication tool. And for some reason, despite our innate intelligence, we think that our dogs can understand us. Sure, we know Muffy isn't a big fan of Milton, but when we go on ad nauseam about why peeing in the dining room is a very, very bad thing to do and isn't she *ashamed* of herself and hasn't she been told before that she's supposed to go outside? . . . Well, we think she's hanging on every word and taking notes.

Here's a little note for you: English — or Spanish, French, Chinese or, well, even Greek, for that matter — is Greek to your dog. Sure, he may know a few commands you've taught him, but his primary way of understanding you and what you want isn't through what you say, it's through how you say it and how you move your body.

I hear what you're saying, man

Your Yorkie can learn to understand certain words: her name, the commands you use, maybe the names of other people and pets in your house, and probably "no," because as a puppy, she's liable to hear it often. How quickly she learns these words and how adept she is at responding appropriately to them depends on your tone, inflection, and how consistent you are in your phrasing.

- ✔ **Tone:** Whether you talk in a happy-happy baby voice, a sharp annoyed voice, or a wussy are-you-gonna-behave-for-mama-please voice directly affects how your Yorkie responds to your command. The best tone to use is calm, firm, and all-business: It's not scary (which a sharp voice can be) or overly dramatic (which can overexcite your dog and make settling her down to business harder). And remember, you're giving a command. Leave the begging request for your attempts to control your kids' behavior.

  Don't yell at your dog, especially when she's excited and barking herself. Her interpretation? You're excited and barking, too. Yelling at her just reinforces her over-the-top response.

- ✔ **Inflection:** Some sounds — short, repeated notes — seem to naturally spur activity; others — long, single notes — naturally slow it down. (Think of a horse rider who uses "hup hup hup" or clicking sounds to get the horse to go, and a deep, slow "Whooooaaaa" to slow it down.) You can use the same techniques. When you want your Yorkie to come to you, say her name and slap your thigh encouragingly. When you're done playing, on the other hand, but your Yorkie is having a hard time settling down, you'd use the long, drawn out "Se-t-t-t-l-e" or "Whoooooooaaaaa, girl."

✔ **Phrasing:** The command "Down" sounds a lot different than the command "Down, down, down, get down now, you're on my cashmere throw, I said DOWN!" Your Yorkie may understand the first command, but the second is sure to confuse her and leave her wondering, comfortably I might add, on that cashmere throw, exactly what you want her to do. Bottom line: Never repeat a command. Say it once, maneuver your dog into compliance if you need to, and then reward her.

Getting body and tongue in sync

When processing the commands you give, your Yorkie listens to what you say and watches what you do. The input that has the most meaning for him? Your movements — conscious or not. So make sure that your movements don't contradict your spoken message. Consider the following actions and how your dog interprets them:

✔ **Leaning forward:** Your dog interprets leaning forward as a signal to stay put. Use this movement if you've given your dog the Stay command and he's making a move out of the stay position. Leaning forward is an effective way you can reinforce your command with a nonverbal cue.

If, on the other hand, you lean forward when you're calling him to come, you're just confusing him. Your movement is telling him to stay put, but your words are telling him to move forward.

✔ **Using your hands:** Humans use their hands to draw things toward them and push them away. When you reach for your dog, however — even if your intent is to push his paws off the sofa because you don't want him in your lap — he interprets this action as attention. If he's excited, he may interpret it as an invitation to play.

To stop your dog from claiming space, block the space he wants or is moving toward. You can block the space by moving your body — not your hands — in that direction. You don't have to actually occupy the space; simply moving in that direction is usually enough to signal to your dog that that space is off-limits.

You want your Yorkie to always associate your hands with good stuff: soft pats, soothing strokes, and goodies. So never, ever use your hands to punish or strike your Yorkie. If you do, you undermine his trust in you and his willingness to submit to whatever care or attention you want to give him.

✔ **Turning or looking away:** The most effective way to disengage from your dog is to turn away from him. Simply by turning your head, chin up, and looking away, you dismiss him.

Equally effective is turning away. Withdrawing all your attention — visual, physical, and vocal — sends a very strong message: You've had enough. Turning away is a great technique to use when he's demanding attention or yipping and jumping himself into a frenzy upon your arrival. Stand still, arms crossed over your chest, head turned away and chin slightly up. If he moves into your line of sight, hold the stance, but turn away. Keep doing this technique until he settles down. As soon as he does, say "Settle," and then praise him for being such a good boy.

Pick the right time and place

Training is actually a great way to spend quality time with your Yorkie. To make these sessions something you look forward to rather than something you dread, pick the right time and place.

When you think about a good time for training, think about when your Yorkie is most receptive to learning (or practicing) new commands. Pick a time when she's calm but fully awake. An excited dog who'd rather play fetch or run around chasing butterflies won't keep her mind on business, and a tired dog will lose interest quickly.

Next, think about how long the training session should last. Although you want her to have time to practice the command, if you turn training into a marathon session, your dog's going to hate it. (Think back to your own school days and how *long* English class seemed when you were learning the distinctions between a predicate nominative and an appositive.) So break your training into short sessions (five or ten minutes, tops) and schedule two or three of them each day. Or skip setting a time altogether and sprinkle the opportunities throughout the day. You can practice Sit commands, for example, just about any time and anywhere: when you feed her, when she wants to go out, periodically during a walk, before you toss the ball into the yard . . . whenever.

And where's a good place to train her? Depends on what you're teaching. If your Yorkie's just beginning to learn basic commands and manners, as explained in Chapter 15, pick a quiet area, inside or out, that doesn't offer a lot of distractions. For other training tasks (like walking on a leash or behaving well in public), select areas suitable for those lessons.

Don't go to the same place for every training session. You may inadvertently be teaching your dog that Sit commands apply only in the living room. So vary the training locations so that your dog learns that wherever she is when you give the command, she needs to obey.

A few other bits of advice

By following a few simple guidelines, you can avoid sending signals that can confuse your dog and undermine your training efforts:

- **Be consistent with your expectations.** Don't waffle. If you aren't clear about what your Yorkie can and can't do, how is he supposed to figure it out? Also make sure that everyone in your family knows the rules, knows how you want them enforced, and knows the command word you associate with the behavior.

- **Pick simple command words with clear meanings.** Keep the command to one or two words (Sit, Down, Stay, and so on), use them consistently, and make sure they're different enough so your dog doesn't get confused. Chapter 15 is all about basic commands.

- **Pick appropriate rewards.** Good rewards are treats (small ones that your Yorkie really likes), praise (short and sweet is best), toys (pick a favorite), or an activity (one that your dog likes). Sometimes the reward can be simply letting him have what he wanted in the first place. If your Yorkie wants to go outside and you make him sit before you open the door (a good way to teach manners and patience), just letting him outside is reward enough.

In the early stages of training, you're going to be handing out a lot of treats. So that you don't completely blow your Yorkie's diet or your budget (dog treats can get expensive), consider getting a different kind of dog food than the one your dog eats regularly (a semi-moist brand, for example) and that you can easily dole out in little pieces. If you feed your dog this food only during training sessions or when he does something especially praiseworthy, your dog will think that he's getting the crème-de-la-crème of dog treats.

Chapter 14

Housetraining

For obvious reasons, the first training task you tackle as a dog owner is housetraining. Before your young puppy can reliably control his bladder or bowel, you want to make sure *you* give him the access he needs to the appropriate bathroom area. Making sure he can get to the bathroom when he has to go is the first step of housetraining: It lays the groundwork for your later training efforts and begins as soon as you bring your puppy home (see Chapter 8 for details).

When your puppy is old enough to begin controlling his bathroom urges (usually around 8 weeks), then you can begin housetraining him in earnest. In this chapter, I explain what you need to know about housetraining in general and about housetraining Yorkies in particular, and I give you step-by-step instructions. And because every dog — even a fully housebroken one — occasionally has accidents, I tell you how to deal with that, too.

Housetraining Fundamentals

Yorkies get a bad rap when it comes to housetraining. People may tell you that the breed is practically impossible to housetrain, that housetraining takes forever, that these dogs refuse to go outside to do their business, and so on, and so on, and so on.

First up, you *can* housetrain Yorkies. They have the same instinctive reluctance to soil their homes that all dogs — even the housetraining champions of the world — have. Beginning at around 12 weeks, Yorkies are physically able to hold their bladders and bowels, just like any other dogs. And, like all other dogs, they live for rewards and attention. By using these traits to your advantage, you have the first tools to ensure potty-training success.

Having said that Yorkies can be housetrained, the breed does offer some challenges to housetraining. Yorkies can be stubborn — especially when housetraining requires your Yorkie to trot out into 2 inches of snow. If you live in a region with cold weather, (remember, Yorkies are small and don't get much protection from their coats in cold weather), you may want to train your puppy to use an indoor area and then slowly transition her to outside potty areas as the weather gets warmer.

Expect to housetrain your dog until she's about 6 months old and continue restricting her free-roaming time until she's about a year old. A year may sound like a long time, but I contend that no dog under a year is truly ready to be given free rein — and free access — to the house she lives in. By the end of this time, however, if you've been diligent and consistent, you'll probably have a dog who knows just what she's supposed to do when she has to go the bathroom and reliably does it.

Whether or not your housetraining efforts are successful depends almost solely on how you proceed. You can't take a slap-dash approach. If you're inconsistent, don't give her the access she needs to the areas you want her to go, or let her roam unsupervised all over your house before she's ready for that freedom, you undermine your efforts. But by picking the right time to begin housetraining, knowing your Yorkie's strengths and weaknesses, and following the guidelines in the following sections, you can put together a plan that's sure to succeed.

Using the positive approach

In Chapter 13, I explain the fundamental principles of positive dog training. Basically, you teach your dog appropriate behaviors by giving him rewards (attention, praise, treats) for good behavior and withdrawing rewards for bad behavior. This strategy works for two reasons: Dogs, as a species, want to get good things and avoid bad things. And they're intelligent enough to learn how to modify their behavior so that they can have what they want and avoid what they dislike. In addition, this approach doesn't use pain or force to elicit the appropriate behaviors.

In housetraining, the positive approach uses these tactics:

✔ **You set your puppy up for success.** Chances are your puppy isn't going to know where the good bathroom areas are, so you have to show him. When he has to go to the bathroom, take him immediately to the area you identified as a bathroom area (see the next section, "Identifying bathroom areas" for details). Do this every time he has to go to the bathroom.

✔ **You reward success.** When your puppy goes in the bathroom area, reward him every single time. You can reward him with praise and/or a small treat, but you need to give it to him immediately. To a dog, a delayed reward is the same as no reward at all.

✔ **You interrupt and redirect mistakes.** Instead of yelling and screaming — or worse, physically punishing your dog — when you find him peeing or pooping where he isn't supposed to, simply stop the misbehavior and redirect it. Say "No!" firmly to interrupt the behavior, say "Outside," and then physically move your puppy to that location where he can finish. See the section "Oops, I did it again" later in this chapter for more info on how to handle accidents.

Identifying bathroom areas

Fortunately for you, dogs don't like to soil their homes. Unfortunately, dogs and humans have different definitions of home. To you, your entire house is home — even the rooms, like the guest bedroom or the formal dining room, that you're rarely in. Your Yorkie identifies home a little differently. She doesn't use floor plans and plaster walls; she uses her nose. Her home is where the family smells are. If you spend lots of time in the kitchen or the family room with her, she identifies that place as a place she lives. If you're never in the guest bedroom, that place isn't home to your dog, and she may view it as a suitable bathroom area — reason number one for absolutely not letting an untrained Yorkie (or any dog for that matter) wander freely through your house.

Yorkies who come from pet stores may not have this aversion to soiling their living areas because they were kept in cages and had no place else to go except in their homes. In some puppy mills, where the cages are stacked, the situation can be even worse because feces from the dogs in the top cages simply falls onto the dogs in the lower cages. You may never be able to fully housetrain dogs who spent the first weeks of their lives in these conditions.

So what's a good place for a bathroom? Depends on who you ask. You'd probably say any place not in the house or, if in the house, somewhere out of the way, like the laundry room or the unfinished part of your basement, so that you (or your guests) don't have to look at or stumble over your dog's ecological contributions every time you turn around.

Your Yorkie, on the other hand, identifies good bathroom areas by smell: places where the family smell is absent and — ding! ding! ding! We have a winner! — any place that already smells like urine or feces. This is reason number two for absolutely not letting an untrained Yorkie wander freely through your home.

So here's what you do to help your dog recognize the bathroom areas you approve of and to identify those areas that are off-limits:

✔ **Spend time in every room of your house with your dog.** Pick a room a night if you have to, and take in a book, sit on the floor, and keep your Yorkie with you. The more she associates a room with you and the family, the less likely she's going to think of it as an outhouse. Another way to broaden your Yorkie's concept of home is to keep her attached to you and, as you go about the everyday business of tending house, she goes along. See Chapter 5 for details on using a tether to keep your puppy near.

✔ **Identify the bathroom area you want her to use (inside or out) and take her there** *every time* **she has to go to the bathroom and treat her when she's done.** As she goes in the right spot, she leaves a bit of her scent — even if you clean it up. Pretty soon the smell, the repetition of going to the same place every time, and the reward she gets for doing well teach her where the best bathroom area is.

✔ **If she has an accident, clean up the mess and use an enzyme-based cleaning solution to eliminate the smell that will lure her back.** (Don't use ammonia, which to a dog, smells like urine.) Then spend some time with your dog in that room to supplant any lingering bathroom smell with your smell.

Restricting his freedom

You can't housetrain a Yorkie if you let him roam freely and unsupervised around your house. With access to everything and no oversight, he does what any self-respecting dog would do when he feels the call of nature: Finds a good spot ("good" according to him; see the earlier section "Identifying bathroom areas") and goes. If this situation happens, housetraining becomes more difficult, and if it happens a lot, you have real challenges ahead of you. To avoid these potty problems, limit your Yorkie's freedom until he proves that you can trust him and you're confident that he won't pull a fast one. In essence, confining your Yorkie to small areas and crate training him are essential.

Using your dog crate

If your Yorkie sleeps in a crate (always a good idea; head to Chapter 7 for reasons why), you're a step ahead of folks who don't use a crate, for the simple reason that the first step in crate training is getting your dog used to the crate so that he considers it his home within a home. After you accomplish this task (see Chapter 15 for instructions), you use your dog's instinctive need to keep his home clean.

How you use the crate for housetraining depends on your preferences. Some people keep their Yorkie pups in their crates pretty much all the time, letting them out at designated times to eat, piddle, and play. The thinking behind this approach is that, when they're frequently confined, they're less likely to have an accident because they want to keep their homes clean. I prefer to use the crate in the same way I use the confinement area: as the place my pups go at night and when I can't be around to watch them; otherwise, they're with me, attached, literally, at the hip.

Confining your dog to a crate teaches him patience and control. Because he doesn't want to soil his sleeping area, he'll wait to go to the bathroom until you let him out. Your dog will wait to go whether you use the crate during the night, during the day when you can't be around or can't keep an eye on him, or most of the time as your main training tool.

Nighttime crating without bathroom breaks works only with puppies who are physically mature enough to have control over their bladders and bowels. Before that, you're setting your pup up for failure and undermining the very instinct that your housetraining relies on. Head to Chapter 7 for scheduling nighttime bathroom breaks for very young puppies.

Confining your Yorkie

Confinement may sound a little oppressive to people who like bad prison movies — "Throw him in solitary!" — but in housetraining, *confinement* simply means keeping your pup in a small area. In essence, you're confining your dog when you keep him tethered to you or when you station him in the room that you're in (you can find out about these techniques in Chapter 8). Both these strategies are good to use when housetraining because your dog is with you and you can watch him for signs that he needs a bathroom break.

When you're not around or can't watch him, you can confine him to a small area, such as a laundry room, kitchen, or bathroom. The right place to confine your pup is one that's safe, not carpeted (simply because cleaning up is easier in case he does have an accident), and enables him to see what's going on (so he doesn't feel isolated); see Figure 14-1.

Keep these points in mind:

- ✔ If you're training your Yorkie to go outside, he's not ready to be confined to a small area until he understands the rules of housetraining (that is, he knows where he's supposed to go and reliably goes there) and has developed enough control to wait until you can let him out before he goes. Until he can do those things, he needs to be close to you or in his crate.

- ✔ If you're training your Yorkie to go in a specified place indoors, make sure that his bathroom area is in the area you've confined him to. Initially, you may want to cover the whole area with newspapers (so that if he goes, he can't help but be successful) and then slowly begin to eliminate some of the papers to narrow the toilet area.

Being consistent

Let's face facts. Fact 1: Yorkies are small and cute. Fact 2: Many people go a little easier on small and cute than they do on big and brawny. It's human nature. The same mess you may be willing to clean up for your Yorkie would leave you aghast if you had a Great Dane. And so, if you had a Great Dane, you'd move heaven and earth to ensure that the Great Dane knew the bathroom rules, but with Yorkies . . . well, their messes are little and easy to clean up anyway, so what does it really matter if they periodically go where they're not supposed to?

©Isabelle Francais

Figure 14-1: Keeping your Yorkie comfortably confined to a small area when you can't watch him helps your housetraining efforts.

It matters because if your dog thinks that anywhere she wants to go is acceptable (even if it's acceptable only sometimes, like when you don't have the energy to keep her near and supervised), she won't ever be fully house-broken and, therefore, you can never completely trust her to be left alone. The only way to avoid this scenario is to be absolutely consistent and committed to your Yorkie's house-training. Yes, housetraining is a lot of work during the first weeks, when you can never relax because your Yorkie is always looking for a place to go (which she is, because Yorkie puppies have bladders the size of a peanut when full). But take heart: As she learns the rules — which she can only do if you enforce them — and applies them more consistently, the task becomes easier.

Your puppy deliberately choosing to go to an alternative — and unapproved — bathroom area isn't an accident; it's a training issue. An accident happens when your Yorkie simply can't hold it any longer and can't get to the bathroom area. How you deal with accidents is different from how you deal with non-accidental messes. See the section "When Accidents Happen" for details.

Training Your Yorkie

When you train your Yorkie, you have two goals: to *never* let him go to the bathroom where he's not supposed to and to teach him where he's *supposed* to relieve himself. Sounds easy enough, and truth be told, the process really isn't that hard — but it does take commitment from you (your dog is basically along for the ride). To achieve these goals, keep your dog close or confined (see the earlier section "Restricting his freedom" for information), set up a potty-training routine, and then follow that routine religiously, making adjustments to it as your dog grows and gets more adept at the whole training thing.

Getting your Yorkie to the point of being completely housetrained and thoroughly trustworthy in your absence and with your new carpets takes months. Months may sound like a long time, but they're really not, so don't rush it.

To housetrain your Yorkie, follow these steps *every single time* he has to go potty:

1. **Say "Outside" (or whatever term you use to denote the bathroom area) and take your Yorkie to the bathroom area.**

   Here's when you need to make these bathroom runs:

   • **First thing in the morning, as soon as you let your Yorkie out of his crate, last thing before bed at**

night, and any time you let him out of his crate or out of the confinement area. If your pup is very young, carry him to the bathroom spot in the morning; if you don't, he'll squat and pee on the way there because of how full his bladder is and how little control he has. As he grows, gains more control, and becomes more accustomed to the routine, you can let him walk to the bathroom area.

- **After every meal.** Young puppies usually need to go to the bathroom pretty quickly after they eat. Wait no more than five or ten minutes before you head that-a-way. Older dogs can wait longer.

- **Regularly throughout the day.** How frequently you take him to the bathroom area depends on his age. If you have a very young puppy, head out every hour if you can; if you can't (because you work, for example) try to arrange for someone to come in periodically to take your pup out. If that's impossible, too, keep him confined in a small area while you're gone and begin the regimen when you get home and on the weekends. As your puppy gets older, gradually increase the time between bathroom breaks.

- **Any other time he needs to.** To be able to take him to the bathroom whenever he has to go, you have to keep him close by and under supervision so that you can see the tell-tale signs. More experienced dogs usually devise a way to let you know (by standing at the door, for example, or bobbing around with their back legs crossed).

2. **As soon as he begins to go to the bathroom, give a bathroom command.**

    Use "Go" or "Do it" or any other word/phrase you can utter without embarrassing yourself or your neighbors when they're within earshot. Essentially, you're training him to go on cue. Once your Yorkie associates the word with the action, you simply give the command, and he'll go — a very useful trick when it's raining or you're in a hurry to leave.

3. **When he's done, say "Good boy," "Yes," or "Okay," and give him a treat.**

    Following the phrase by the treat lets your Yorkie know that he did what he was supposed to and that you're pleased. When you use these words consistently to mean "you're done and you did well," this phrase becomes an important training marker for your dog (see Chapter 15).

Remember these tips as you housetrain:

✔ If you take your puppy to an outside bathroom area, have him on a leash and don't allow him to wander or play. He's there for business. For indoor potty breaks, the idea is the same but you don't need the leash.

✔ Take your dog out the same door every time you head to the outdoor bathroom spot. Otherwise, he may get confused and think that he gets to play.

✔ Consider hanging a small bell near the door or from the door handle, just above your dog's nose level. Every time you open the door to let him out, give the bell a little jingle. Any time your Yorkie rings the bell, take him out to go potty. Eventually, he'll learn to use the bell to signal when he has to go to the bathroom.

When Accidents Happen

All dogs — even housetrained dogs — periodically have accidents. Accidents can happen for any number of reasons:

✔ **Your dog isn't fully house-broken yet.** Although you try your hardest to avoid them during training, accidents do happen. Make sure you're adequately supervising your dog and that you confine her when you can't supervise.

✔ **You missed the signs that she needed to go.** Dogs can't hold it forever, and if you find a mess near the back door, chances are the mess wasn't your dog's fault.

✔ **Your dog isn't feeling well.** Sometimes your digestive tract can give you quite the surprise. If your dog has diarrhea or runny stool, she may have been taken up short and is probably just as dismayed at the mess as you are. (*Note:* If the diarrhea continues, call your vet; refer to Chapter 12.)

✔ **She's stressed.** Some dogs react to changes (a new animal in the house, for example) or emotional turmoil in the house by soiling in places they don't normally. Sometimes they soil out of defiance. If your Yorkie has suddenly taken to leaving gifts and you don't have any other explanation for it, talk to your vet. He can help you uncover the causes and figure out how to fix it.

Oops, I did it again

How you respond to an accident depends on when you discover it. If you happen upon your Yorkie in the middle of his transgression, do the following steps:

1. **Say "No" or clap your hands once sharply.**

   Your intent is to startle your dog into stopping, not to scold. You don't have time for a lecture, and he wouldn't understand it anyway.

2. **Say "Outside," and immediately pick him up, take him to the bathroom area, and give him the bathroom command.**

   When he finishes in the right spot, reward him.

If you find the accident after the fact, just clean it up and resolve to keep a better eye on your Yorkie in the future.

You may wonder where the punishment comes in. To be blunt, it doesn't — at least not in the way you may be thinking: the rolled up newspaper, the nose-rubbing, or the cursing. Punishing after the fact doesn't work. Once the deed is done (and it may have been done ten minutes or four hours ago), dogs don't associate your reaction with the problem you're reacting to. They associate your reaction with the here and now. And in the here and now, they can't figure out what you're getting all worked up about.

"But he knows he isn't supposed to do that! Just look how guilty he acts!" you may say. What you see isn't guilt, it's apprehension. Your acting like a maniac scares him. Plus dogs are good at routines. If your dog knows that anytime you come home, see a little pile of brown stuff on the floor, and start ranting and raving, he can expect the same reaction whenever, lo and behold, a brown pile awaits you. But he doesn't make the connection between his actions that produced the nugget and your reaction to finding it. He just wants you to calm down and be the happy, loving human you normally are.

When re-training is necessary

If your previously housetrained Yorkie suddenly begins having accidents, talk to your vet first. Your dog may have health issues that you need to be aware of. If your dog is healthy, however, and you have no other reasonable explanation for her behavior, she may have simply fallen out of good habits and into bad ones. Maybe you've been too lax in enforcing the rules. If this situation occurs, you have to retrain her. Although she's (probably) not a puppy anymore, use the same techniques I describe earlier in this chapter.

Chuck E. Cheese
07/06/05

My Trip to Chuck E. Cheese's

Chapter 15

Teaching Basic Commands

In This Chapter

▶ Instructing your pooch using a simple training technique

▶ Training your Yorkie to follow basic, but important, commands

▶ Helping your Yorkie be a good family member

*L*ike all of us, dogs are creatures of habit. Instill good habits, and you have a nice, well-behaved dog. Let bad habits form, and you end up in the principal's office because your baby was caught smoking behind the jungle-gym.

To help your Yorkie form good habits, take the time to train him. He doesn't need to push a stroller while wearing a tutu, but he does need to know the basic behaviors common to well-mannered dogs. These lessons are important for two reasons: First, they keep you in control and keep your Yorkie safe (try to stop your Yorkie from chasing a cat into the street by jumping up and down and saying "Ooh! Ooh! Ooh!"). Second, these lessons make your dog more pleasant to be around. Even the sweetest dog can become pretty annoying when he whines constantly for attention or pretty scary when he turns into a demon protecting his food dish.

Training Technique

To successfully train your dog, you need a technique. Here's one that works:

1. **Get your Yorkie's attention.**

   She can't learn anything if she's busy trying to coax the cat off the bookshelf while you issue commands. For this reason, make sure that you pick a good time and place to train. Refer to Chapter 13.

2. **Elicit the behavior and, as your Yorkie moves into the position you want, say the corresponding command.**

You can either capture the behavior (that is, note when your Yorkie naturally does what you want her to do, such as sit) or you can gently coax her into the position you want. The reason you add the command *as* your dog takes the position and not before is because you want her to associate the command with the position. Later, you'll be able to say the command (or give a nonverbal cue) to elicit the behavior.

3. **As soon as she's in the position you want (or doing what you asked), verbally note her success (say "Good girl," or "Okay," for example).**

   Some people use a clicker (a device that makes a clicking sound) to give this verbal marker, but you don't have to. Giving some audible confirmation that your Yorkie did what she was supposed to do *as soon as she does it* is the important thing.

4. **Give her the reward.**

   When you're just beginning, treats are probably the most powerful reward. But they're certainly not the only rewards that can be effective when you're training. Refer to Chapter 13 for other ideas.

5. **Keep practicing until your Yorkie gets the command right nearly all the time.**

   If you're using yummies, gradually decrease the times that you offer them as your Yorkie becomes more adept at following the command. As she approaches mastering the command, give them to her only occasionally. Of course, you don't have to wean her from "Good boy" or "Good girl" — a kind word is always appreciated.

Commands for Control and Safety

By having a few basic commands at your disposal, you can effectively direct your Yorkie's behavior.

Teach one command at a time. Don't move on to the next one until your Yorkie has the hang of the first one.

His name

Okay, so teaching your Yorkie his name seems almost unnecessary. I mean, after all, he probably already knows it, right? Well, the key here is that you want him to look at you *every single time* you say his name. He doesn't necessarily need to come, but he needs to turn his attention to you. Being able to respond to his name is the first step toward any other training. Fortunately, teaching this command is phenomenally simple:

1. **Say your Yorkie's name.**

2. **As soon as he looks at you (makes eye contact), say "Good boy," and give him a treat.**

   If he doesn't look at you, _don't_ repeat his name. Make some kissie noises (dogs can't resist this ridiculous noise), and when he turns to find out what the noise is about and makes eye contact, then say "Good boy" and give a treat.

3. **Repeat these steps a few times.**

   You know he's got the command when you say his name while he's paying attention to something else and he snaps his attention to you.

Come

Come is an important command because it lets you call your Yorkie to you. You'll find it particularly helpful when she's approaching something that you want her to stay away from, like the creek in your backyard or the prize pansies she's taken to sleeping in.

1. **Call your Yorkie's name to get her attention; when she turns toward you, pat your thigh a few times to spur her forward.**

   If you use a treat cup (a little cup filled with dog treats), you can shake the cup instead of patting your thigh. You're just trying to motivate her to move to you.

2. **As she begins to run toward you, say "Come" in a happy voice.**

3. **When she arrives, say "Good girl" and then reward her.**

Begin these lessons with your Yorkie nearby and in an area that has few distractions. As she begins to come more reliably, increase the distance and the distractions. Once your Yorkie understands the command, add variables into the training sessions. For instance, as she plays with another family member, say "Name, come." When she interrupts her game to come to you, give her a treat, praise her, and then allow her to return to her game. Doing so encourages her to interrupt anything she's doing when you call. Keep this training up and before you know it, she'll come from wherever whenever you call her.

Because you want your Yorkie to come *every single time you call*, never call her to you in order to scold her. You want coming to you to be one of the highlights of her life.

Sit

Sit is a great command because, even if your Yorkie never graduates to Settle or Down, Sit helps him calm down — even though his little tail may be wagging under him and his body quivering from the motion. Take a few treats to a quiet place and follow these steps:

1. **Say your Yorkie's name to get his attention.**

2. **When he's facing you, hold a treat under his nose and slowly lift it up over his head.**

   This motion generally lures your dog into a sit position (see Figure 15-1). If it doesn't, gently coax his bottom down. If, on the other hand, your guy jumps the gun and sits before you even have to lure him into it, say "Sit" and jump to Step 4.

3. **As he begins to sit (even if you're coaxing him), say "Sit."**

4. **When he's in the Sit position, say "Good boy," and then give him the treat.**

©Isabelle Francais

Figure 15-1: The Sit command is one of the first your Yorkie should learn.

This command is one of the easiest to learn and one you can practice anywhere: Put your Yorkie in a sit before you give him his food dish, before you open the door for him to go outside, whenever he comes up and wants to be petted.

Down

You can teach Down (see Figure 15-2) after your Yorkie has mastered Sit. Follow these steps:

1. **Say your Yorkie's name to get her attention and give the Sit command.**

2. **When she's sitting, hold a treat in front of her nose; slowly lower the treat between her paws.**

   If all goes well, she'll lower her body to follow the treat. If she doesn't, gently coax her down by cradling her elbows and lowering her.

3. **As she moves into position (or as you lower her), say "Down."**

4. **As soon as her elbows touch the ground, say "Good girl," and then give her the treat.**

©Isabelle Francais

Figure 15-2: The Down command is a good way to manage and protect your Yorkie when you're busy and she's underfoot.

Stay

When you put your Yorkie in a Stay, your goal is to keep him in that position until you release him. This command is great, for example, when a Girl Scout comes to the door to deliver your cookies and you don't want your Yorkie spoiling the moment by incessantly barking and dashing over the threshold. To teach your Yorkie Stay, take him to a quiet room with no distractions and do the following:

1. **Say your Yorkie's name to get his attention and give the Sit command.**

2. **When he's sitting, stand in front of him and flash your hand, palm out, and say "Stay."**

3. **Stay in your position for a few seconds; then say "Okay," and wave your hand to release him. Give him a treat.**

   Repeat Steps 1 through 3 until he can stay in position throughout the pause.

4. **Command Sit again; again say "Stay" as you give the signal, and take one step away from your Yorkie.**

5. **Wait for a few seconds and then say "Okay," and wave your hand to release him. Give him a treat.**

   Again, repeat Steps 4 and 5 until he holds the Stay.

6. **Repeat the process outlined in the preceding steps; as your Yorkie successfully holds the position, move farther away and hold the Stay for longer periods of time.**

   As you practice Stay, gradually add distractions.

   Don't increase the distance or the duration until your Yorkie can successfully remain in the Stay position at each interval.

Settle

Yorkies are so happy to see you when you return home, they just can't contain themselves. So you have to help them with the Settle command. Essentially, this command means "Stop jumping around like a lunatic and sit still so that I can pet you." You can use this command any time you want to calm your dog down. When your Yorkie races toward you and jumps up demanding attention, do the following:

1. **Stand still but ignore her by crossing your arms and looking away, with your chin tilted upward (see Figure 15-3).**

2. **As she starts to quiet down, hold your stance, but say "Settle."**

©Isabelle Francais

Figure 15-3: Withhold your attention when your Yorkie demands it; when she's calm, give her all the attention you want.

3. **When she's still (she may even be sitting), turn your head to her, say "Good girl," and give her the attention she wants.**

When you first teach Settle, you may want to use a treat, in addition to giving her your attention. But after she gets the hang of it, you don't need the treats anymore. What your dog is really after is your attention. That's reward enough.

Drop It

Drop It is useful because every dog periodically picks up something — like a baby toy, a dead mouse, or a dropped pork chop — you don't want him to have. In these situations, the last thing you want to do is initiate a game of tug-of-war. Trying to pry a prize from your dog's clenched mouth can quickly escalate into a true power struggle (and a bite) and result in a dog who's very protective of his things — never a good thing. The solution is to teach your Yorkie that when you say "Drop it," he's in line for a really neat treat, even better than the object he already has. So gather a toy your Yorkie really likes and a handful of treats, and do the following:

1. **Encourage your dog to play with the toy; when he has it in his mouth, say his name to get his attention and hold out a treat.**

   He'll probably come up for a sniff and, when he figures out it's a yummy, he'll open his mouth to take it.

2. **As he opens his mouth to take the treat, the toy will fall out; at that point, say "Drop it," pick up the toy, and give him the treat.**

   If he manages to keep a hold of the toy as he goes after the treat, don't relinquish the treat until he releases the toy. Let him nibble on the treat but don't' give him the whole thing until the toy is out of his mouth. Then pick it up and give him the whole treat.

3. **Give him back the toy and repeat these steps.**

   Giving back the toy is important because he learns not only that he gets a treat for releasing the toy, but he also gets his toy back. What could be better than that?

After he gets the hang of Drop It, you can give the command before you show the treat. Gradually progress from toys to forbidden, but safe, objects (like tissue balls, socks, and kid toys). When you do, don't encourage him to play with the object (you don't want to send the wrong message), but drop it "accidentally" near him so that he can't help but notice and be intrigued. After he has it in his mouth, say "Drop it," and when he does, give him the treat. (If you have to, show him the treat to encourage him to let go of the forbidden object.)

If, after the initial training, you only use the Drop It command when you need to take something away from your Yorkie that he'll never get back, he'll catch on pretty soon to what's really going down and won't give up the prize. So periodically practice this command just for fun and with your Yorkie's toys — things he'll get back after he gives them up.

Wait

If you don't teach her any better, your Yorkie's going to dash in and out of doors ahead of you, up and down stairs ahead of you, and in essence leave you bringing up the rear. Which isn't always a problem. I mean, if you're heading out into your safe, fenced backyard to water the garden, whether you or your Yorkie precedes or follows doesn't much matter. But, when you open the front door to get the paper or when you get out of the car to go to the vet's office, the last thing you want is a quick-as-lightning dog dashing ahead of you. So teach her to wait.

For this command, you don't need any treats. If she wants to go outside, for example, simply being able to go out is reward enough. (*Note:* If you're practicing this command at a door that leads to an unfenced area, be sure that your Yorkie is on a leash, just for safety's sake, but don't use the leash to control her). Follow these steps:

1. **At the door, move your body in front of your Yorkie's so that you're standing between her and the door.**

   Your Yorkie should be 3 or 4 feet away from the door. If she's pressed against the door, herd her back with your body; don't use the leash (if you have one on her). If she tries to dash around you, move your feet to deflect her forward motion.

2. **When she's settled and no longer trying to make an end run around you, say "Wait" and partially open the door.**

3. **If your Yorkie is like most, she's going to make a run for it; block her with your body or shut the door. *Don't* repeat the command.**

   If you close the door, be sure not to shut it on your dog as she makes her bid for freedom. The lesson you're teaching her is: If I wait patiently, I can go outside. If I don't or if I try to make a break for it, I'm stuck in here.

4. **As soon as she pauses, even just a little bit, say "Okay," and open the door to let her out.**

For Yorkies who are just learning the Wait command, you want to reinforce the first sign of good behavior. With practice, your Yorkie will become more adept at holding her horses. After she learns this command around doors, practice around stairs and in cars.

Minding Manners

Some training lessons aren't so much about control and safety as they are about being good members of the family.

Walking on a leash

Taking walks with your Yorkie can be an enjoyable, relaxing time, as shown in Figure 15-4, or a royal pain in the posterior — for both you and your dog. To make these times enjoyable, follow one simple rule: No tugging. Taking walks isn't any fun for you when your Yorkie dashes hither and yon and back again. And your Yorkie has no fun when you spend the entire walk giving little jerks to his leash to bring him in line.

To teach your Yorkie to walk politely on a leash without racing ahead only to be jerked back again, follow these steps:

1. **Attach the leash but don't budge until he stops straining ahead.**

   Your arm may get a little tired, and you may worry a little bit what the neighbors are thinking, but stay completely still until your dog stops pulling.

2. **As soon as your Yorkie stops straining at the leash, take a step forward.**

   I say a step because any forward movement on your part is like a starting shot at the racetrack for your dog. He'll be off again — or off as far as the leash lets him go.

©Isabelle Francais

Figure 15-4: A calm dog and calm human make for an enjoyable walk around the neighborhood.

3. **If he starts tugging ahead again, stop; when he stops trying to yank you forward, resume your walk, one step at a time, if you have to.**

   Continue this training until he learns that you two aren't going anywhere until he walks calmly beside you.

When you're on a walk, give him a little slack. Let him sniff the things he wants to, pause around the fire hydrants, and walk a little ahead. As long as he isn't pulling like a sled dog, he's doing fine, and you can relax.

Nipping yipping in the bud

Yorkies, as a rule, can be yippy little dogs. Which makes them good watchdogs. For that reason, you don't want to (and frankly, can't) eliminate the barking entirely. But, if your Yorkie yips all the time or gets herself worked into a frenzy whenever someone comes to the door or passes by the window, you can try the following; you'll need a willing friend and a penny can (an aluminum can filled with a few pennies) or a squirt bottle with water:

1. **Have your friend ring the doorbell or knock.**

2. **When your Yorkie starts barking, shake the can or spray her discreetly with water.**

   Either of these methods should startle her into a second's worth of silence.

3. **Immediately say "Quiet" or "Shhh," and then give the Sit command.**

4. **Open the door, keeping your Yorkie behind you.**

5. **Repeat these steps until she has the hang of it.**

Dealing with food protectiveness

Dogs who are protective of their food are dangerous, especially to small children who often don't know to stay away from the dog dish. Even adults can be in danger if the dog is also aggressive. The best way to avoid this problem is to get your Yorkie used to people being around his food dish and touching his food, even while he's eating (see Figure 15-5). To help your puppy associate you and your hands with getting food, not taking it away, try these strategies, and begin them as soon as your puppy comes home:

✔ Feed your puppy his kibble a few pieces at a time directly from your hand.

✔ Fill your puppy's bowl up a handful of kibble at a time while he's eating.

✔ Sit beside him as he eats and periodically stroke his head. If he accepts that, stroke his muzzle and under his chin.

✔ When your dog is so used to your presence around his food bowl that he is oblivious to it, take some kibble out and then put it back, praising him as you do.

If your dog is already showing signs of aggressiveness around his food dish (like deep growling or raised hackles), ask your vet for advice. Once the problem is started, you need professional help to deal with it. Your vet can either suggest a course of action or direct you to an animal behaviorist who can help you modify your dog's behavior.

©Isabelle Francais

Figure 15-5: You can train your Yorkie to happily accept your presence while he eats.

Part V
The Part of Tens

" Hey – that's a record! Honey, I just clocked
the Yorkie at 28 mph coming through the
living room."

In this part . . .

*I*f you love Yorkies — and my bet is that you do or soon will — you'll want to know as much about them as you possibly can. In this part, I offer you ten Web sites devoted to Yorkies and ten fun Yorkie facts. And because you may hanker for a turn in the show ring, you can also find ten pointers for showing your Yorkie.

Chapter 16

Ten (or So) Fun and Useful Yorkie Web Sites

In This Chapter

▶ Yorkie organization sites

▶ Yorkie rescue group sites

▶ General Yorkie information sites

▶ Fun 'n' games Yorkie sites

*Y*ou can find a lot of information about Yorkshire Terriers on the Internet. Simply go to any search engine, type in "Yorkshire Terrier" and wait to be amazed at the various listings your search generates. Among the results are sites offering general information on Yorkies and ones devoted to specific topics, such as grooming tips or housetraining techniques. Yorkie organizations and breed clubs, commercial enterprises, breeders (reputable and otherwise), as well as Yorkie lovers all over the world maintain these sites.

In this chapter, I list 10 (okay, 11) Web sites that contain interesting, useful, and informed comments about Yorkshire Terriers. Use these sites as a starting point in your quest to find out more about your little dog and to connect with others who love them as much as you do.

Yorkshire Terrier Club of America (YTCA)

The *Yorkshire Terrier Club of America (YTCA)* is the national breed club for Yorkies. Whether you already own a Yorkshire Terrier or are still in the throes of making a decision, you can't beat the YTCA's

Web site for information, pointers, and interesting tidbits of all things Yorkie. Here's just a sampling of the information you can find on this site:

- ✔ **Breed information:** You can find the complete breed standard as well as general information about owning and caring for a Yorkie. If you need general grooming tips or want to try your hand at trimming, the grooming links are especially helpful.

- ✔ **Breeder referral:** Although the YTCA doesn't recommend any particular breeders, the club does offer a list of breeders by region. The breeders listed are YTCA members and, as such, agree to abide by the club's policies and code of ethics and conduct. You can also find rescue information if you're interested in adopting an older Yorkie.

- ✔ **Competition information:** You can find information on competitions open to Yorkshire Terriers as well as a bulletin board of events on the Web site. Keep in mind, however, that various regional clubs submit the events, so a club from your area may not be included in the information.

- ✔ **Club information:** Several links are devoted to information about the club itself, including a link to the YTCA code of ethics and conduct, a list of club officers, the requirements of membership, and the general information about the club's mission. You can also find links to regional clubs and information about the YTCA Foundation, an organization that's devoted to improving breeding practices and the health of the breed through research and education.

To access the Web site, go to www.ytca.org.

Yorkie.org

At Yorkie.org (www.yorkie.org), the home page for Rhapsody Yorkshire Terriers, a Yorkie breeder, you can find a great deal of information about Yorkies in general. An excellent site to go to *before* you decide whether or not to adopt a Yorkie, you can find out about both the joys and challenges of adopting this breed. For particularly good information, click the Puppies Tips, Grooming Tips, and Health Issues links.

American Kennel Club (AKC)

The American Kennel Club's (AKC) mission is to "advance the study, breeding, exhibiting, running and maintenance of purebred dogs." So, the AKC includes scores of breeds, not just the Yorkshire Terrier. Although the site isn't solely devoted to Yorkies, you can still find a lot of information about the breed and its group (the Toy Group). Through the site's links, you can also access information about breeders. Other general information you may find helpful includes a listing of dog events, regional breed clubs, and AKC registration information and forms.

To access the AKC site, go to www.akc.org.

Yorkshire Terrier National Rescue, Inc., and Yorkshire Terrier Rescue Network, Inc.

Yorkshire Terrier National Rescue, Inc., and Yorkshire Terrier Rescue Network, Inc., are both organizations dedicated to caring for and finding homes for Yorkies who've been abandoned, relinquished, or removed from their previous homes. If you want to adopt a Yorkie who needs a second (or third) chance at happiness, you can find information and guidance at either of these sites:

- **Yorkshire Terrier National Rescue, Inc.:** www.yorkshire terrierrescue.com

- **Yorkshire Terrier Rescue Network, Inc.:** www.yorkshire. terrierrescue.net

Yorkshire Terrier Connection

The Yorkshire Terrier Connection (www.doggies.com/Yorkshire_ Terrier) offers links to great information; simply click the topic you want to know more about. The site covers competitive events, training, where to find dog supplies and accessories, how to raise a Yorkie pup, picking a name (including thousands of names to choose from), dog-biscuit recipes, and more.

Shooter Dog.com

Shooter is a dog who lives in California with his humans, who seem to have a great deal of time on their hands and a pretty wacky sense of humor. With their help, Shooter has posted a Web site where you can, among other things, find Yorkie horoscopes, see artwork with

Yorkies substituted for people (think Mona Lisa as a Yorkie), find answers to the world's problems from a dog's perspective, and read news stories featuring the adventures of Yorkies hobnobbing with celebrities both dead and alive. Beyond all the silly stuff, which frankly is so over-the-top you can't help but chuckle, you can find real information that's very detailed and helpful.

To access the fun stuff, just go to www.shooterdog.com. To find the real meat of the site, click the Visit Alex link (Alex, it seems, is Shooter's more cerebral pal) and then click Alex's Yorkie Care FAQ.

Yorkieland

By going to the Yorkieland home page (http://members.tripod. com/Yorkieland_One/yorkieland_one.htm), you can join a discussion group dedicated to people who love and own Yorkies. Simply click the Yorkieland banner to join in. Scroll down the home page, and you can find links to breeders, rescue groups, and recommended books.

Yorkies Direct

From the Yorkies Direct home page (www.yorkiesdirect.com), you can access all sorts of information about Yorkshire Terriers. The site offers info on health issues, training, and general care. You can even join a Yorkie chat room.

Animal Stamps.com

Who knew that Yorkies adorn stamps around the world? Well, now you do. Antigua, Barbados, Bulgaria, the Central African Republic, the Island Republic of Monserrat, and more. If you're a Yorkie lover *and* a stamp collector, you're in for a treat. Browse or buy the stamps at Animal Stamps.com (www.animalstamps.com).

Not in My Backyard!

Not in My Backyard! is a comic strip by Dale Taylor, featuring Yorkshire Terriers, among other dog breeds. The Yorkie characters are long on attitude and short on sense. To see strips from 1998 to 2001, go to www.notinmybackyard.com.

Chapter 17

Ten Things to Know about Showing Yorkies

*Y*our Yorkie can compete in many events (agility, tracking, obedience, and more; refer to Chapter 9 for a complete list), but dog shows, also known as *conformation events,* are probably the most popular event for Yorkies and their humans. If you're unfamiliar with conformation events, you may think that they're simply beauty contests for dogs. But in these shows, the judges evaluate the breeding stock of each breed. The winners are those dogs who most closely match the breed standard (for more on breed standard, see Chapter 2) and the breeders whose breeding programs produced them.

Participating in conformation events either as an *exhibitor* (that is, someone who's showing her dog) or a spectator is one of the most enjoyable things you can do. In this chapter, I give you ten bits of info that can help you understand what goes on at these shows.

Although conformation events are basically the same all around the world, in this chapter, I focus on the conformation events sponsored by the American Kennel Club (AKC). If you live or plan to show your Yorkie in another country, contact national or local breed clubs in that country for information and guidance.

Eligibility Requirements

The eligibility requirements to enter a dog show are pretty straight-forward: Your Yorkie must be

- ✔ Registered with the American Kennel Club (AKC) or the breed club sponsoring the event.

- ✔ At least 6 months old on the day of the show.

- ✔ A member of the breed being judged.

- ✔ *Unaltered* (that is, neither spayed or neutered). If your Yorkie is fixed, he or she can compete only in the stud dog and brood bitches classes (classes for dogs who were previously bred). To find out more about which surgical procedures are and aren't acceptable for conformation events, go the section "Cosmetic and Surgical No-Nos."

Cosmetic and Surgical No-Nos

Because the purpose of conformation events is to evaluate the breeding stock, the only allowable cosmetic and surgical procedures are those that restore the health of a dog or are mentioned in the breed standard. Yorkies, for example, can have their tails docked and their dewclaws removed because those are mentioned in the Yorkshire Terrier breed standard. But you're not allowed to cosmetically or surgically change your dog's appearance solely for the purpose of making him a better representative of the breed.

Types of Shows

There are three types of conformation shows: specialty, group, and all-breed. The type of show determines which dogs can compete:

- ✔ **Specialty shows:** These shows are limited to one breed of dog. You can't (and probably wouldn't want to anyway) enter your Yorkie in a specialty show for Rottweilers, for example.

- ✔ **Group shows:** Only dogs belonging to a particular AKC group (Sporting, Hound, Working, Terrier, Toy, Non-Sporting, and Herding) can enter group shows. In these competitions, your Yorkie competes with other members of the Toy group, which is happily populated with breeds such as the Pekingese, Miniature Pinscher, Chinese Crested, Brussels Griffon, and more.

  ✔ **All-breed shows:** These shows are open to all 150 breeds
    that the AKC recognizes. These shows are the ones — like the
    premiere Westminster Kennel Club Dog Show (in the United
    States) and Crufts (in the United Kingdom) — that you usually
    see on TV.

Point Shows Versus Fun Matches

Beyond the three types of conformation shows (specialty, all-breed,
and group; see the preceding section), conformation events can
either be

  ✔ **Fun matches:** These events are put on strictly for fun; no points
    are earned, although you and your dog may get a pretty ribbon
    for your winning efforts. Just because these shows don't award
    points toward a championship, however, doesn't mean that
    they're a waste of time. In addition to meeting lots of other
    people who share your passion, participating in fun matches
    is an excellent way to practice your exhibiting skills. Before
    you know it, you'll be an exhibitionist extraordinaire.

  ✔ **Point shows:** In these shows, your Yorkie can earn points
    toward the "Champion" title. If you're working for a title, you
    want to participate in point shows. For information on how
    points are awarded and how many points your Yorkie needs
    to achieve the coveted title, see the section "Pointers on the
    Point System" later in this chapter.

Competition Categories

Your Yorkie can compete in one of six regular classes, depending
on her age and whether she's earned previous titles or points:

  ✔ **Puppy:** The Puppy class is open to dogs between 6 and
    12 months old who aren't champions yet.

  ✔ **Twelve-to-eighteen months:** This class is open to dogs
    between 12 and 18 months old who aren't champions yet.

  ✔ **Novice:** This class is open to any dog over 6 months old who
    hasn't

      • Won any points toward her championship

      • Won three first prizes in the Novice class

      • Won any first prizes in the Bred-by-Exhibitor, American-
        Bred, or Open classes

✔ **Bred-by-Exhibitor:** This class is for dogs who aren't champions and are shown by their owner-breeders.

✔ **American-Bred:** This class is for U.S.-bred dogs who aren't champions yet.

✔ **Open:** This class is for any dog of the breed who's at least 6 months old.

Dog shows aren't mixers. The males (dogs) competing for their Championship titles are shown with other male dogs. The females (bitches) are shown only with other female dogs when competing for Championship points. Males and females only compete against each other in the Best of Breed Class, which includes a Best of Winners between the Winners Dog and the Winners Bitch classes.

Pointers on the Point System

To become an official AKC champion, your Yorkie has to earn a total of 15 points at point matches. At each match, your Yorkie can earn between 1 and 5 points. How many points are actually awarded at each event depends largely on the number of dogs competing. More dogs equal more points. (Where the show is located, the sex of the dogs competing, and the breed can also impact how many points are awarded.)

The AKC has different divisions, and a single division can encompass several states. The AKC mandates how many dogs have to complete in each division.

Of course, you can't have your Yorkie compete and win in 15 different one-point matches and consider him a champion. Nor can you show him in front of a single judge who just loves him to pieces and keeps awarding him all the points. To earn the title "Champion," a chunk of the 15 total points has to come from two major wins under two different judges. A *major win* is one in which 3, 4, or 5 points are awarded.

Marching through the Match

Here's what happens during a dog show. First comes the breed competition, in which judges judge the dogs — boys first and then girls — by breed.

Each class of a particular breed, from Puppy to Open, (refer to the section "Class Acts: Competition Categories) is evaluated. Some dogs in each class are awarded ribbons; others aren't. First-place winners in each class remain in competition; everyone else goes home or sits back and enjoys the rest of the show.

When all the classes of a single breed have been evaluated, the first-place winners of each class are brought back to compete in the Winners class. The dog who wins the Winners class competition is awarded the points. The male winner is called Winners Dog; the female winner is the Winners Bitch. The runners up in the winners class are awarded Reserve Winners Dog (male) and Reserve Winners Bitch.

When the Winners class competition is completed, all the current champs (any dogs who hold the title champion) — both males and females — join the Winners Dog and Winners Bitch in the ring. Now the judges evaluate them again (boys and girls together this time) to determine Best of Breed. If the Best of Breed is a male, the judges select a female to be Best of Opposite Sex; if the Best of Breed is female, a male is chosen Best of Opposite Sex. At this time, a Best of Winners is also chosen between the Winners Dog and Winners Bitch.

At all-breed shows, all the Best of Breed winners compete in their groups (Sporting, Hunting, Toy, and so on). When all the seven groups have been judged, the seven first-place winners from the Group competition vie for Best in Show.

All the Pretty Ribbons

Judges give out a slew of ribbons that indicate the type of award the dog's won:

Color	Place
Blue	First place in class competitions and often as a rosette in group competitions
Red	Second place in class competitions and often as a rosette in group competitions
Yellow	Third place in class competitions and often as a rosette in group competitions

Color	Place
White	Fourth place in class competitions and often as a rosette in group competitions
Purple	Winners Dog and Winners Bitch classes
Purple and white	Reserve Winners (essentially runners up to Winners Dog and Winners Bitch)
Purple and gold	Best of Breed
Blue and white	Best of Winners
Red and white	Best of Opposite Sex
Red, white, and blue	Best in Show

Conformation and Kids

The AKC offers Junior Showmanship classes that get kids involved in agility, obedience, conformation events, and more. In Junior Showmanship events, the kids compete against others in their age groups and are evaluated on how well they present their dogs. In these events, the kids are the ones evaluated, not the dogs. For that reason, any AKC-registered dog is eligible to compete, provided that the child or the child's family owns the dog. Neither the quality of the dog nor the breed being handled matters; even a dog who's been fixed can compete because it's the handler being judged.

Junior Showmanship, open to children between the ages of 10 and 18, is divided into the following classes:

- ✔ **Novice Junior:** 10–14 years old who haven't won 3 first places against competition

- ✔ **Novice Senior:** 14–18 years old who haven't won 3 first places against competition

- ✔ **Open Junior:** 10–14 years old who have won 3 first places in Novice classes

- ✔ **Open Senior:** 14–18 years old who have won 3 first places in Novice classes.

To find out more about Junior Showmanship, go to the AKC Web site (www.akc.org) and click "Dog Events," then "Junior Showmanship," and browse around from there. You can also call 919-816-3814.

Getting Started

If you've never shown a dog before and you want to get started with your Yorkie, the best place to start is by joining a local kennel club. In addition to meeting other people who share your interests, you're sure to find a wealth of useful information about local shows, training classes, grooming for the show ring, and much, much more. Many local clubs also sponsor fun matches where you can hone your skills as an exhibitor. To find Yorkshire Terrier clubs in your area, go to the Yorkshire Terrier Club of America Web site (www.ytca.org) and click "Regional Clubs and Their Show Results." For a list of general breed clubs, go to the AKC site (www.act.org), click "Clubs," and then click "Club Search." You can also call the AKC at 919-233-9767.

Another good starting place is to attend dog shows as a spectator, just to see how they work and to gather information from the booths that are set up and from the exhibitors. Many of the exhibitors are more than happy to answer your questions. Get a program in advance so that you know when Yorkies are showing.

Chapter 18

Ten Fun Facts and Interesting Claims about Yorkies

In This Chapter

▶ Stories about real-life Yorkies

▶ Yorkies in literature and folklore

▶ Yorkies in the record books

▶ Other obscure Yorkie facts

*T*his chapter contains absolutely nothing that you positively *must* know to care for and love your Yorkie. It's purely fun stuff: trivia, a few little-known facts, and some interesting claims that people have made about the Yorkshire Terrier.

Yorkie Firsts in the U.S. and U.K.

The Yorkshire Terrier started off as an English-Scottish dog. In fact, the breed was originally called a "Broken-Haired Scottish Terrier." But the breed quickly made its way to the U.S. (refer to Chapter 2 if you want more Yorkie history). Here are a few interesting firsts for Yorkies in the U.S. and the U.K.:

✔ **1872:** The first Yorkie was born in the U.S., shortly followed by the first major U.S.-led "Awwwww" at the sight of the little guy.

✔ **1874:** The first Yorkies were registered in the British Kennel Club stud book.

✔ **1885:** The American Kennel Club (AKC), first established in 1884, recognized Yorkies as a breed.

> ✔ **1886:** The AKC first officially recognized Yorkshire Terriers as an individual breed, separate from other Scottish Terriers.
>
> ✔ **1889:** Bradford Harry was the first Yorkie to become an American Champion.
>
> ✔ **1898:** In the U.K., the first Yorkshire Terrier breed club was formed.

Rich and Famous Yorkie Owners

Several celebrities have owned Yorkies, including heads of state, royal family members, entertainers, and athletes. Here are just a few: Queen Victoria, Richard Nixon, Princess Masako of Japan, Audrey Hepburn, Tara Reid, Joan Rivers, Elizabeth Taylor, Eva Gabor, and Serena Williams.

Toto Was a Yorkie (Maybe)

Some folks claim that the character Toto in L. Frank Baum's *The Wonderful Wizard of Oz* was a Yorkie. According to Frank, Toto was "a little black dog, with long silky hair and small black eyes that twinkled merrily on either side of his funny, wee nose." This description, you have to admit, can apply to several breeds of dogs. But the Wizard of Oz's original illustrator, W.W. Denslow, owned a Yorkie and very well may have used his dog as a model for the illustrations in the book. So Toto may or may not be a Yorkie. But he definitely wasn't a Cairn Terrier, which is the type of dog cast in the 1939 movie version. But what do you expect? Hollywood studio execs also wanted Shirley Temple to play the role of Dorothy and ended up "settling" for Judy Garland.

War Hero Yorkie

Yorkies are definitely hardy little dogs, but did you know that one is even considered a war hero? During World War II, American soldier William Wynne found a Yorkshire Terrier in a shell hole near the Japanese lines in New Guinea. No one knew who she belonged to, and she didn't seem to understand commands in English or Japanese. Wynne adopted her, and she went with him on 150 air raids and several air-sea rescue missions. She even jumped from a 30-foot tower, wearing her own special parachute. Her most amazing feat, however, was tunneling a wire through a 70-foot-long, dirt-clogged pipe underneath an air strip. Through the rest of the war, she continued to travel in Wynne's backpack, sleep in his tent, and share his C-rations. After the war, she lived a long and happy life, traveling around the country and showing off her skills.

Greyfriar's Bobby Was a Yorkie

Greyfriar's Bobby was a small Scottish dog who stayed faithfully at his master's grave for years following the man's death. Some folks claim that this dog was a Yorkshire Terrier; others (including the folks in the town where the tale unfolded and where a monument of the dog was erected) claim that he was a Skye Terrier (a close kin to the Yorkshire Terrier; refer to Chapter 2).

Here's the story: John Gray was a Scottish farmer who died in 1858. He was buried in the Greyfriar's Kirkyard (churchyard). His dog, Bobby, made his home by his master's grave and stayed there until his own death 14 years later. Townsfolk fed Bobby, built a shelter for him near the grave, and even paid the annual dog-license fee that his dead master would have paid had he lived. After Bobby's death, he was buried in the same churchyard with his master.

Yorkies in Mines

In addition to chasing vermin away from looms, participating in rat-baiting contests, and running small game to ground, Yorkies worked in the coal mines, too. Their job was to carry wire through underground tubes. Some say that their coloring was a result of the miners' needs. Completely black dogs were too hard to see, and completely white dogs got too dirty. The black and gold coat of the Yorkie, however, made them ideal for working in the mines: The black camouflaged the soot of the coal, and the gold made them easy to see in the dark mines.

The Smallest Dog Recorded

The smallest dog ever recorded was a Yorkie, even though Yorkies themselves aren't the smallest breed (that prize goes to the Chihuahua). Her name was Sylvia, and Arthur Marples of England was her owner. Sylvia was 2 ½ inches tall, 3½ inches long, and, at full size, weighed a mere 4 ounces. The poor little thing died shortly after her second birthday in 1945.

Westminster Best in Show, 1978

The Westminster Kennel Club Dog Show, hosted in New York City, is the premiere dog show in the U.S. Only nine times since 1907 (the first year that the show included a Best-in-Show competition) has a dog in the Toy group won Best in Show at the Westminster Dog show. In 1978, a Yorkshire Terrier named Ch Cede Higgins, owned by Barbara and Charles Switzer, took the top prize.

Huddersfield Ben: Father of Modern Yorkie

Huddersfield Ben was one of the most famous early Yorkies. Born in 1865, he was quite a bit larger than today's Yorkies, weighing in at 12 pounds. Still, he had a huge influence on *setting type* (that is, contributing important characteristics to the breed). In his relatively short life (he died in 1871, when he was only 6), Ben won several prizes in the show ring and sired many other dogs. Nearly all accounts of the history of the Yorkshire Terrier go back to Ben and his contributions.

Gaining Popularity

According to AKC statistics, small dogs are growing increasingly popular. Ten years ago, no small breeds broke the top ten most popular dogs in the U.S. Today, three Toy dogs — the Chihuahua, Shih Tzu, and Yorkshire Terrier — are in the top ten. In 2003, the Yorkie was recorded as the sixth most popular of the 150 AKC-recognized breeds.

Index

• **C** •

• D •

FOR DUMMIES®

A world of resources to help you grow

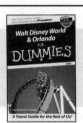

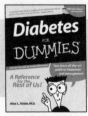